WRITER: **JONATHAN HICKMAN**

ISSUES #18-21
ARTIST: **VALERIO SCHITI** WITH SALVADOR LARROCA (#21)
COLOR ARTIST: **FRANK MARTIN** WITH PAUL MOUNTS (#20-21)
COVER ART: **DUSTIN WEAVER & JASON KEITH**

ISSUES #22-23
ARTIST: **KEV WALKER**
COLOR ARTIST: **FRANK MARTIN**
COVER ART: **DALE KEOWN & JASON KEITH** (#22) AND
CHRISTIAN WARD (#23)

LETTERER: **VC'S JOE CARAMAGNA**
ASSISTANT EDITOR: **JAKE THOMAS**
EDITORS: **TOM BREVOORT** WITH **WIL MOSS**

AVENGERS CREATED BY **STAN LEE & JACK KIRBY**

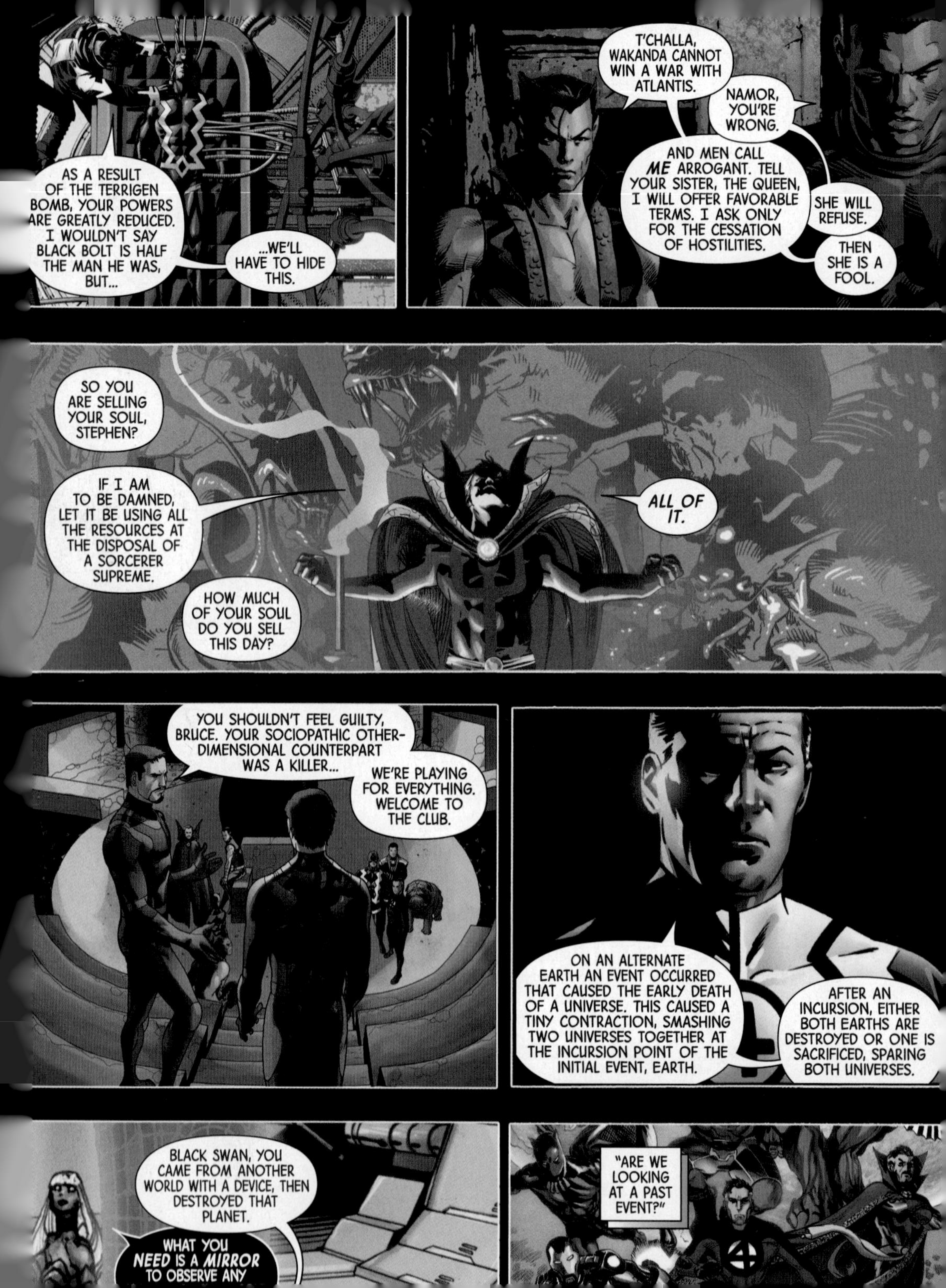

AS A RESULT OF THE TERRIGEN BOMB, YOUR POWERS ARE GREATLY REDUCED. I WOULDN'T SAY BLACK BOLT IS HALF THE MAN HE WAS, BUT...
...WE'LL HAVE TO HIDE THIS.
T'CHALLA, WAKANDA CANNOT WIN A WAR WITH ATLANTIS.
NAMOR, YOU'RE WRONG.
AND MEN CALL *ME* ARROGANT. TELL YOUR SISTER, THE QUEEN, I WILL OFFER FAVORABLE TERMS. I ASK ONLY FOR THE CESSATION OF HOSTILITIES.
SHE WILL REFUSE.
THEN SHE IS A FOOL.
SO YOU ARE SELLING YOUR SOUL, STEPHEN?
IF I AM TO BE DAMNED, LET IT BE USING ALL THE RESOURCES AT THE DISPOSAL OF A SORCERER SUPREME.
HOW MUCH OF YOUR SOUL DO YOU SELL THIS DAY?
ALL OF IT.
YOU SHOULDN'T FEEL GUILTY, BRUCE. YOUR SOCIOPATHIC OTHER-DIMENSIONAL COUNTERPART WAS A KILLER...
WE'RE PLAYING FOR EVERYTHING. WELCOME TO THE CLUB.
ON AN ALTERNATE EARTH AN EVENT OCCURRED THAT CAUSED THE EARLY DEATH OF A UNIVERSE. THIS CAUSED A TINY CONTRACTION, SMASHING TWO UNIVERSES TOGETHER AT THE INCURSION POINT OF THE INITIAL EVENT, EARTH.
AFTER AN INCURSION, EITHER BOTH EARTHS ARE DESTROYED OR ONE IS SACRIFICED, SPARING BOTH UNIVERSES.
BLACK SWAN, YOU CAME FROM ANOTHER WORLD WITH A DEVICE, THEN DESTROYED THAT PLANET.
WHAT YOU *NEED* IS A *MIRROR* TO OBSERVE ANY
"ARE WE LOOKING AT A PAST EVENT?"

THE ILLUMINATI

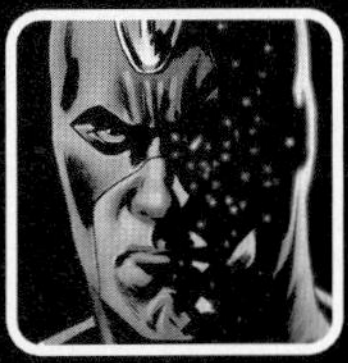

BLACK BOLT
Celestial Messiah

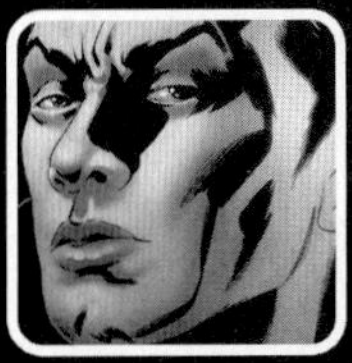

NAMOR
Imperius Rex

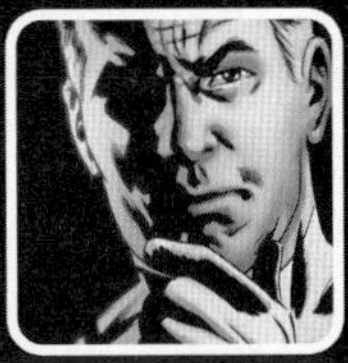

REED RICHARDS
Universal Builder

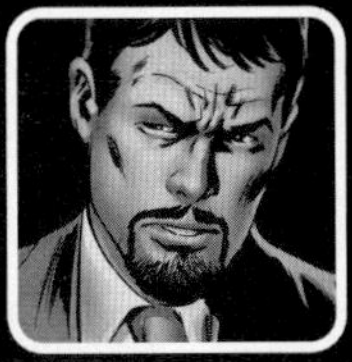

IRON MAN
Master of Machines

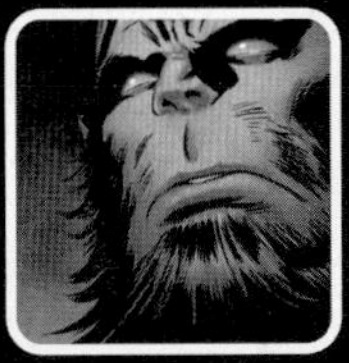

BEAST
Mutant Genius

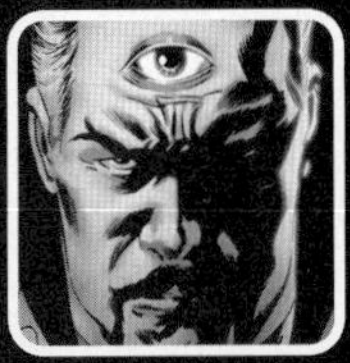

DOCTOR STRANGE
Sorcerer Supreme

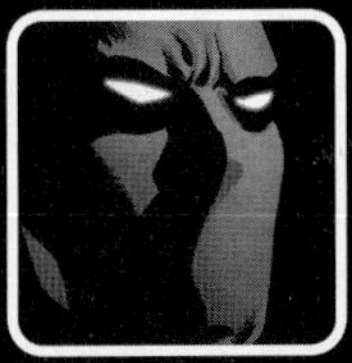

BLACK PANTHER
King of the Dead

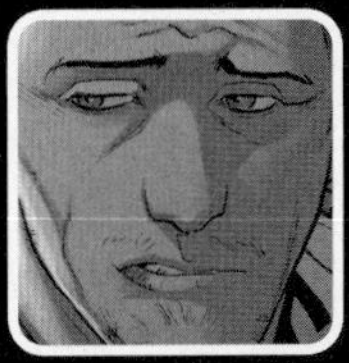

HULK/BRUCE BANNER
Strongest There Is

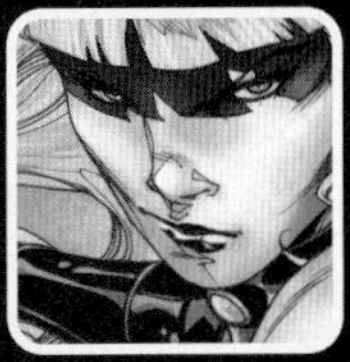

BLACK SWAN
Incursion Survivor

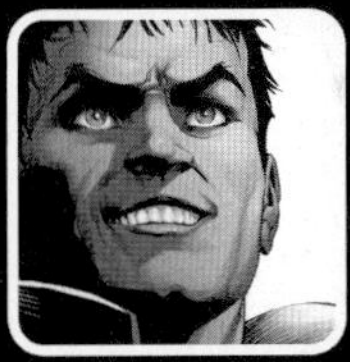

MAXIMUS
Inhuman Madman

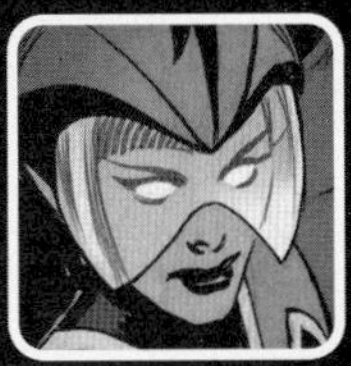

BOUNDLESS

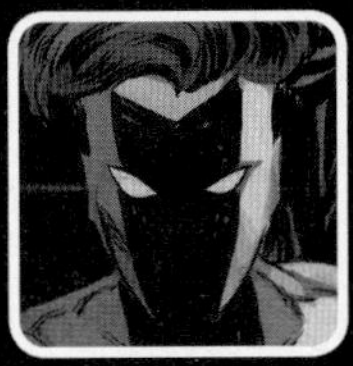

DR. SPECTRUM

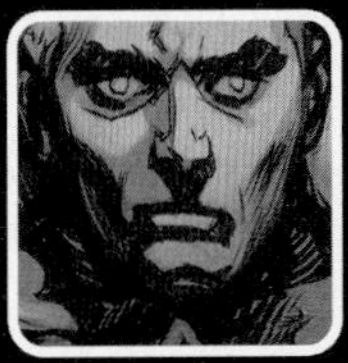

SUN GOD

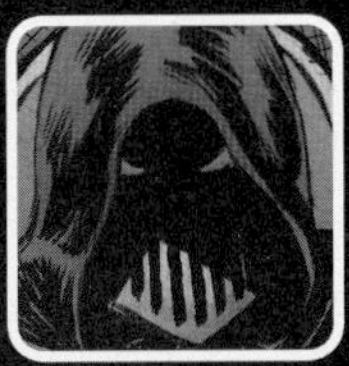

THE RIDER

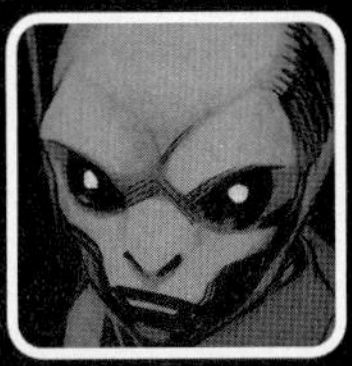

THE JOVIAN

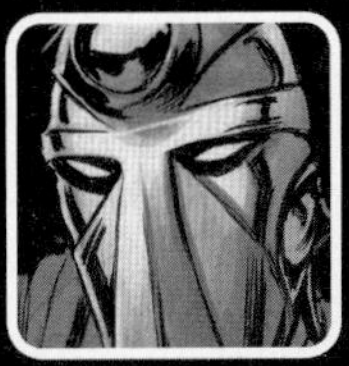

THE NORN

"INTO THE BREACH"

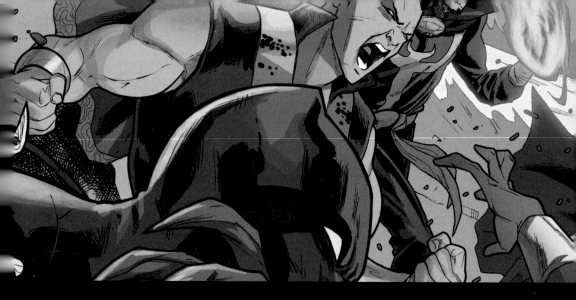

COLLECTION EDITOR: **JENNIFER GRÜNWALD**
ASSISTANT EDITOR: **SARAH BRUNSTAD**
ASSOCIATE MANAGING EDITOR: **ALEX STARBUCK**
EDITOR, SPECIAL PROJECTS: **MARK D. BEAZLEY**
SENIOR EDITOR, SPECIAL PROJECTS: **JEFF YOUNGQUIST**
SVP PRINT, SALES & MARKETING: **DAVID GABRIEL**
BOOK DESIGN: **JEFF POWELL**

EDITOR IN CHIEF: **AXEL ALONSO**
CHIEF CREATIVE OFFICER: **JOE QUESADA**
PUBLISHER: **DAN BUCKLEY**
EXECUTIVE PRODUCER: **ALAN FINE**

NEW AVENGERS VOL. 4: A PERFECT WORLD. Contains material originally published in magazine form as NEW AVENGERS #18-23. First printing 2015. ISBN# 978-0-7851-8960-2. Published by MARVEL WORLDW INC., a subsidiary of MARVEL ENTERTAINMENT, LLC. OFFICE OF PUBLICATION: 135 West 50th Street, New York, NY 10020. Copyright © 2015 MARVEL No similarity between any of the names, characters, pers and/or institutions in this magazine with those of any living or dead person or institution is intended, and any such similarity which may exist is purely coincidental. **Printed in the U.S.A.** ALAN FINE, Presic Marvel Entertainment; DAN BUCKLEY, President, TV, Publishing and Brand Management; JOE QUESADA, Chief Creative Officer; TOM BREVOORT, SVP of Publishing; DAVID BOGART, SVP of Operations & Procurem Publishing; C.B. CEBULSKI, VP of International Development & Brand Management; DAVID GABRIEL, SVP Print, Sales & Marketing; JIM O'KEEFE, VP of Operations & Logistics; DAN CARR, Executive Directe Publishing Technology; SUSAN CRESPI, Editorial Operations Manager; ALEX MORALES, Publishing Operations Manager; STAN LEE, Chairman Emeritus. For information regarding advertising in Marvel Comics c

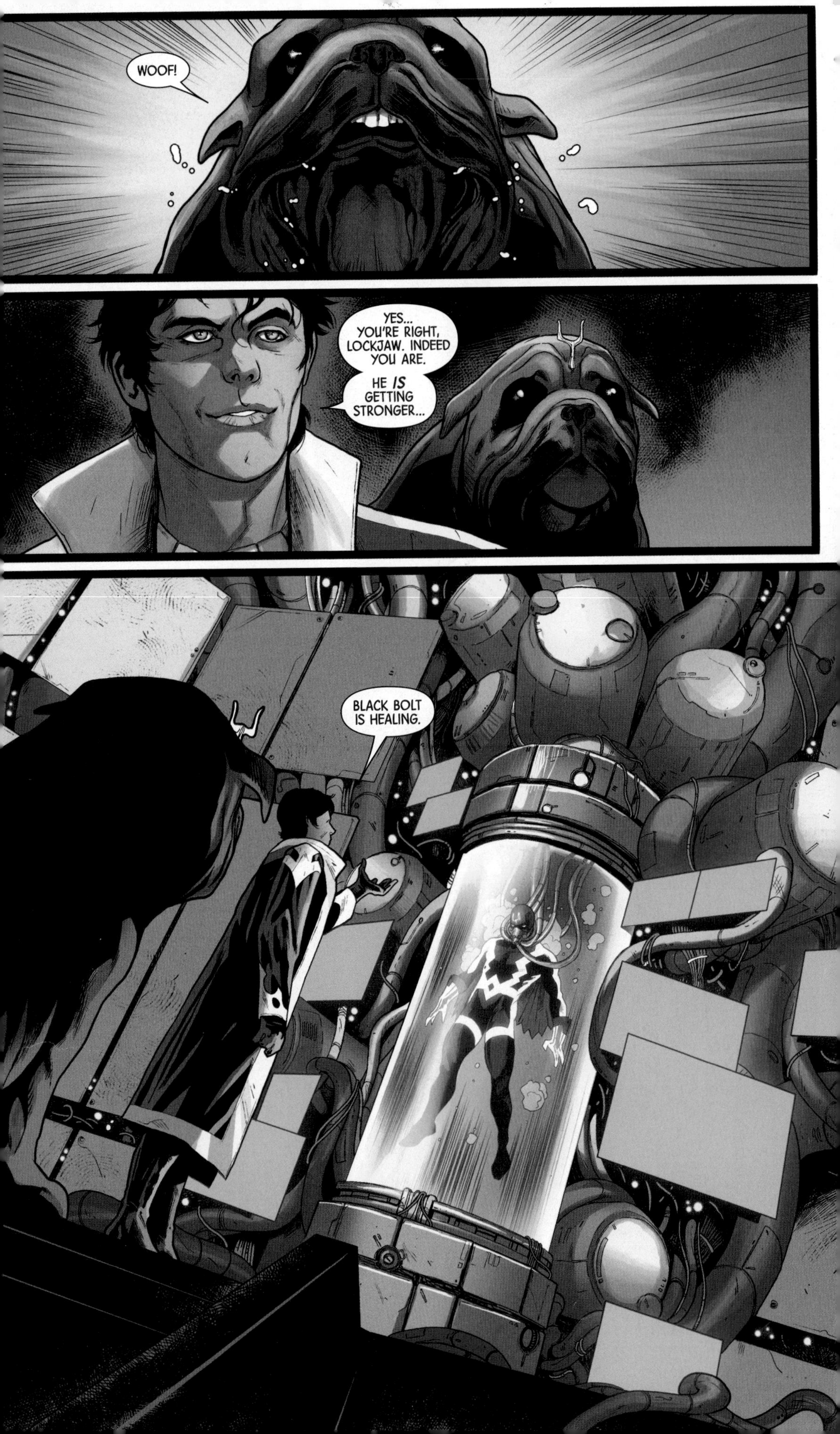
WOOF!
YES... YOU'RE RIGHT, LOCKJAW. INDEED YOU ARE.
HE *IS* GETTING STRONGER...
BLACK BOLT IS HEALING.

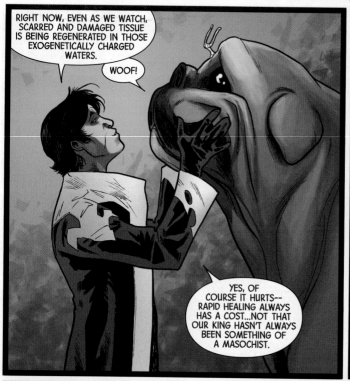

RIGHT NOW, EVEN AS WE WATCH, SCARRED AND DAMAGED TISSUE IS BEING REGENERATED IN THOSE EXOGENETICALLY CHARGED WATERS.

WOOF!

YES, OF COURSE IT HURTS-- RAPID HEALING ALWAYS HAS A COST...NOT THAT OUR KING HASN'T ALWAYS BEEN SOMETHING OF A MASOCHIST.

MY BROTHER, YOU SEE--THE CELESTIAL MESSIAH--HUNG HIMSELF ON THE CROSS SO THAT OUR PEOPLE MIGHT BE SAVED THROUGH GLOBAL TERRIGENESIS.

AND NOW WE'RE ALL ONE HAPPY UNIVERSAL FAMILY OF INHUMANS.

WELL, WE ARE IF YOU OVERLOOK THE FACT THAT, RIGHT NOW, EVERYONE THINKS WE DIED IN THE FALL OF ATTILAN.

STILL, WE HAVE OUR PLANS... AND NOW WE HAVE A FIT AND FULLY HEALED KING.

ALL HE HAS TO DO IS RETURN VICTORIOUS FROM THE ILLUMINATI'S WAR TO ANSWER THE NIGHTLY PRAYERS OF HIS PEOPLE.

THEY WILL ACCEPT OUR RESURRECTION WITH OPEN ARMS...

FOR WHAT SANE PERSON WANTS TO COMMUNE WITH THE DEAD?

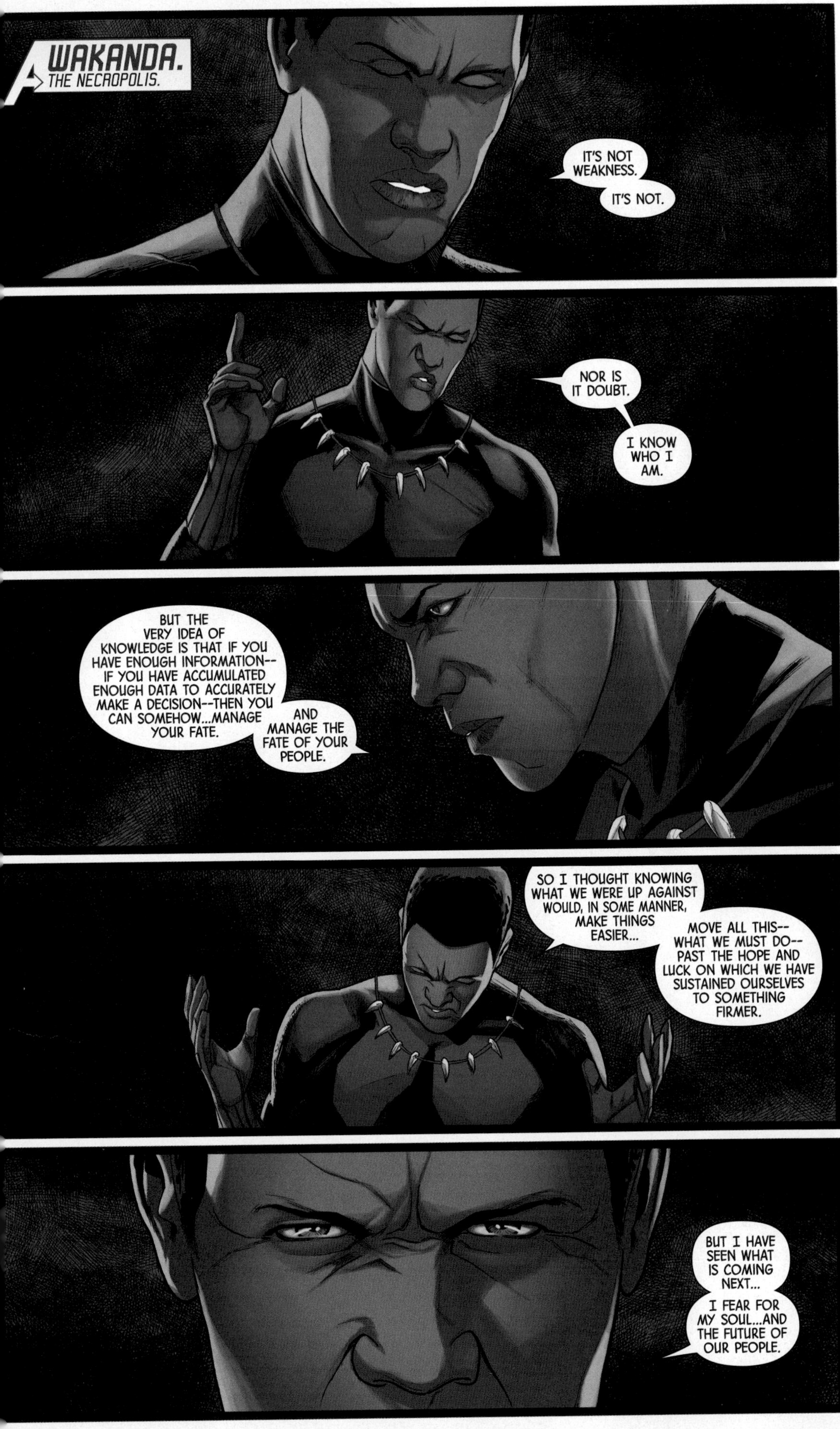
WAKANDA.
THE NECROPOLIS.
IT'S NOT WEAKNESS.
IT'S NOT.
NOR IS IT DOUBT.
I KNOW WHO I AM.
BUT THE VERY IDEA OF KNOWLEDGE IS THAT IF YOU HAVE ENOUGH INFORMATION-- IF YOU HAVE ACCUMULATED ENOUGH DATA TO ACCURATELY MAKE A DECISION--THEN YOU CAN SOMEHOW...MANAGE YOUR FATE.
AND MANAGE THE FATE OF YOUR PEOPLE.
SO I THOUGHT KNOWING WHAT WE WERE UP AGAINST WOULD, IN SOME MANNER, MAKE THINGS EASIER...
MOVE ALL THIS-- WHAT WE MUST DO-- PAST THE HOPE AND LUCK ON WHICH WE HAVE SUSTAINED OURSELVES TO SOMETHING FIRMER.
BUT I HAVE SEEN WHAT IS COMING NEXT...
I FEAR FOR MY SOUL...AND THE FUTURE OF OUR PEOPLE.

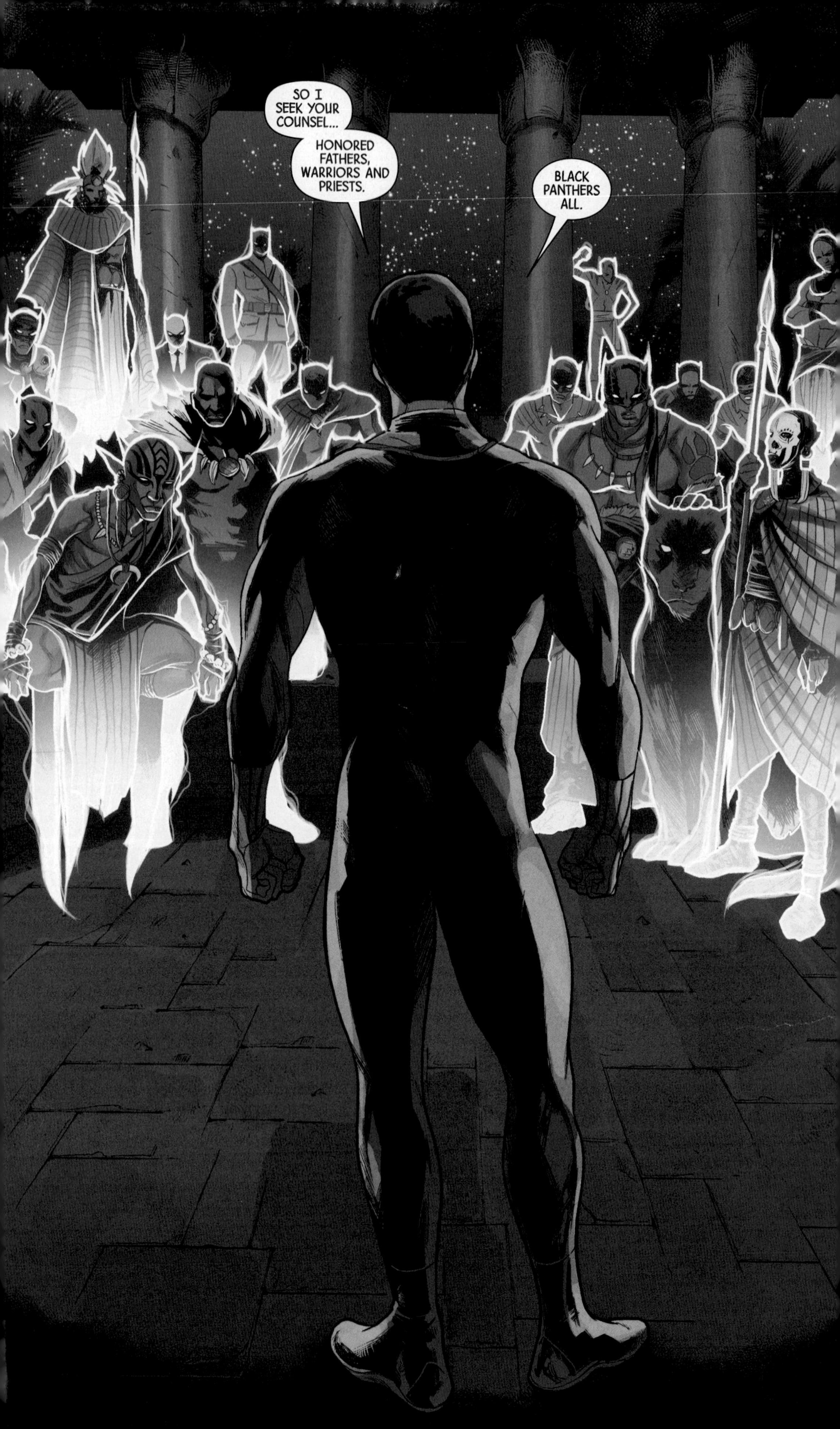
SO I SEEK YOUR COUNSEL...
HONORED FATHERS, WARRIORS AND PRIESTS.
BLACK PANTHERS ALL.

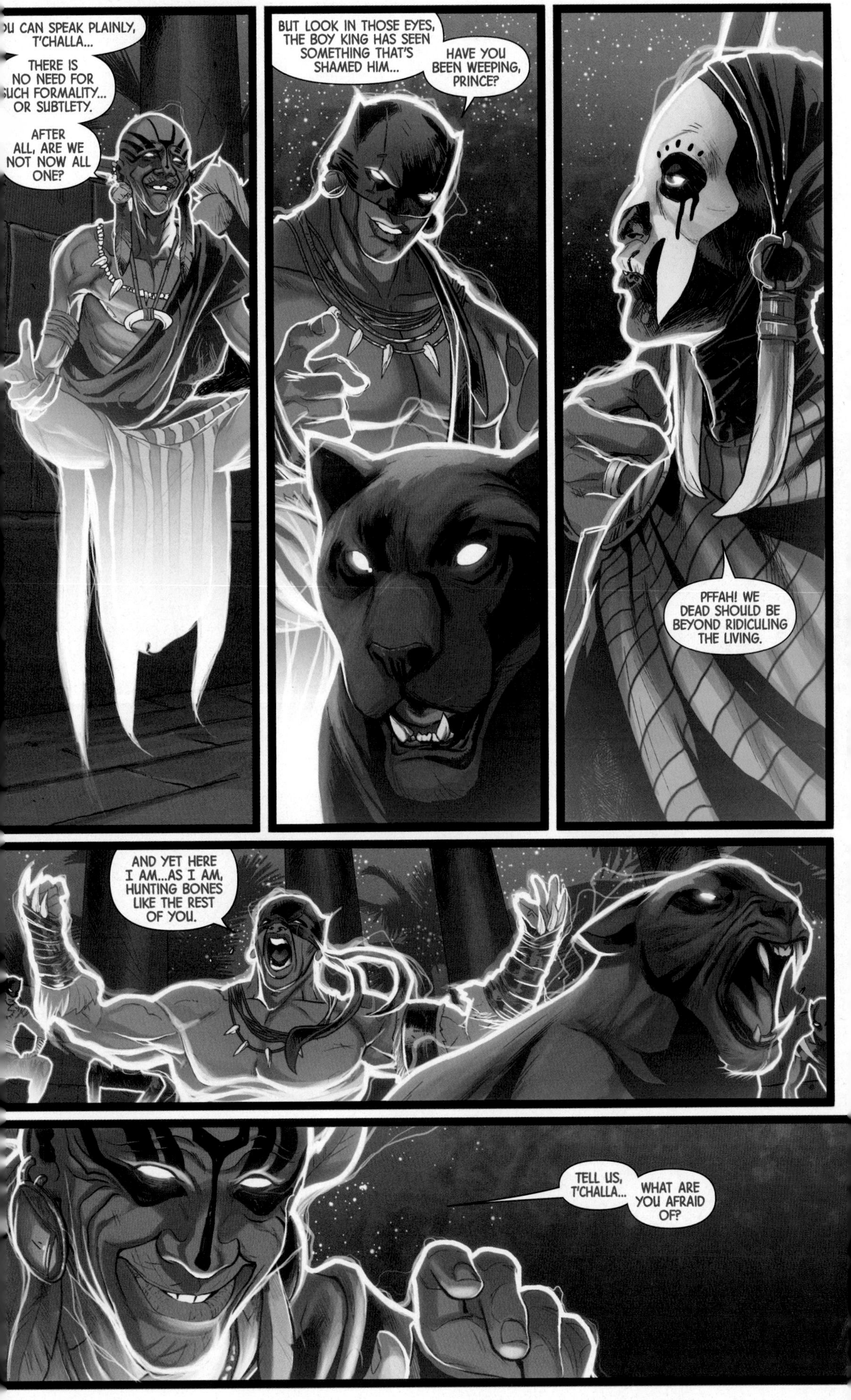

U CAN SPEAK PLAINLY, T'CHALLA...
THERE IS NO NEED FOR SUCH FORMALITY... OR SUBTLETY.
AFTER ALL, ARE WE NOT NOW ALL ONE?
BUT LOOK IN THOSE EYES, THE BOY KING HAS SEEN SOMETHING THAT'S SHAMED HIM...
HAVE YOU BEEN WEEPING, PRINCE?
PFFAH! WE DEAD SHOULD BE BEYOND RIDICULING THE LIVING.
AND YET HERE I AM...AS I AM, HUNTING BONES LIKE THE REST OF YOU.
TELL US, T'CHALLA...
WHAT ARE YOU AFRAID OF?

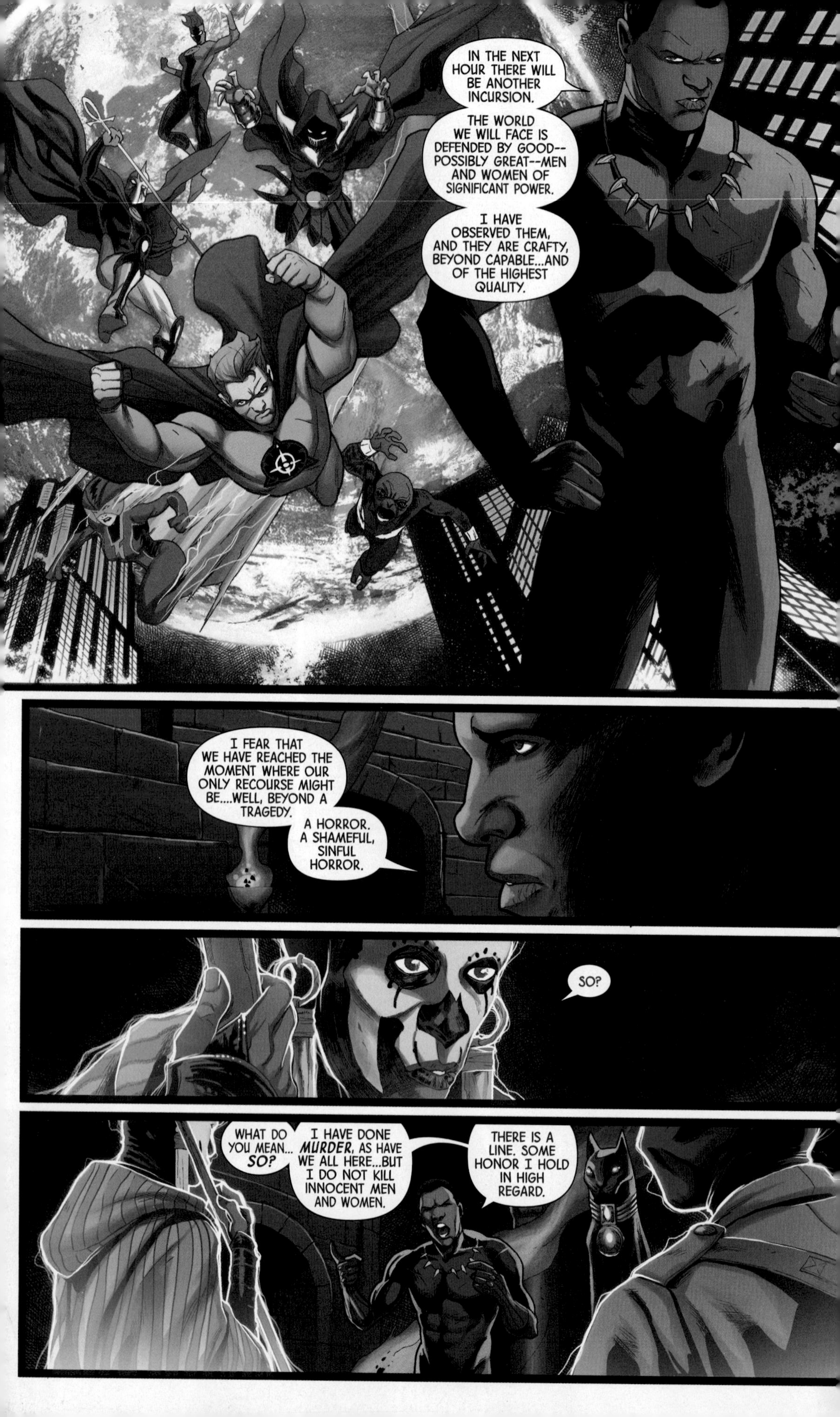
IN THE NEXT HOUR THERE WILL BE ANOTHER INCURSION.
THE WORLD WE WILL FACE IS DEFENDED BY GOOD-- POSSIBLY GREAT--MEN AND WOMEN OF SIGNIFICANT POWER.
I HAVE OBSERVED THEM, AND THEY ARE CRAFTY, BEYOND CAPABLE...AND OF THE HIGHEST QUALITY.
I FEAR THAT WE HAVE REACHED THE MOMENT WHERE OUR ONLY RECOURSE MIGHT BE....WELL, BEYOND A TRAGEDY.
A HORROR. A SHAMEFUL, SINFUL HORROR.
SO?
WHAT DO YOU MEAN... *SO?*
I HAVE DONE *MURDER*, AS HAVE WE ALL HERE...BUT I DO NOT KILL INNOCENT MEN AND WOMEN.
THERE IS A LINE. SOME HONOR I HOLD IN HIGH REGARD.

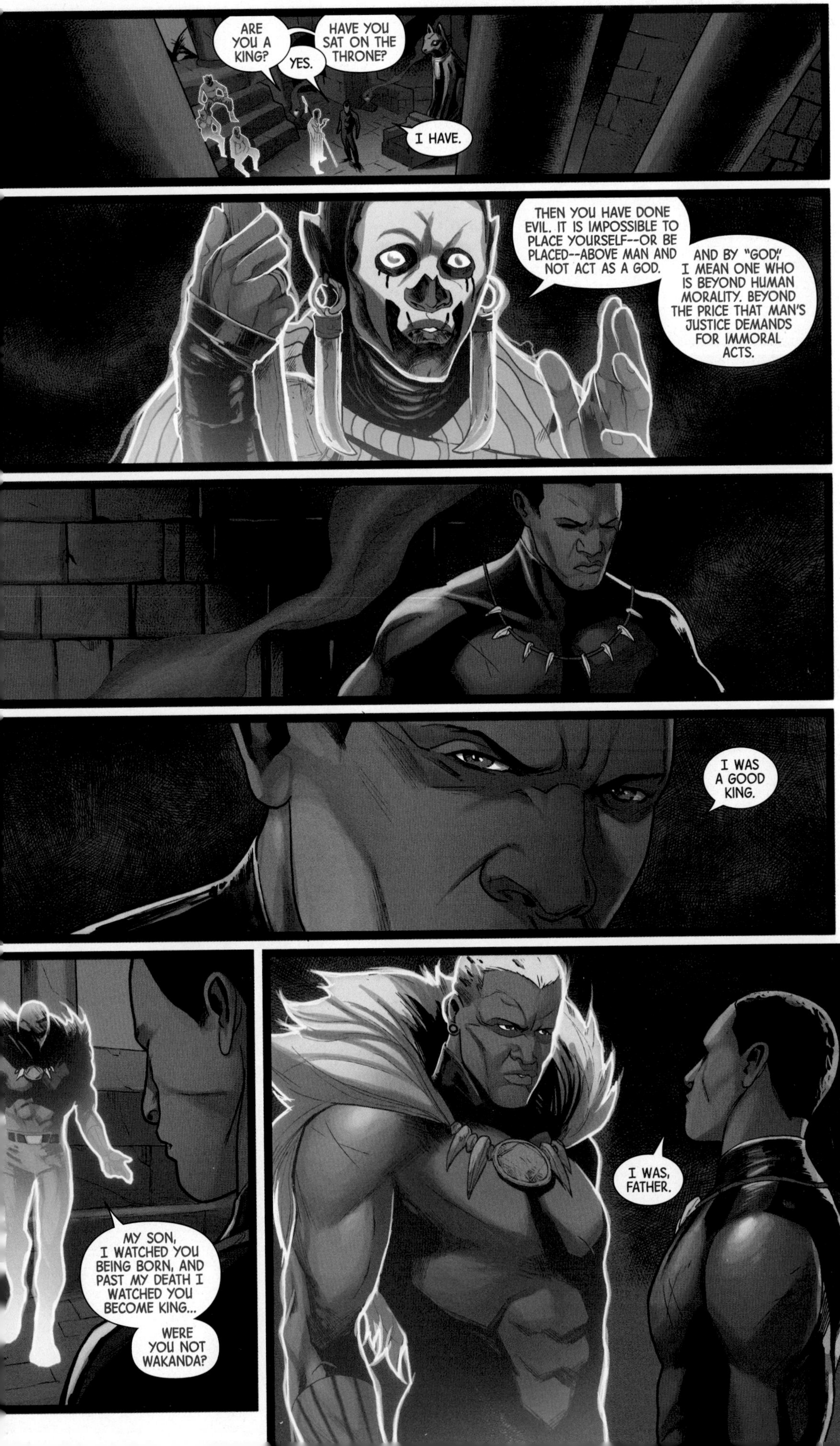
ARE YOU A KING?
YES.
HAVE YOU SAT ON THE THRONE?
I HAVE.
THEN YOU HAVE DONE EVIL. IT IS IMPOSSIBLE TO PLACE YOURSELF--OR BE PLACED--ABOVE MAN AND NOT ACT AS A GOD.
AND BY "GOD," I MEAN ONE WHO IS BEYOND HUMAN MORALITY. BEYOND THE PRICE THAT MAN'S JUSTICE DEMANDS FOR IMMORAL ACTS.
I WAS A GOOD KING.
MY SON, I WATCHED YOU BEING BORN, AND PAST MY DEATH I WATCHED YOU BECOME KING...
WERE YOU NOT WAKANDA?
I WAS, FATHER.

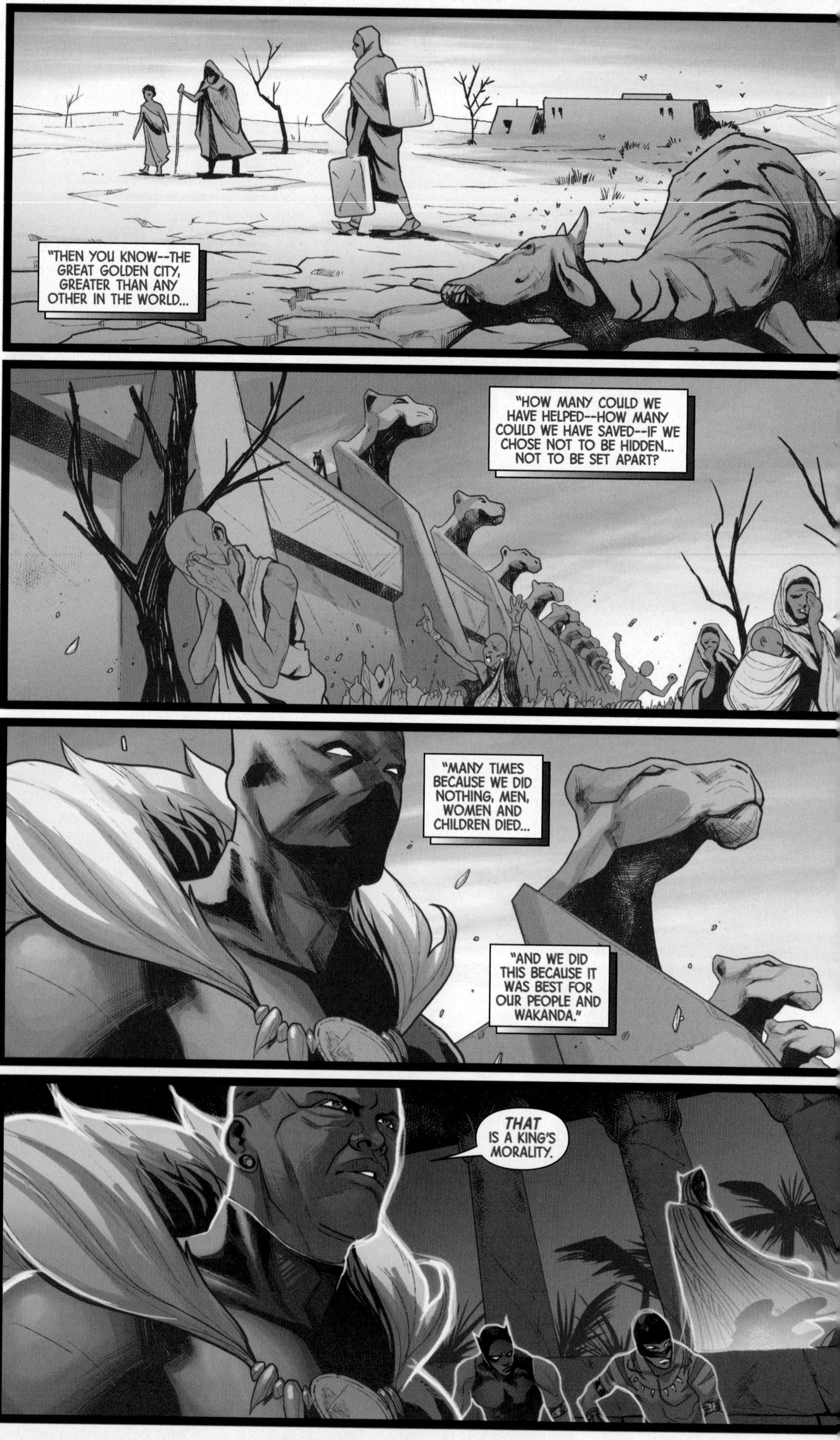
"THEN YOU KNOW--THE GREAT GOLDEN CITY, GREATER THAN ANY OTHER IN THE WORLD...
"HOW MANY COULD WE HAVE HELPED--HOW MANY COULD WE HAVE SAVED--IF WE CHOSE NOT TO BE HIDDEN... NOT TO BE SET APART?
"MANY TIMES BECAUSE WE DID NOTHING, MEN, WOMEN AND CHILDREN DIED...
"AND WE DID THIS BECAUSE IT WAS BEST FOR OUR PEOPLE AND WAKANDA."
THAT IS A KING'S MORALITY.

WE HAVE ALL MADE IMPOSSIBLE CHOICES LIKE THE ONES FACING YOU.

BUT WE SHOULDER THEM WE SHOULD... IT IS OUR BURDEN.

YOU SOUGHT MY COUNSEL AND HERE IT IS:

MEASURE ALL THINGS AGAINST THE SURVIVAL OF OUR PEOPLE. AND THAT SURVIVAL ABOVE ALL OTHERS.

WILL THERE BE A COST? YES.

MIGHT THE UNIVERSE BURN? LET IT.

THESE ARE HARD WORDS TO HEAR, BUT YOU MUST HEAR THEM ALL THE SAME.

YOU WILL KILL THEM ALL IF IT MEANS WAKANDA STANDS.

THE GOLDEN CITY MUST NEVER FALL.

I WILL DO...

...WHAT I MUST.

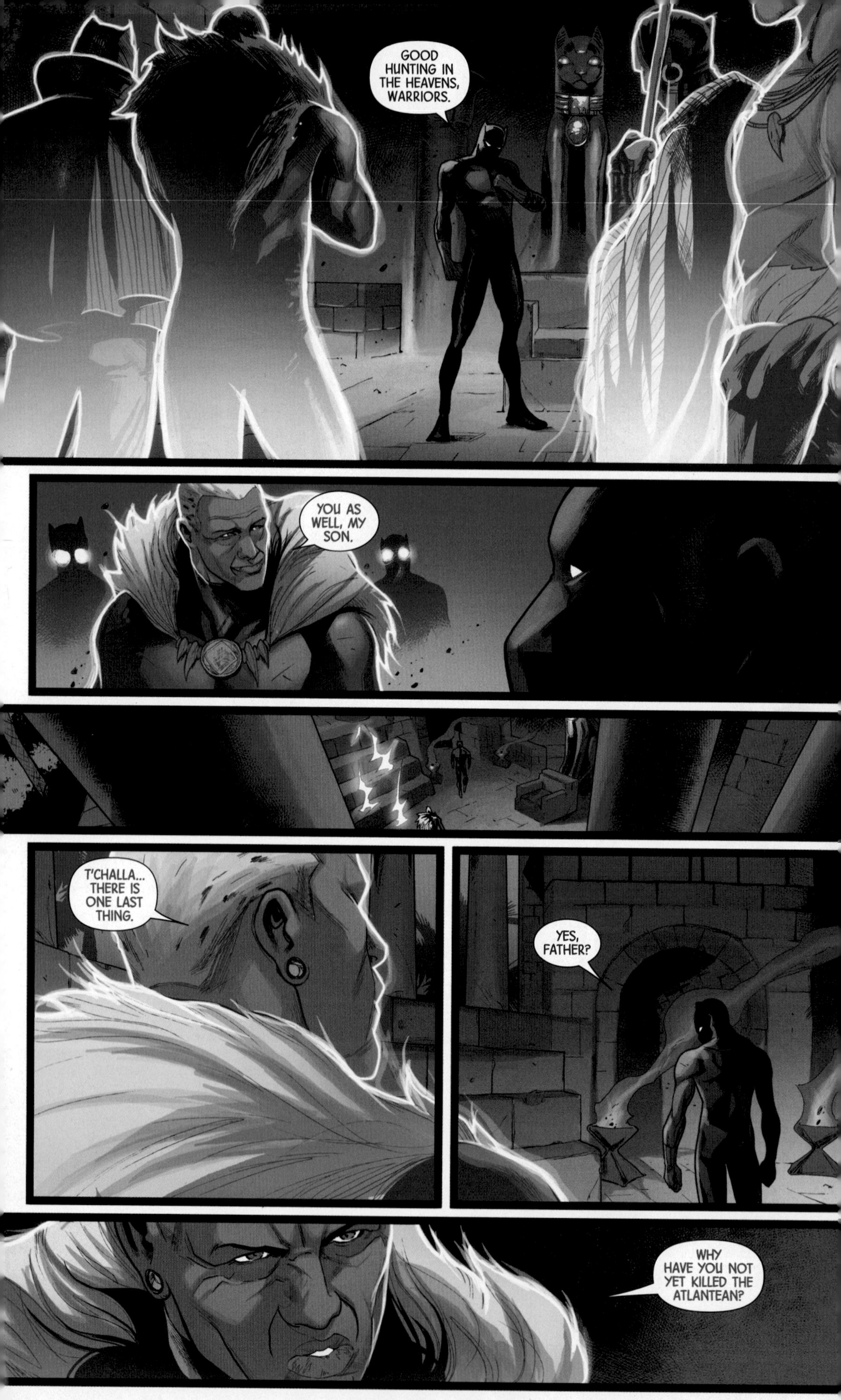
GOOD HUNTING IN THE HEAVENS, WARRIORS.
YOU AS WELL, MY SON.
T'CHALLA... THERE IS ONE LAST THING.
YES, FATHER?
WHY HAVE YOU NOT YET KILLED THE ATLANTEAN?

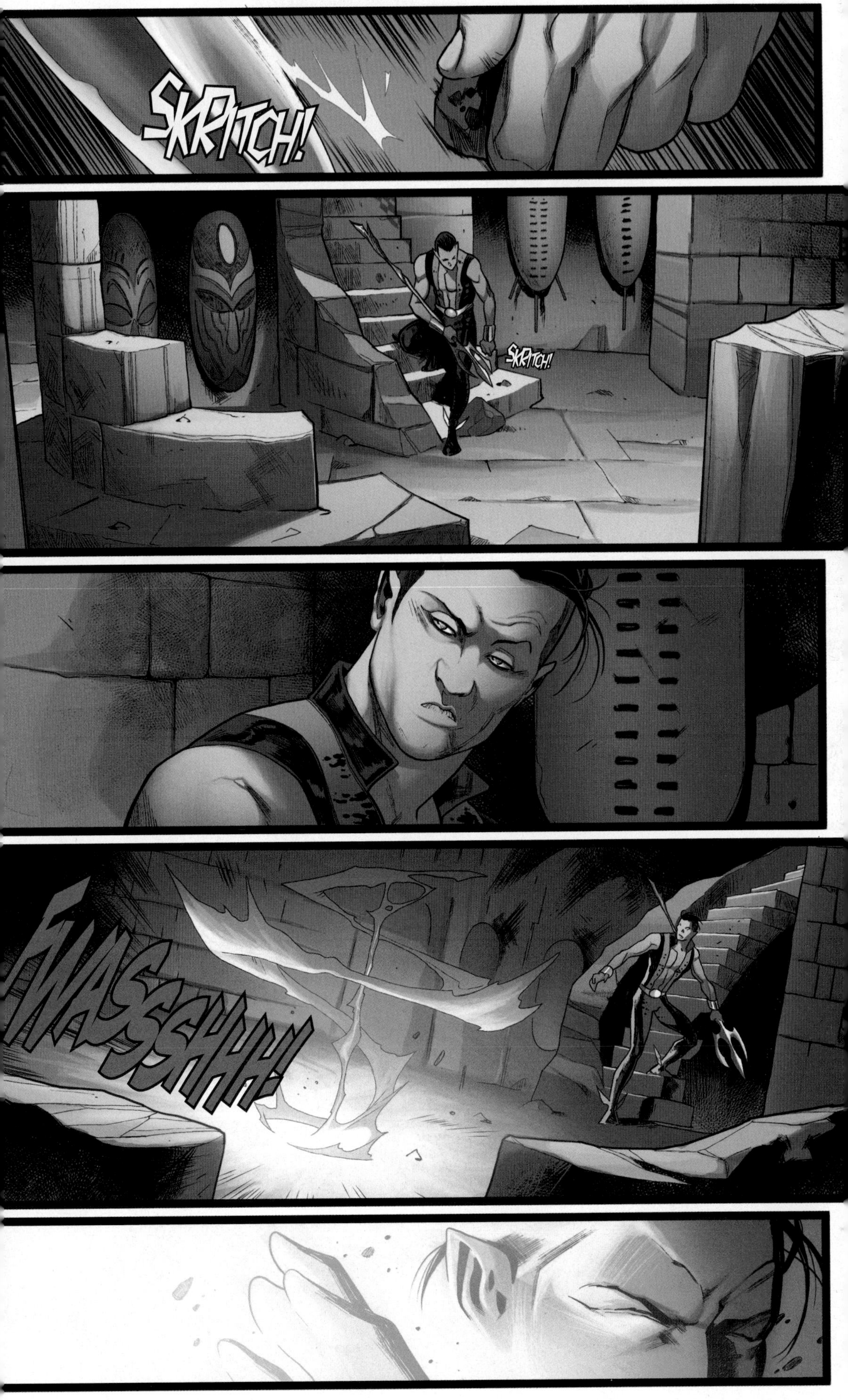
SKRITCH!
SKRITCH!
TWASSHHH!

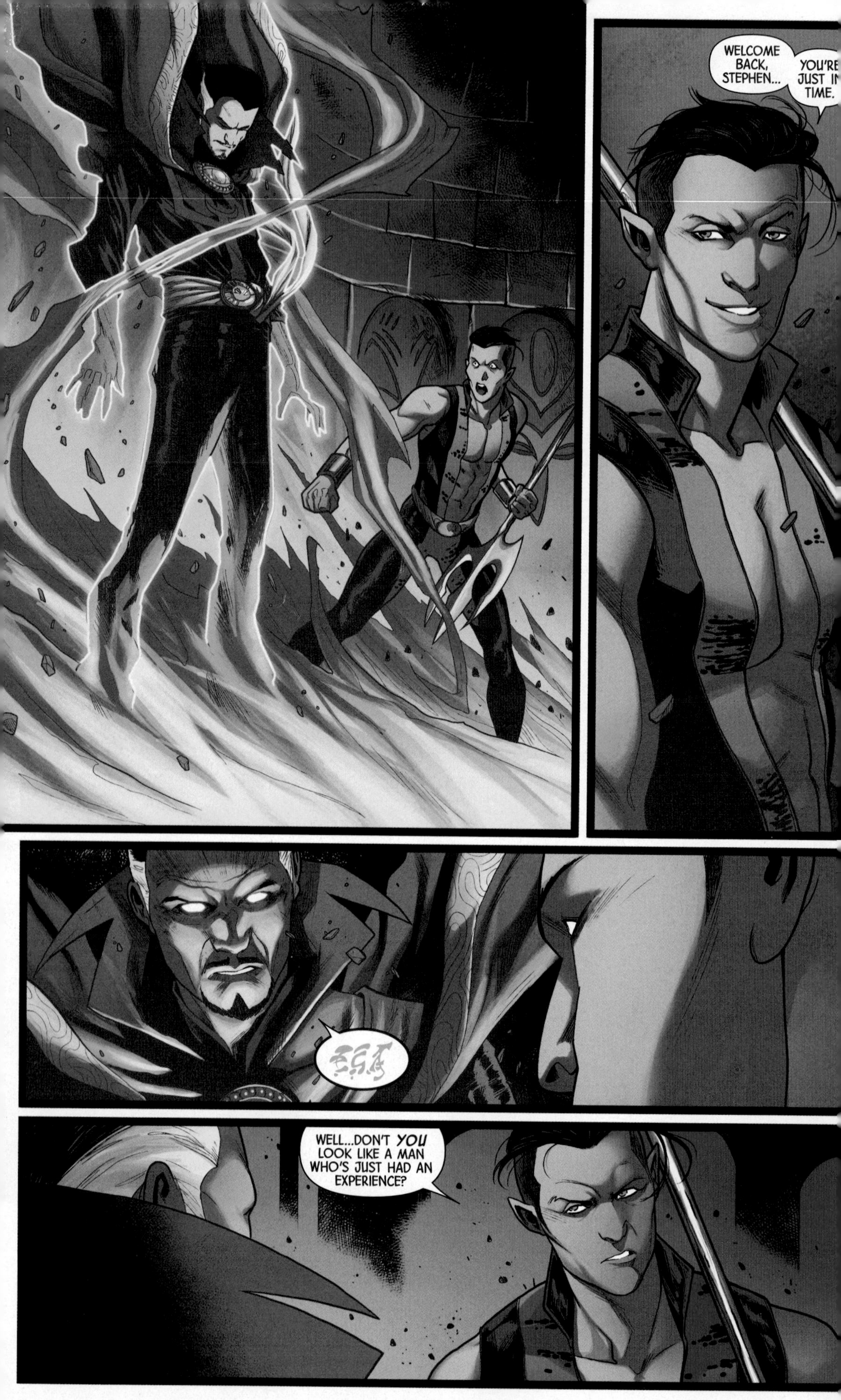
WELCOME BACK, STEPHEN...
YOU'RE JUST IN TIME.
WELL...DON'T YOU LOOK LIKE A MAN WHO'S JUST HAD AN EXPERIENCE?

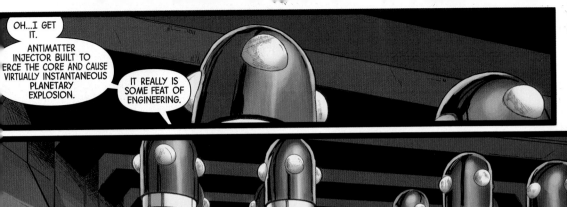

OH...I GET IT. ANTIMATTER INJECTOR BUILT TO PIERCE THE CORE AND CAUSE VIRTUALLY INSTANTANEOUS PLANETARY EXPLOSION.

IT REALLY IS SOME FEAT OF ENGINEERING.

MY QUESTION IS...WHY SO MANY?

AND WHY DO YOU SEEM TO BE ARMING ONE?

I CAN GUESS, OF COURSE...BUT I DON'T THINK I'LL LIKE THE ANSWER.

NO ONE DOES, DOCTOR BANNER.

AND FORGIVE MY OUT-OF-CHARACTER BLUNTNESS AS I EXPAND ON THE THEME...

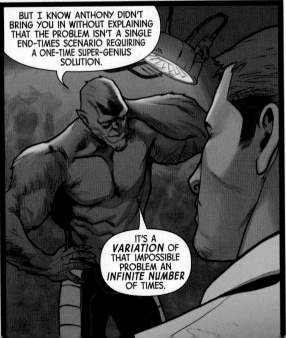

BUT I KNOW ANTHONY DIDN'T BRING YOU IN WITHOUT EXPLAINING THAT THE PROBLEM ISN'T A SINGLE END-TIMES SCENARIO REQUIRING A ONE-TIME SUPER-GENIUS SOLUTION.

IT'S A *VARIATION* OF THAT IMPOSSIBLE PROBLEM AN *INFINITE NUMBER* OF TIMES.

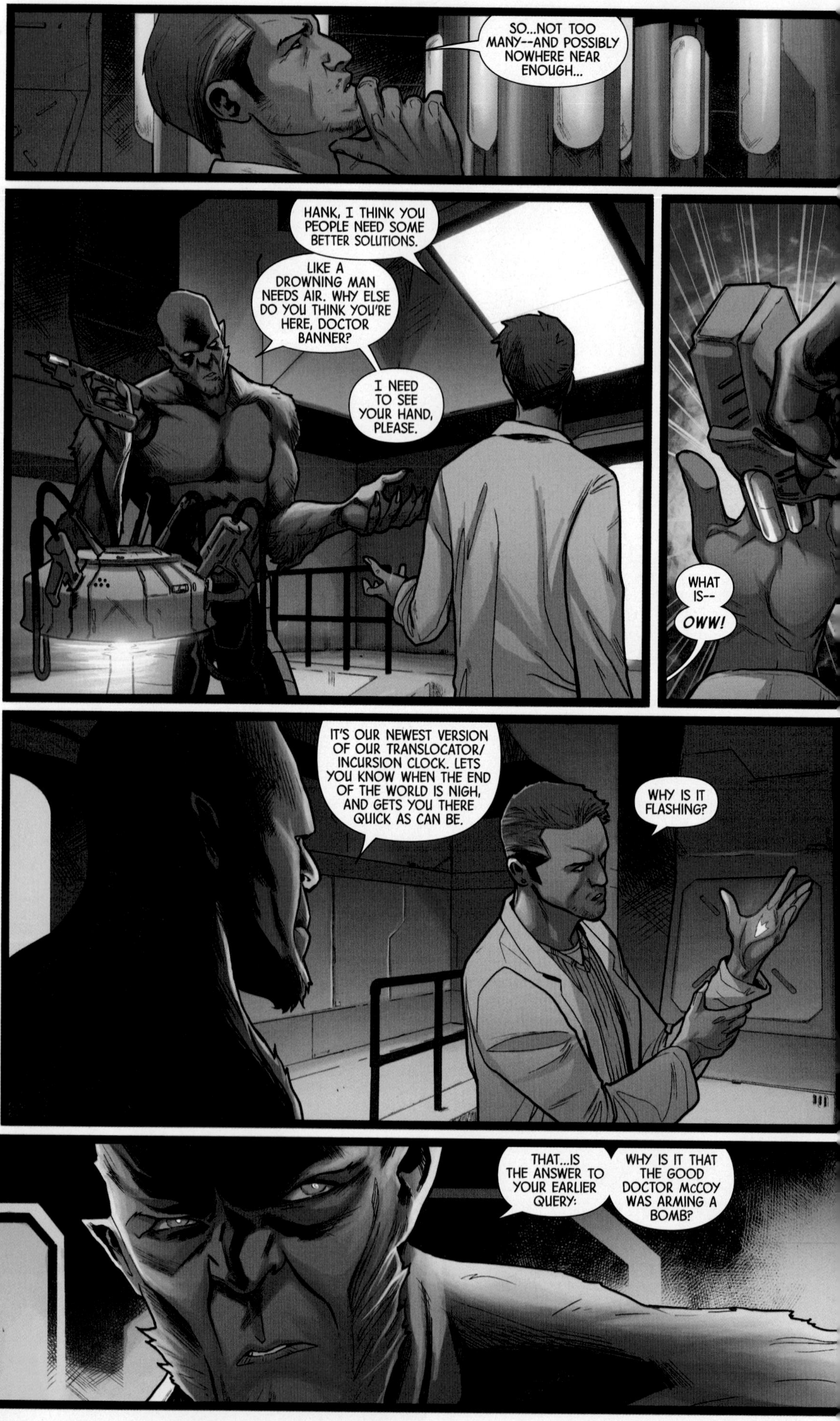
SO...NOT TOO MANY--AND POSSIBLY NOWHERE NEAR ENOUGH...
HANK, I THINK YOU PEOPLE NEED SOME BETTER SOLUTIONS.
LIKE A DROWNING MAN NEEDS AIR. WHY ELSE DO YOU THINK YOU'RE HERE, DOCTOR BANNER?
I NEED TO SEE YOUR HAND, PLEASE.
WHAT IS--
OWW!
IT'S OUR NEWEST VERSION OF OUR TRANSLOCATOR/ INCURSION CLOCK. LETS YOU KNOW WHEN THE END OF THE WORLD IS NIGH, AND GETS YOU THERE QUICK AS CAN BE.
WHY IS IT FLASHING?
THAT...IS THE ANSWER TO YOUR EARLIER QUERY:
WHY IS IT THAT THE GOOD DOCTOR McCOY WAS ARMING A BOMB?

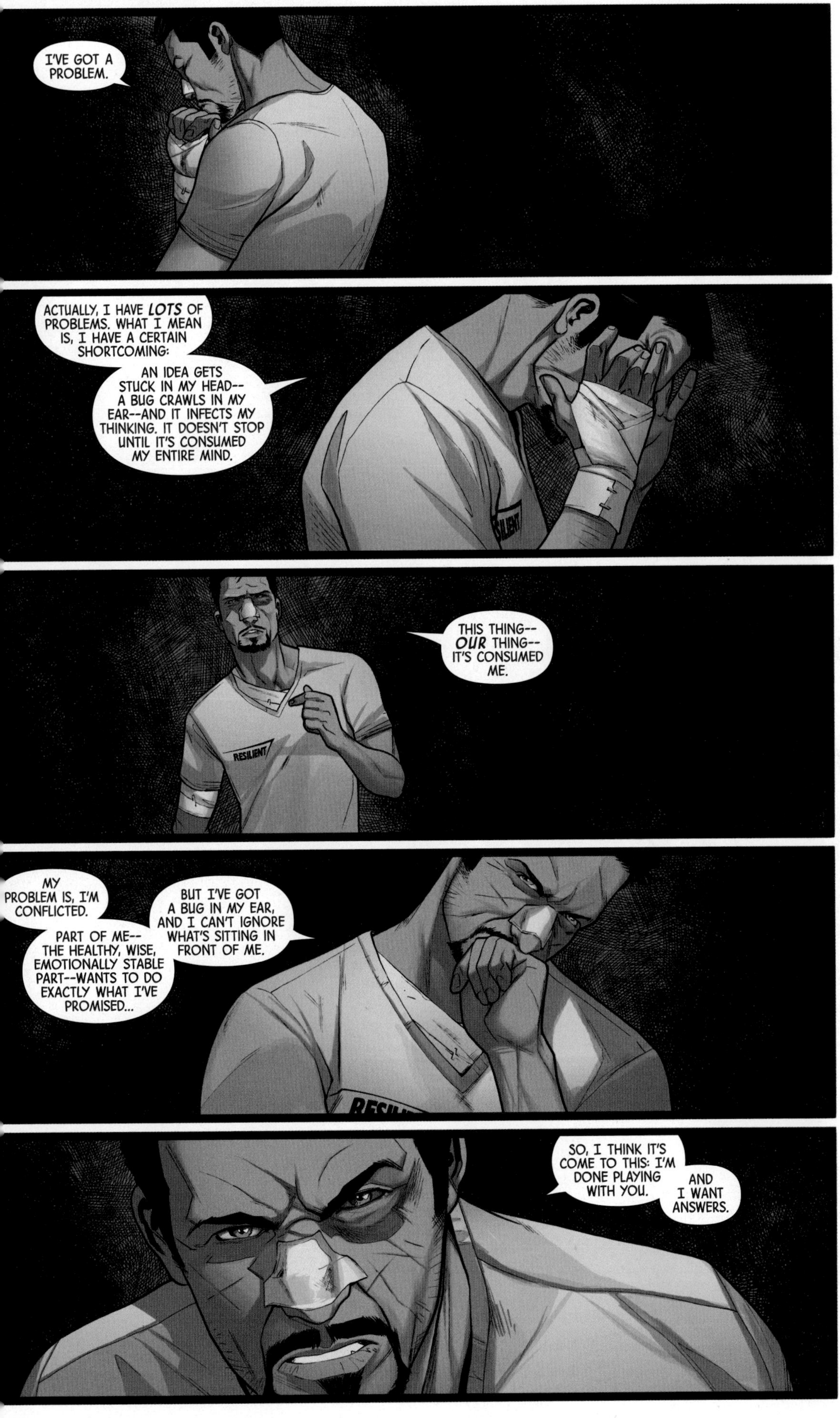
I'VE GOT A PROBLEM.
ACTUALLY, I HAVE LOTS OF PROBLEMS. WHAT I MEAN IS, I HAVE A CERTAIN SHORTCOMING:
AN IDEA GETS STUCK IN MY HEAD-- A BUG CRAWLS IN MY EAR--AND IT INFECTS MY THINKING. IT DOESN'T STOP UNTIL IT'S CONSUMED MY ENTIRE MIND.
RESILIENT
THIS THING-- OUR THING-- IT'S CONSUMED ME.
RESILIENT
MY PROBLEM IS, I'M CONFLICTED.
PART OF ME-- THE HEALTHY, WISE, EMOTIONALLY STABLE PART--WANTS TO DO EXACTLY WHAT I'VE PROMISED...
BUT I'VE GOT A BUG IN MY EAR, AND I CAN'T IGNORE WHAT'S SITTING IN FRONT OF ME.
SO, I THINK IT'S COME TO THIS: I'M DONE PLAYING WITH YOU.
AND I WANT ANSWERS.

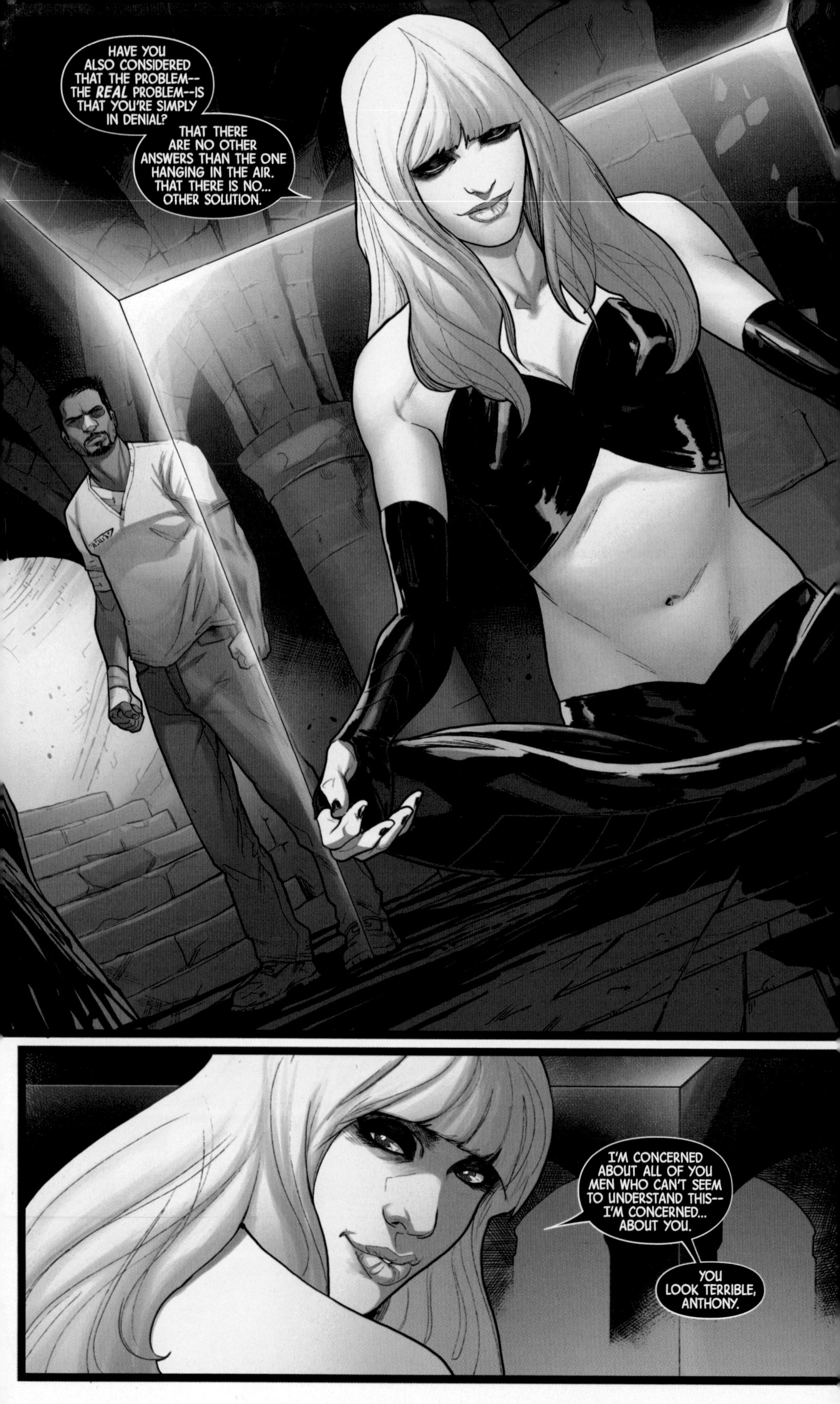
HAVE YOU ALSO CONSIDERED THAT THE PROBLEM-- THE *REAL* PROBLEM--IS THAT YOU'RE SIMPLY IN DENIAL?
THAT THERE ARE NO OTHER ANSWERS THAN THE ONE HANGING IN THE AIR. THAT THERE IS NO... OTHER SOLUTION.
I'M CONCERNED ABOUT ALL OF YOU MEN WHO CAN'T SEEM TO UNDERSTAND THIS-- I'M CONCERNED... ABOUT YOU.
YOU LOOK TERRIBLE, ANTHONY.

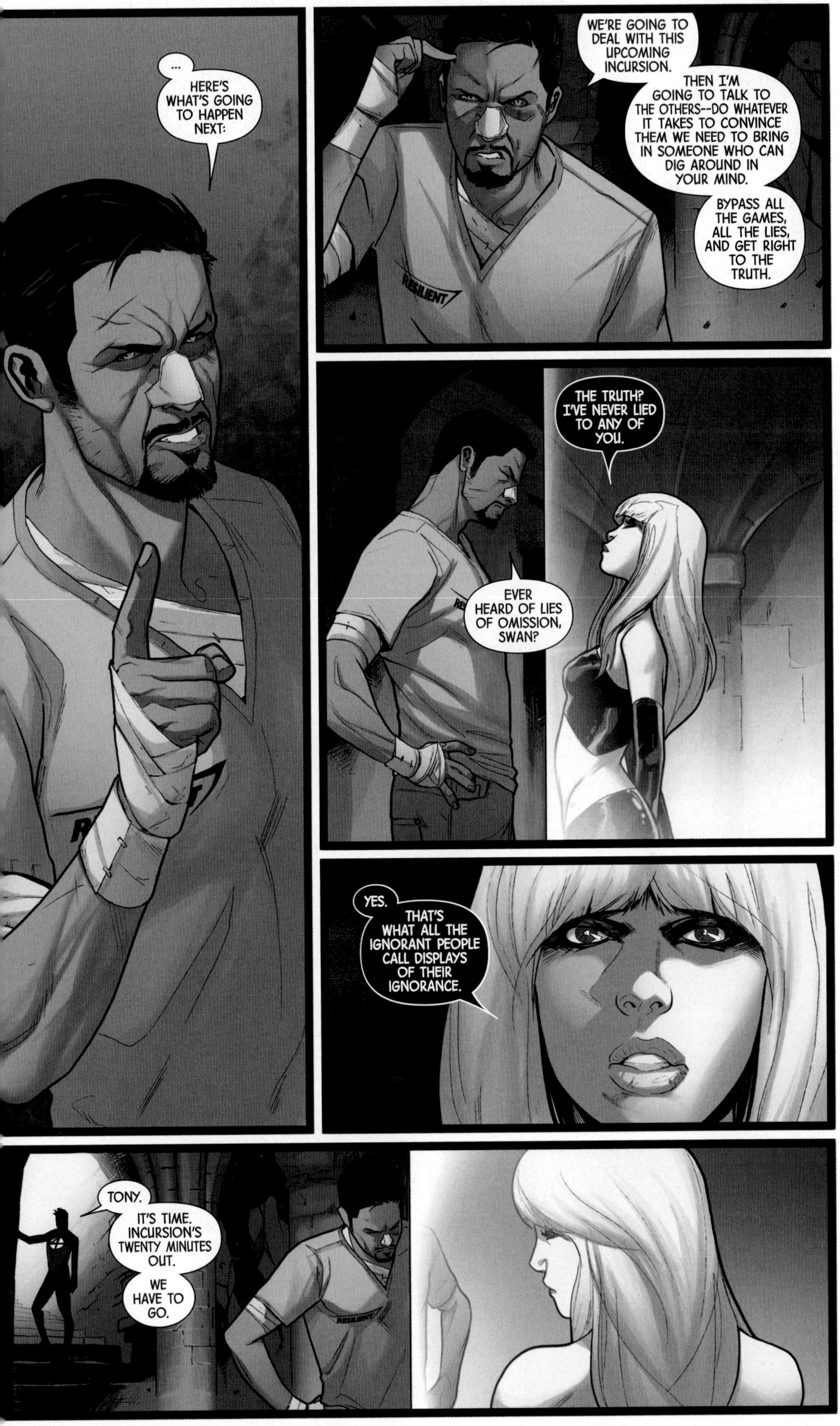
...
HERE'S WHAT'S GOING TO HAPPEN NEXT:
WE'RE GOING TO DEAL WITH THIS UPCOMING INCURSION.
THEN I'M GOING TO TALK TO THE OTHERS--DO WHATEVER IT TAKES TO CONVINCE THEM WE NEED TO BRING IN SOMEONE WHO CAN DIG AROUND IN YOUR MIND.
BYPASS ALL THE GAMES, ALL THE LIES, AND GET RIGHT TO THE TRUTH.
RESILIENT
THE TRUTH? I'VE NEVER LIED TO ANY OF YOU.
EVER HEARD OF LIES OF OMISSION, SWAN?
YES.
THAT'S WHAT ALL THE IGNORANT PEOPLE CALL DISPLAYS OF THEIR IGNORANCE.
TONY.
IT'S TIME. INCURSION'S TWENTY MINUTES OUT.
WE HAVE TO GO.
RESILIENT

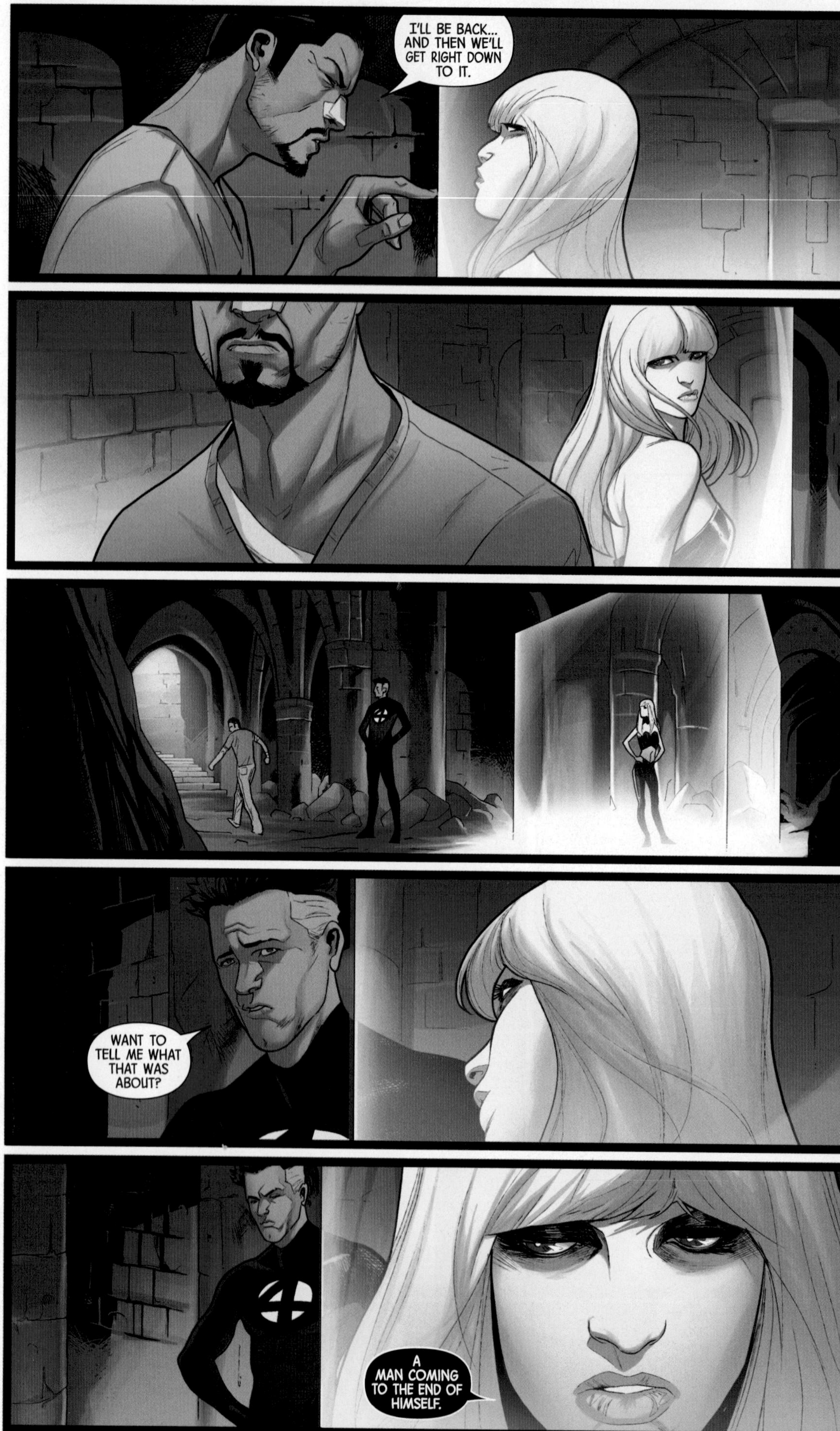
I'LL BE BACK... AND THEN WE'LL GET RIGHT DOWN TO IT.
WANT TO TELL ME WHAT THAT WAS ABOUT?
A MAN COMING TO THE END OF HIMSELF.

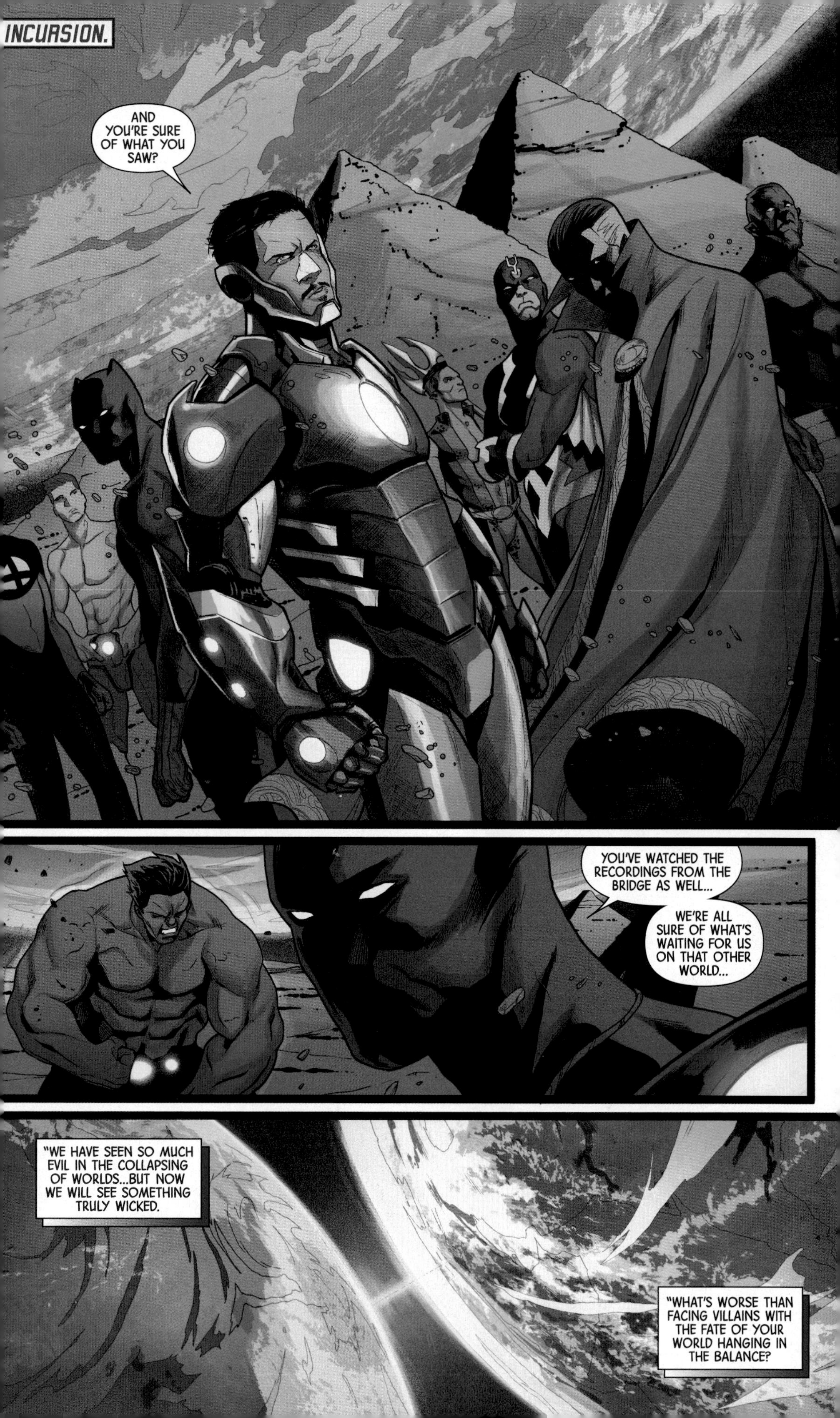
INCURSION.
AND YOU'RE SURE OF WHAT YOU SAW?
YOU'VE WATCHED THE RECORDINGS FROM THE BRIDGE AS WELL...
WE'RE ALL SURE OF WHAT'S WAITING FOR US ON THAT OTHER WORLD...
"WE HAVE SEEN SO MUCH EVIL IN THE COLLAPSING OF WORLDS...BUT NOW WE WILL SEE SOMETHING TRULY WICKED.
"WHAT'S WORSE THAN FACING VILLAINS WITH THE FATE OF YOUR WORLD HANGING IN THE BALANCE?

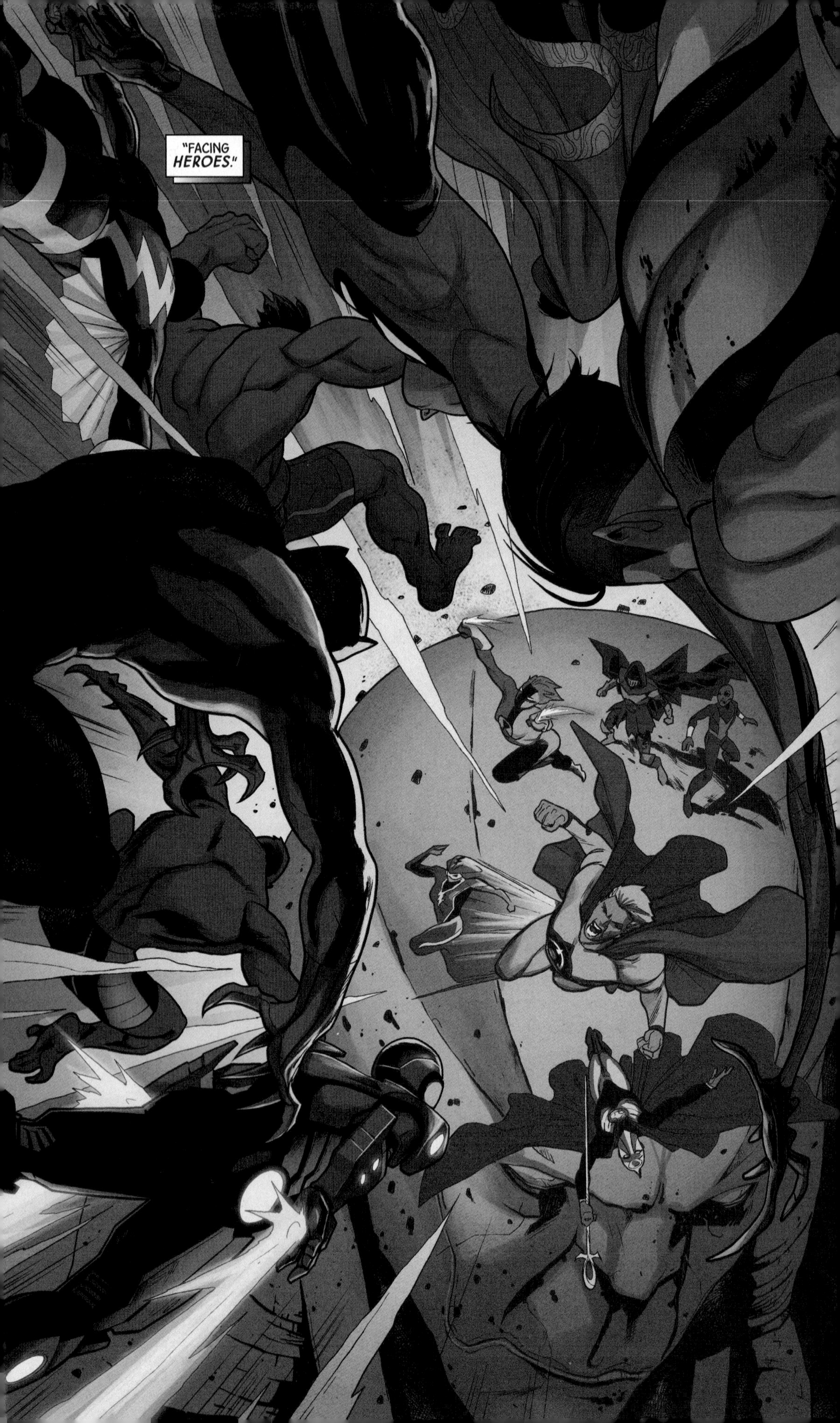
"FACING HEROES."

"WE ARE ALL MONSTERS NOW"

INCURSION.
EARTH-616 : EARTH-4,290,001.

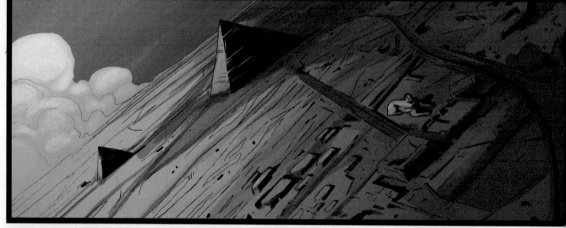

ANYTHING?

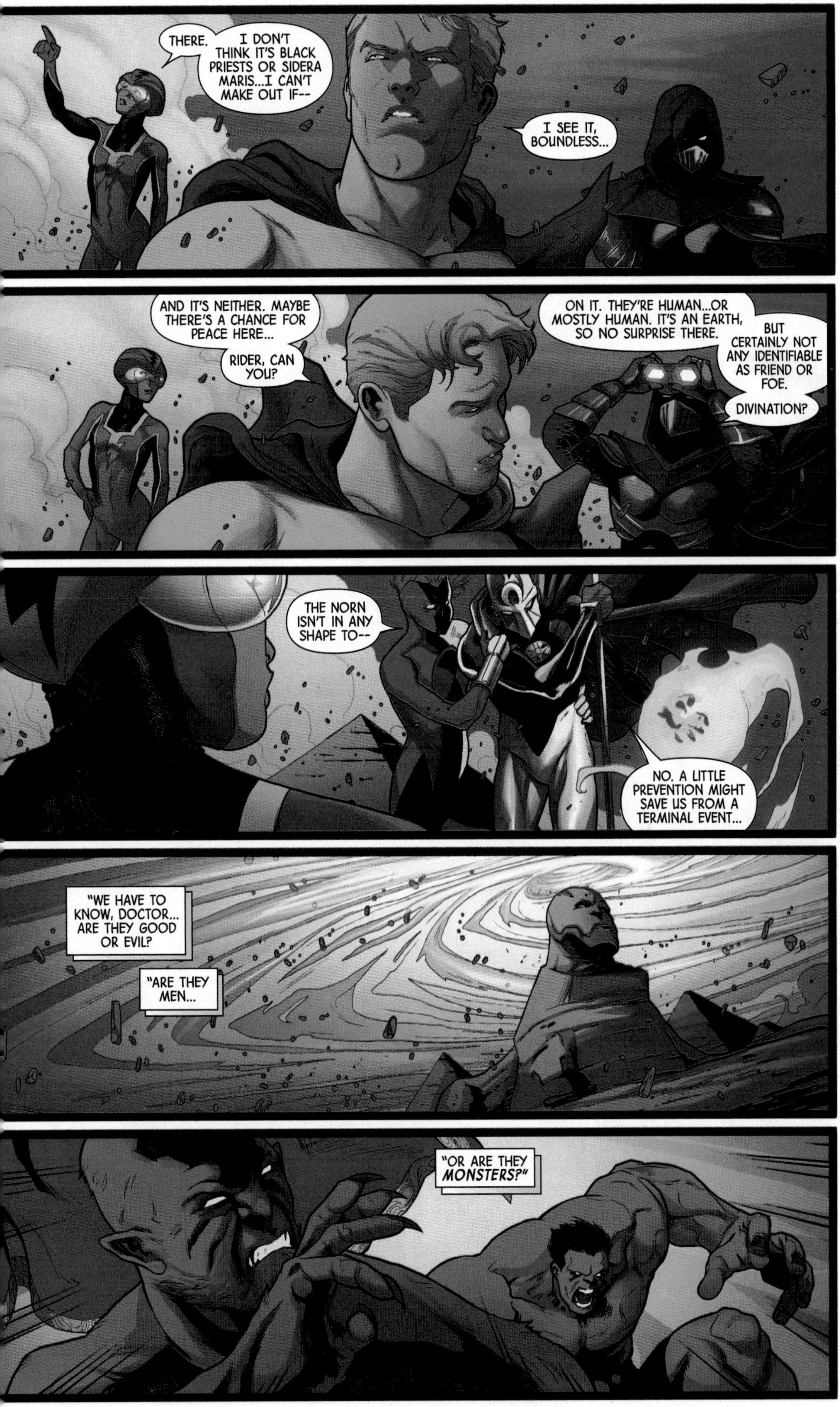
THERE.
I DON'T THINK IT'S BLACK PRIESTS OR SIDERA MARIS...I CAN'T MAKE OUT IF--
I SEE IT, BOUNDLESS...
AND IT'S NEITHER. MAYBE THERE'S A CHANCE FOR PEACE HERE...
RIDER, CAN YOU?
ON IT. THEY'RE HUMAN...OR MOSTLY HUMAN. IT'S AN EARTH, SO NO SURPRISE THERE.
BUT CERTAINLY NOT ANY IDENTIFIABLE AS FRIEND OR FOE.
DIVINATION?
THE NORN ISN'T IN ANY SHAPE TO--
NO. A LITTLE PREVENTION MIGHT SAVE US FROM A TERMINAL EVENT...
"WE HAVE TO KNOW, DOCTOR... ARE THEY GOOD OR EVIL?
"ARE THEY MEN...
"OR ARE THEY *MONSTERS?*"

THEN.

WHAT'S THIS, DOCTOR BANNER?

AN IDEA I GOT FROM THE BRAIN-DAMAGED HULK FROM ANOTHER EARTH...

HIS AVENGERS TEAMMATES COULD CONTROL HIM BY STIMULATING THE EMOTIONAL CENTERS OF HIS BRAIN. THEY BASICALLY CREATED A HULK OVERRIDE SYSTEM--CONTROLLING WHEN HE COULD BECOME THE HULK AND WHEN HE REMAINED BANNER.

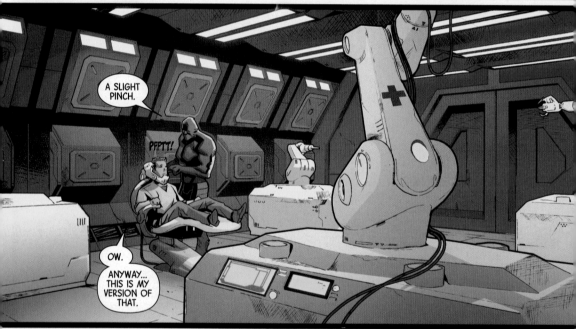

A SLIGHT PINCH.

PFPTT!

OW.

ANYWAY... THIS IS MY VERSION OF THAT.

IT'S A LIMITED WORK-AROUND THAT I'LL USE SPARINGLY...

BUT IT GIVES ME SOME MANNER OF CONTROL OVER WHEN I CHANGE--AND, FOR LACK OF A BETTER TERM, IT ALLOWS ME TO *THROTTLE BACK* WHILE GREEN WITH RAGE.

WELL, PARDON M[E] FOR STATING TH[E] OBVIOUS, BRUCE[...] BUT WHY THE LIMITATION?

IF IT WORKS, IT WORKS... NO?

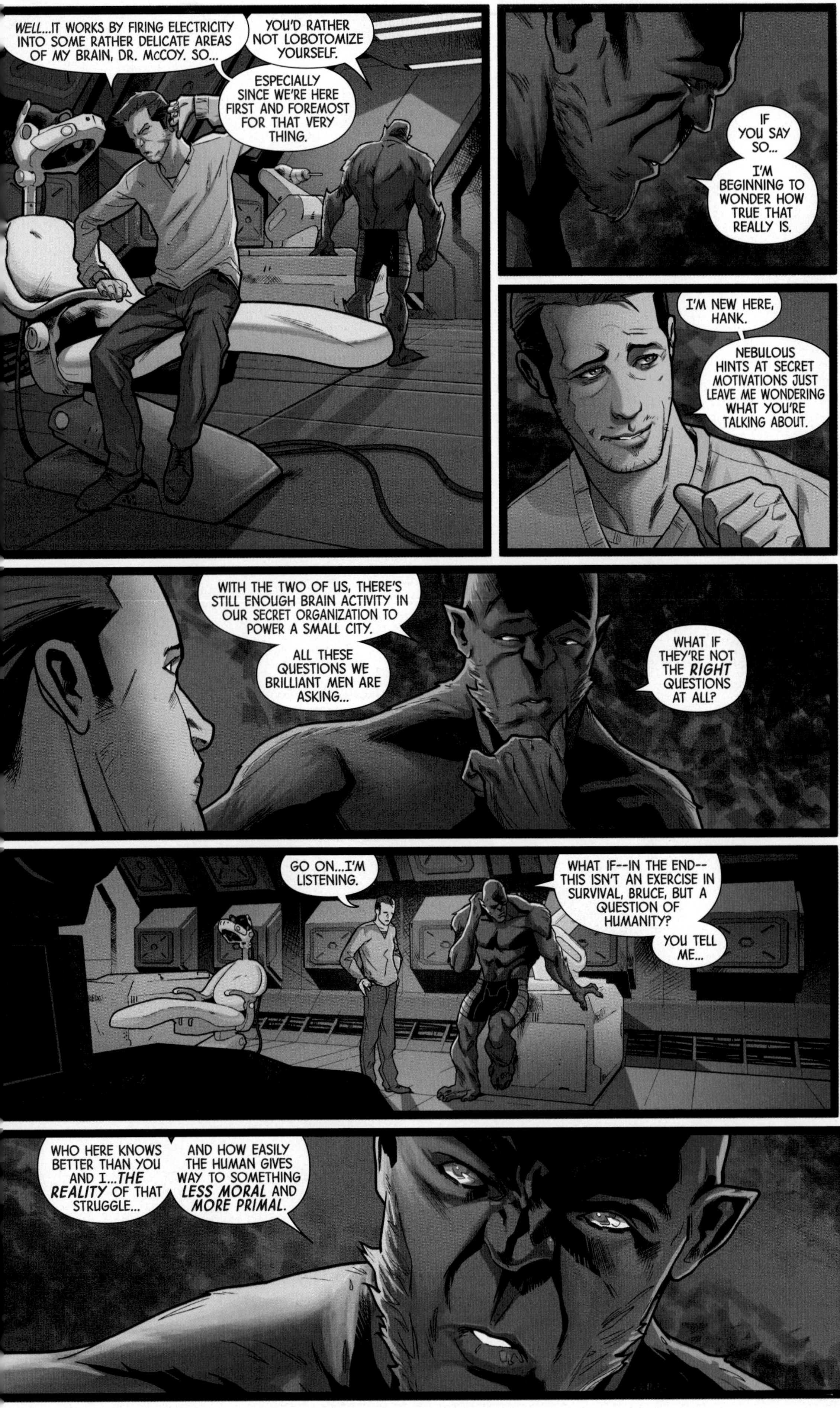
WELL...IT WORKS BY FIRING ELECTRICITY INTO SOME RATHER DELICATE AREAS OF MY BRAIN, DR. McCOY. SO...
YOU'D RATHER NOT LOBOTOMIZE YOURSELF.
ESPECIALLY SINCE WE'RE HERE FIRST AND FOREMOST FOR THAT VERY THING.
IF YOU SAY SO...
I'M BEGINNING TO WONDER HOW TRUE THAT REALLY IS.
I'M NEW HERE, HANK.
NEBULOUS HINTS AT SECRET MOTIVATIONS JUST LEAVE ME WONDERING WHAT YOU'RE TALKING ABOUT.
WITH THE TWO OF US, THERE'S STILL ENOUGH BRAIN ACTIVITY IN OUR SECRET ORGANIZATION TO POWER A SMALL CITY.
ALL THESE QUESTIONS WE BRILLIANT MEN ARE ASKING...
WHAT IF THEY'RE NOT THE RIGHT QUESTIONS AT ALL?
GO ON...I'M LISTENING.
WHAT IF--IN THE END--THIS ISN'T AN EXERCISE IN SURVIVAL, BRUCE, BUT A QUESTION OF HUMANITY?
YOU TELL ME...
WHO HERE KNOWS BETTER THAN YOU AND I...THE REALITY OF THAT STRUGGLE...
AND HOW EASILY THE HUMAN GIVES WAY TO SOMETHING LESS MORAL AND MORE PRIMAL.

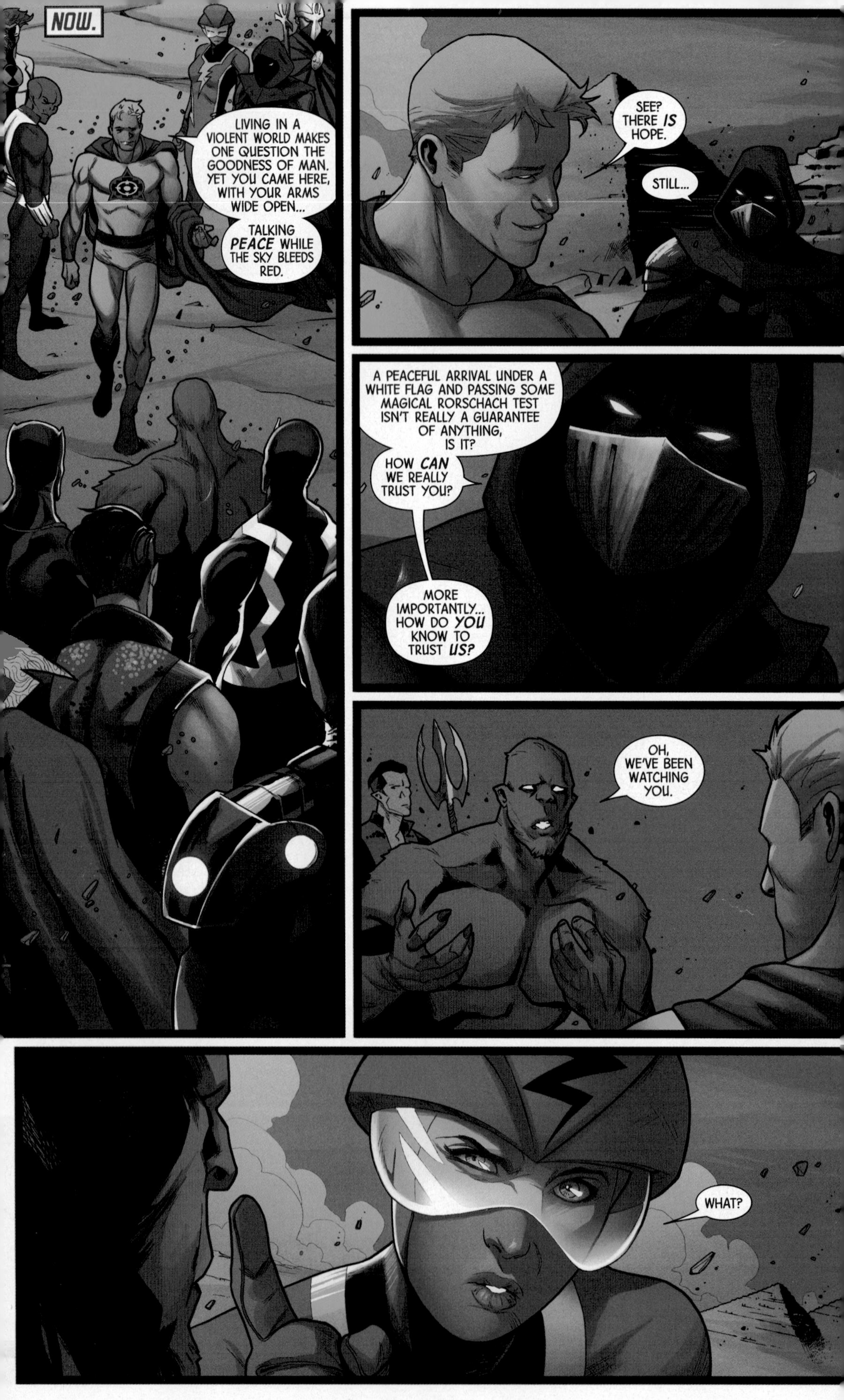
NOW.
LIVING IN A VIOLENT WORLD MAKES ONE QUESTION THE GOODNESS OF MAN. YET YOU CAME HERE, WITH YOUR ARMS WIDE OPEN...
TALKING PEACE WHILE THE SKY BLEEDS RED.
SEE? THERE IS HOPE.
STILL...
A PEACEFUL ARRIVAL UNDER A WHITE FLAG AND PASSING SOME MAGICAL RORSCHACH TEST ISN'T REALLY A GUARANTEE OF ANYTHING, IS IT?
HOW CAN WE REALLY TRUST YOU?
MORE IMPORTANTLY... HOW DO YOU KNOW TO TRUST US?
OH, WE'VE BEEN WATCHING YOU.
WHAT?

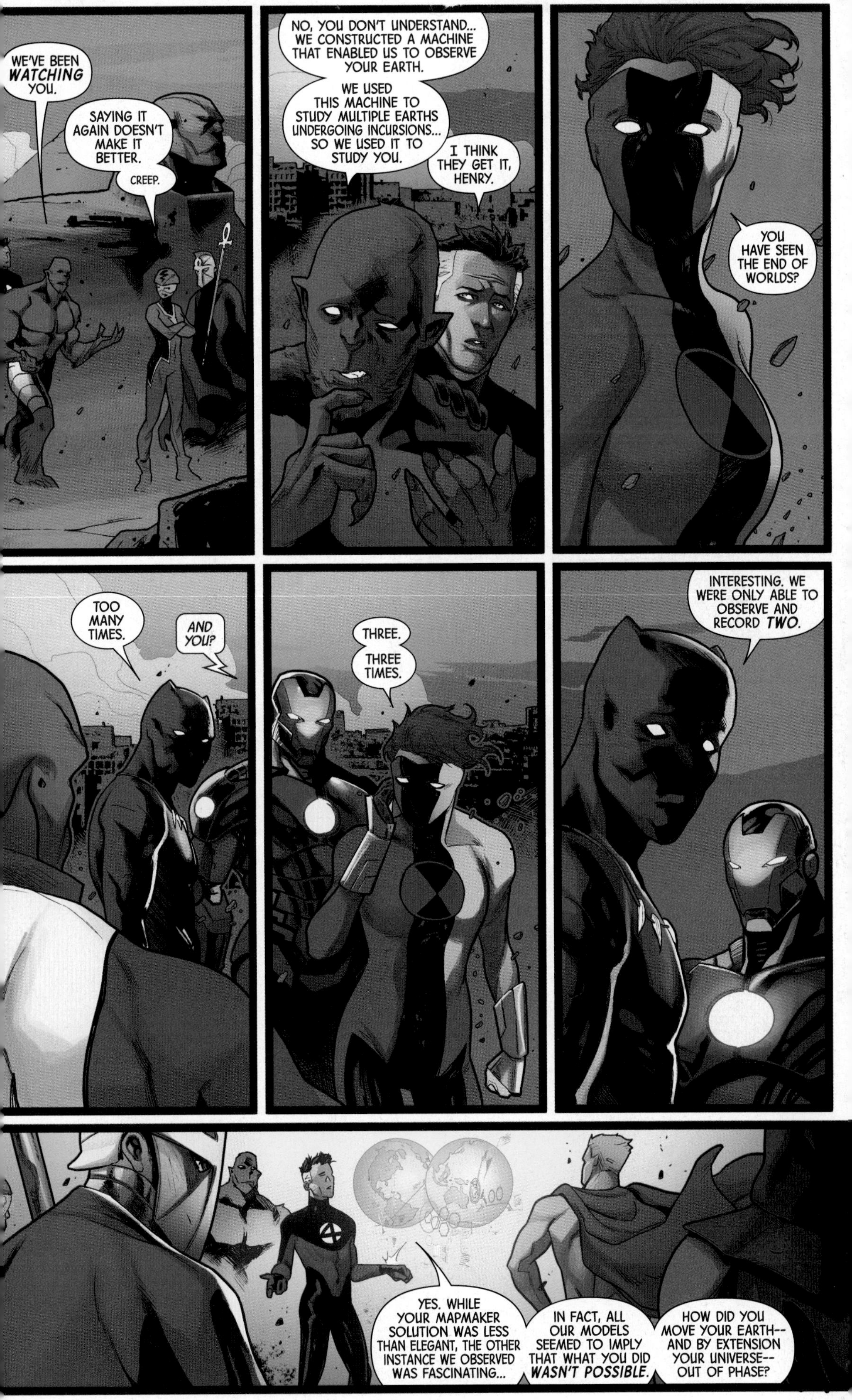

WE'VE BEEN *WATCHING* YOU.
SAYING IT AGAIN DOESN'T MAKE IT BETTER.
CREEP.
NO, YOU DON'T UNDERSTAND... WE CONSTRUCTED A MACHINE THAT ENABLED US TO OBSERVE YOUR EARTH.
WE USED THIS MACHINE TO STUDY MULTIPLE EARTHS UNDERGOING INCURSIONS... SO WE USED IT TO STUDY YOU.
I THINK THEY GET IT, HENRY.
YOU HAVE SEEN THE END OF WORLDS?
TOO MANY TIMES.
AND YOU?
THREE.
THREE TIMES.
INTERESTING. WE WERE ONLY ABLE TO OBSERVE AND RECORD *TWO*.
YES. WHILE YOUR MAPMAKER SOLUTION WAS LESS THAN ELEGANT, THE OTHER INSTANCE WE OBSERVED WAS FASCINATING...
IN FACT, ALL OUR MODELS SEEMED TO IMPLY THAT WHAT YOU DID *WASN'T POSSIBLE*.
HOW DID YOU MOVE YOUR EARTH-- AND BY EXTENSION YOUR UNIVERSE-- OUT OF PHASE?

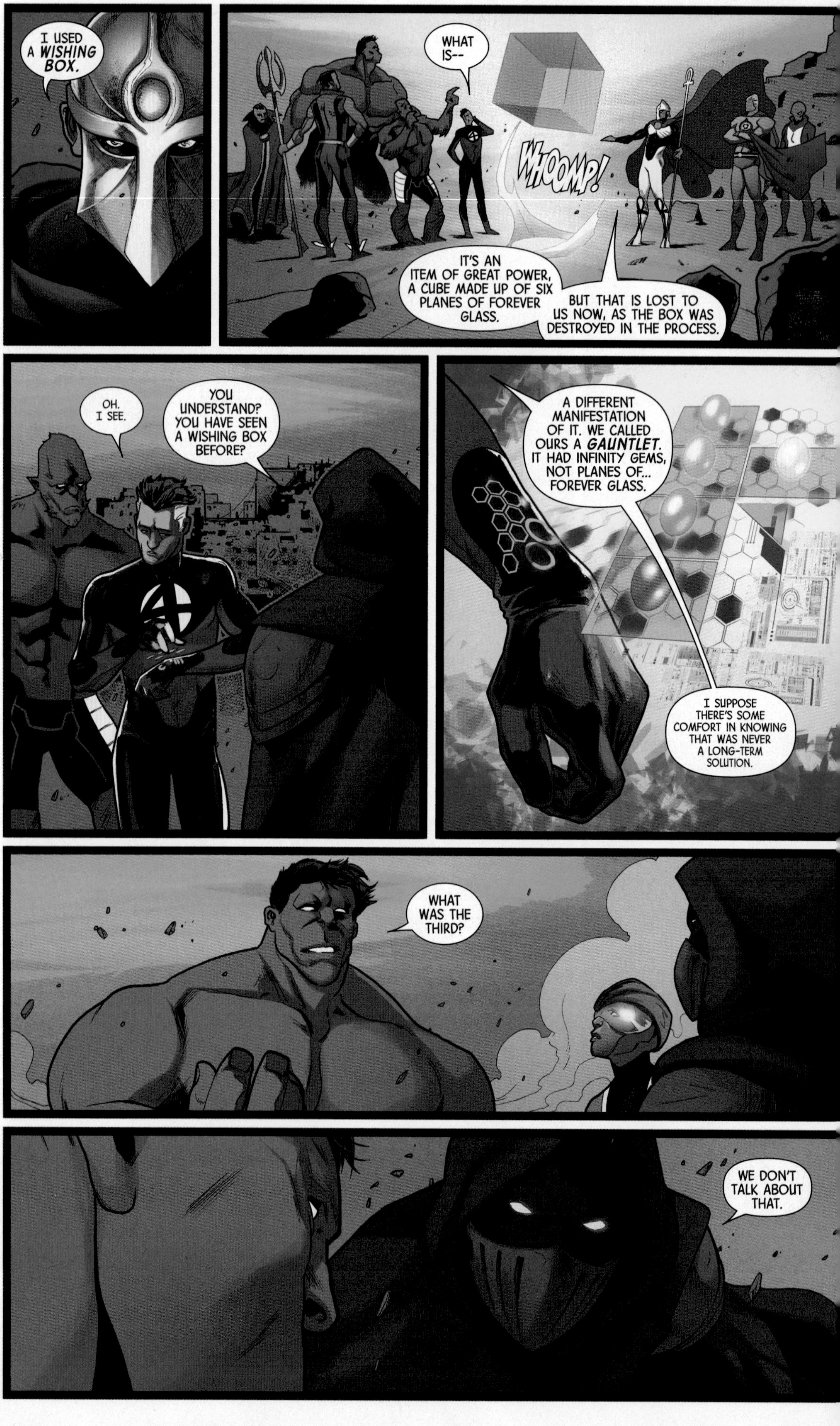
I USED A *WISHING BOX.*
WHAT IS--
WHOOMP!
IT'S AN ITEM OF GREAT POWER, A CUBE MADE UP OF SIX PLANES OF FOREVER GLASS.
BUT THAT IS LOST TO US NOW, AS THE BOX WAS DESTROYED IN THE PROCESS.
OH. I SEE.
YOU UNDERSTAND? YOU HAVE SEEN A WISHING BOX BEFORE?
A DIFFERENT MANIFESTATION OF IT. WE CALLED OURS A *GAUNTLET*. IT HAD INFINITY GEMS, NOT PLANES OF... FOREVER GLASS.
I SUPPOSE THERE'S SOME COMFORT IN KNOWING THAT WAS NEVER A LONG-TERM SOLUTION.
WHAT WAS THE THIRD?
WE DON'T TALK ABOUT THAT.

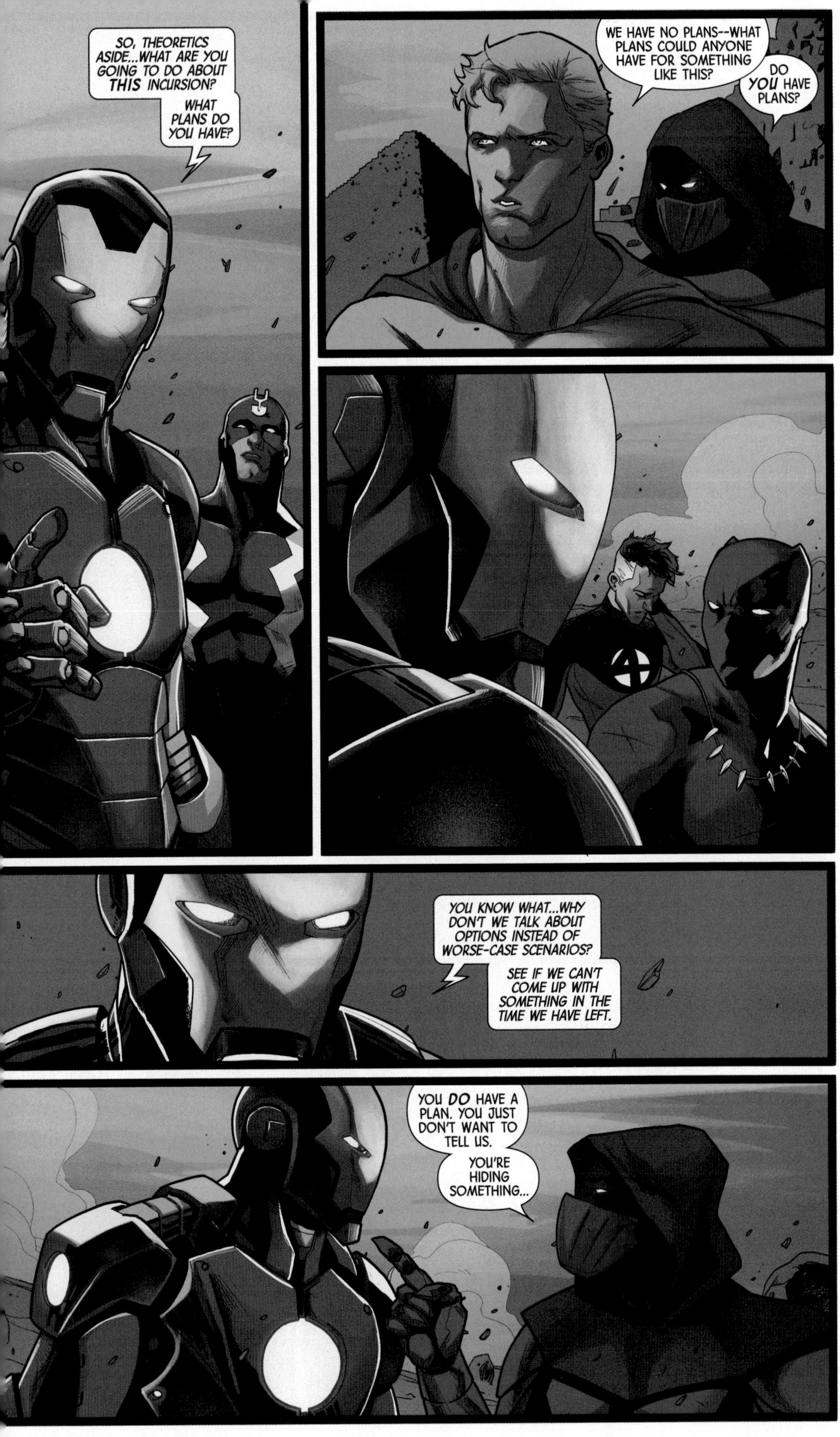
SO, THEORETICS ASIDE...WHAT ARE YOU GOING TO DO ABOUT THIS INCURSION?
WHAT PLANS DO YOU HAVE?
WE HAVE NO PLANS--WHAT PLANS COULD ANYONE HAVE FOR SOMETHING LIKE THIS?
DO YOU HAVE PLANS?
YOU KNOW WHAT...WHY DON'T WE TALK ABOUT OPTIONS INSTEAD OF WORSE-CASE SCENARIOS?
SEE IF WE CAN'T COME UP WITH SOMETHING IN THE TIME WE HAVE LEFT.
YOU DO HAVE A PLAN. YOU JUST DON'T WANT TO TELL US.
YOU'RE HIDING SOMETHING...

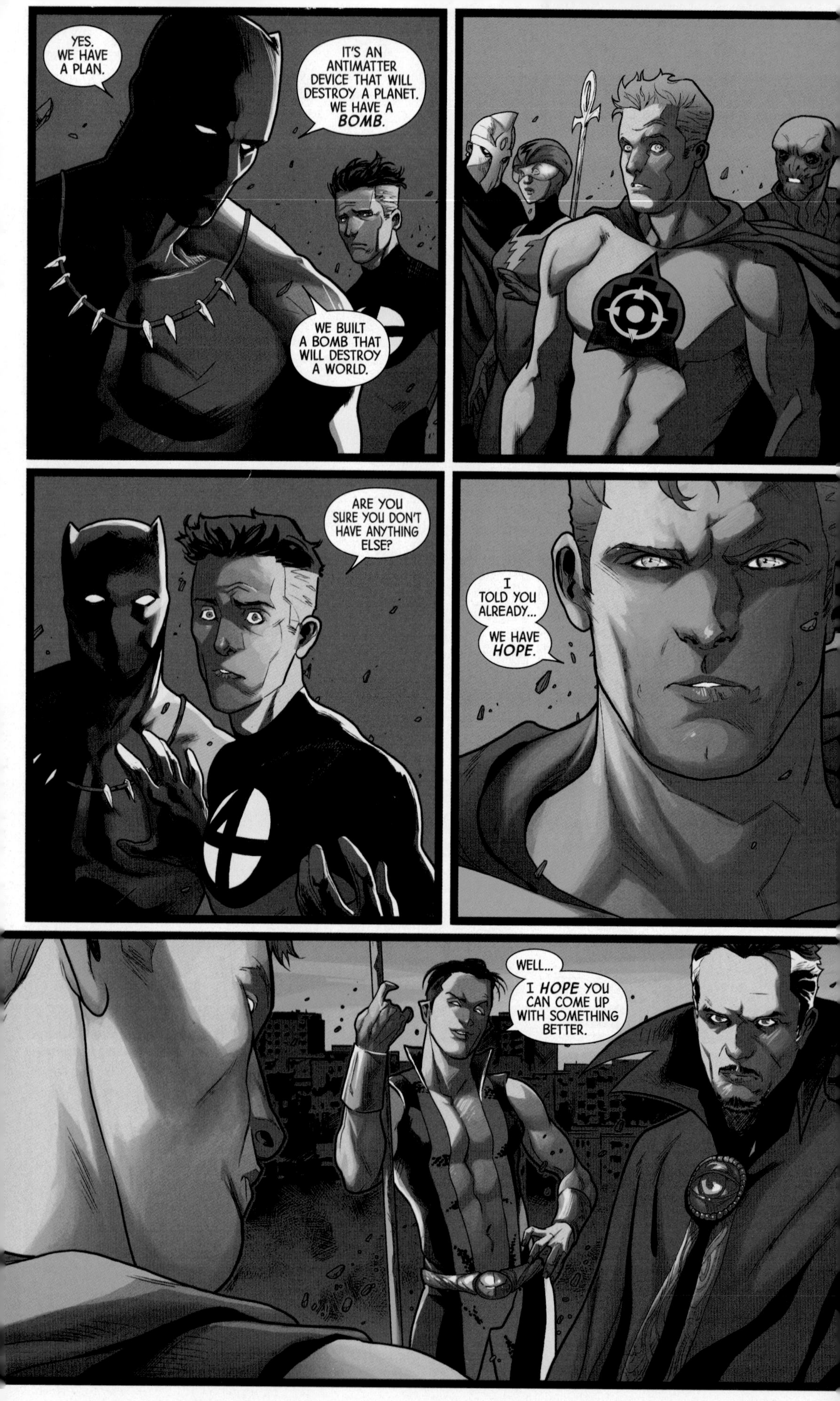
YES. WE HAVE A PLAN.
IT'S AN ANTIMATTER DEVICE THAT WILL DESTROY A PLANET. WE HAVE A BOMB.
WE BUILT A BOMB THAT WILL DESTROY A WORLD.
ARE YOU SURE YOU DON'T HAVE ANYTHING ELSE?
I TOLD YOU ALREADY...
WE HAVE HOPE.
WELL...
I HOPE YOU CAN COME UP WITH SOMETHING BETTER.

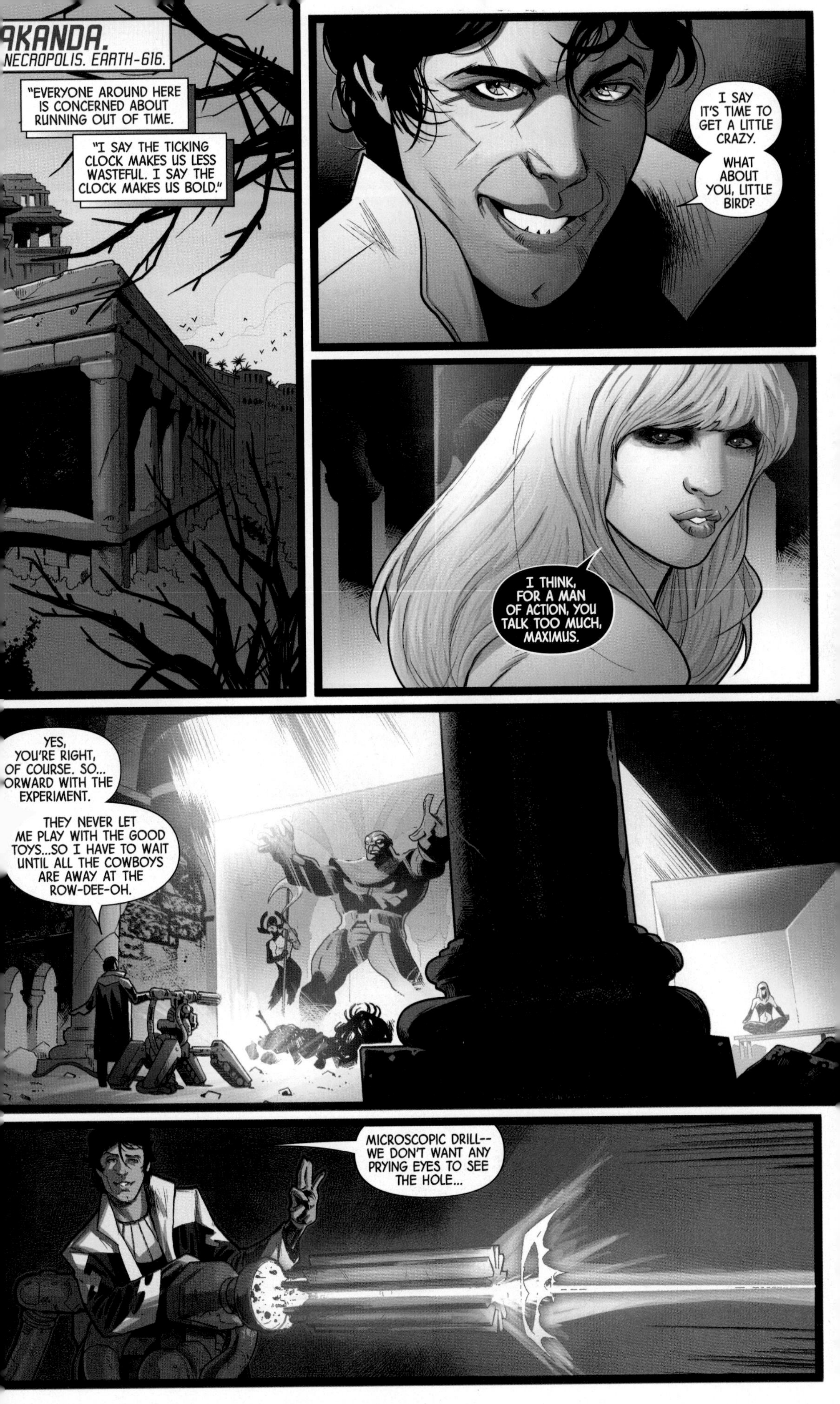
AKANDA.
NECROPOLIS. EARTH-616.
"EVERYONE AROUND HERE IS CONCERNED ABOUT RUNNING OUT OF TIME.
"I SAY THE TICKING CLOCK MAKES US LESS WASTEFUL. I SAY THE CLOCK MAKES US BOLD."
I SAY IT'S TIME TO GET A LITTLE CRAZY.
WHAT ABOUT YOU, LITTLE BIRD?
I THINK, FOR A MAN OF ACTION, YOU TALK TOO MUCH, MAXIMUS.
YES, YOU'RE RIGHT, OF COURSE. SO... ORWARD WITH THE EXPERIMENT.
THEY NEVER LET ME PLAY WITH THE GOOD TOYS...SO I HAVE TO WAIT UNTIL ALL THE COWBOYS ARE AWAY AT THE ROW-DEE-OH.
MICROSCOPIC DRILL-- WE DON'T WANT ANY PRYING EYES TO SEE THE HOLE...

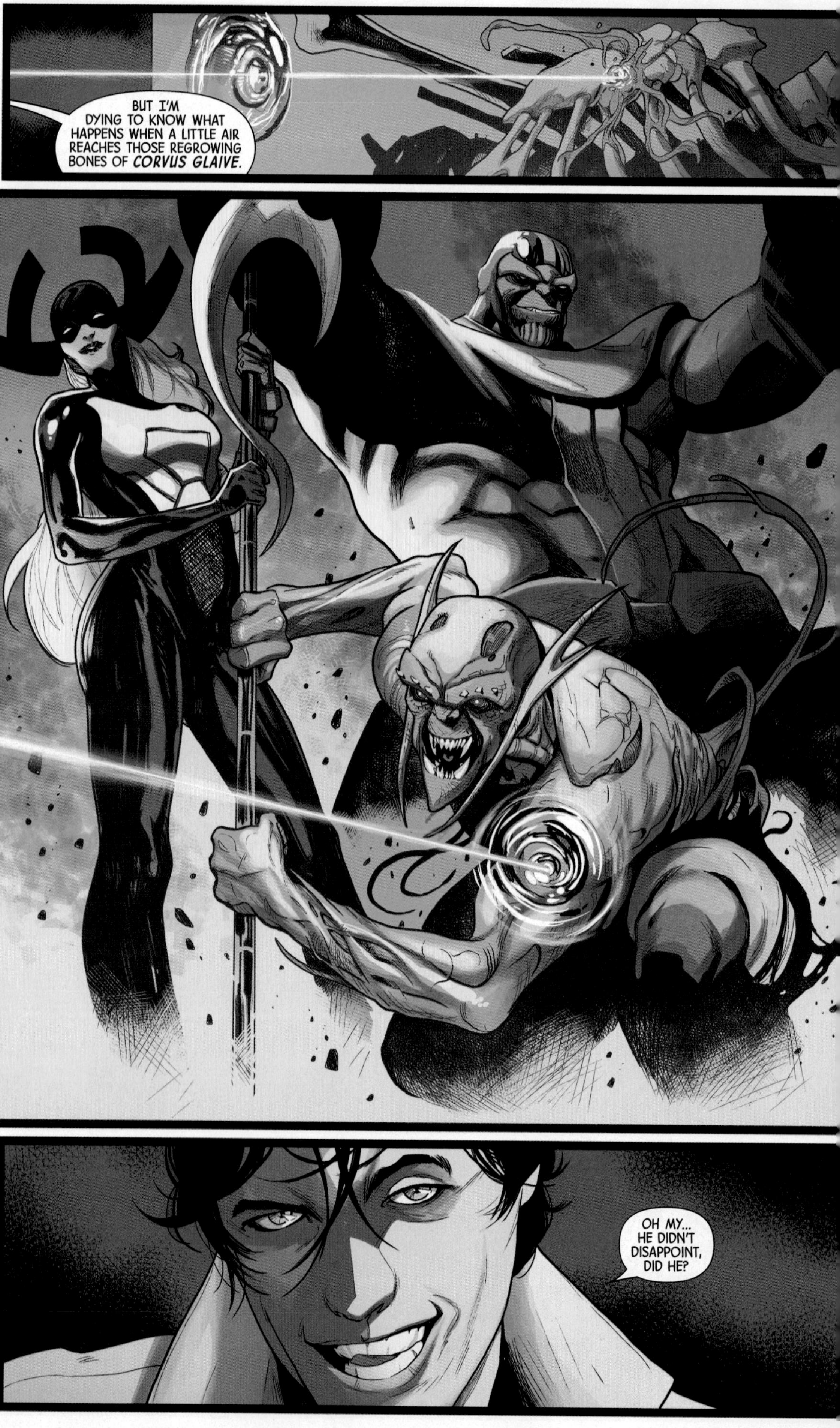
BUT I'M DYING TO KNOW WHAT HAPPENS WHEN A LITTLE AIR REACHES THOSE REGROWING BONES OF *CORVUS GLAIVE*.
OH MY... HE DIDN'T DISAPPOINT, DID HE?

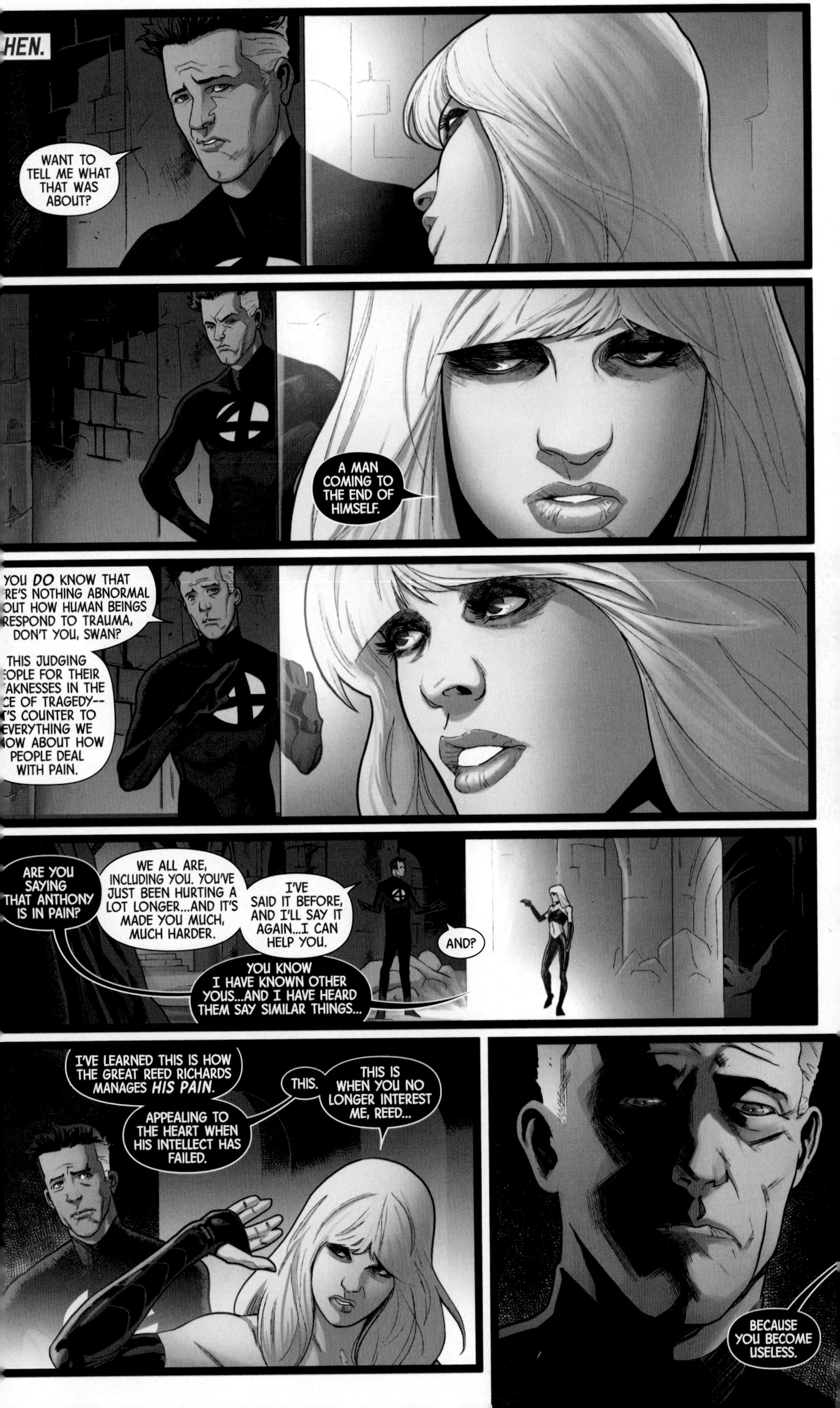

HEN.
WANT TO TELL ME WHAT THAT WAS ABOUT?
A MAN COMING TO THE END OF HIMSELF.
YOU DO KNOW THAT 'RE'S NOTHING ABNORMAL OUT HOW HUMAN BEINGS RESPOND TO TRAUMA, DON'T YOU, SWAN?
THIS JUDGING EOPLE FOR THEIR 'AKNESSES IN THE CE OF TRAGEDY-- T'S COUNTER TO EVERYTHING WE IOW ABOUT HOW PEOPLE DEAL WITH PAIN.
ARE YOU SAYING THAT ANTHONY IS IN PAIN?
WE ALL ARE, INCLUDING YOU. YOU'VE JUST BEEN HURTING A LOT LONGER...AND IT'S MADE YOU MUCH, MUCH HARDER.
I'VE SAID IT BEFORE, AND I'LL SAY IT AGAIN...I CAN HELP YOU.
AND?
YOU KNOW I HAVE KNOWN OTHER YOUS...AND I HAVE HEARD THEM SAY SIMILAR THINGS...
I'VE LEARNED THIS IS HOW THE GREAT REED RICHARDS MANAGES HIS PAIN.
APPEALING TO THE HEART WHEN HIS INTELLECT HAS FAILED.
THIS.
THIS IS WHEN YOU NO LONGER INTEREST ME, REED...
BECAUSE YOU BECOME USELESS.

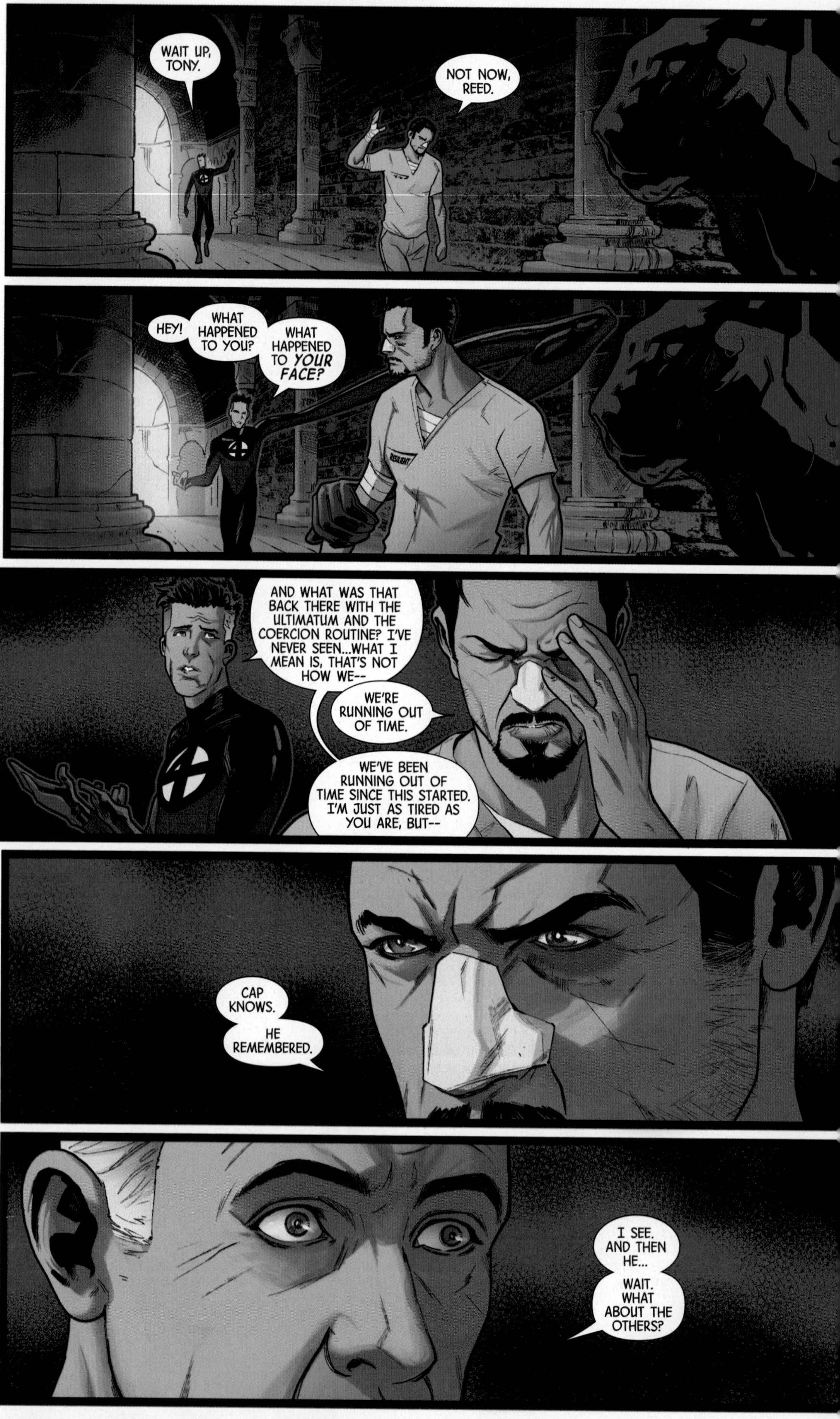
WAIT UP, TONY.
NOT NOW, REED.
HEY!
WHAT HAPPENED TO YOU?
WHAT HAPPENED TO YOUR FACE?
RESILIENT
AND WHAT WAS THAT BACK THERE WITH THE ULTIMATUM AND THE COERCION ROUTINE? I'VE NEVER SEEN...WHAT I MEAN IS, THAT'S NOT HOW WE--
WE'RE RUNNING OUT OF TIME.
WE'VE BEEN RUNNING OUT OF TIME SINCE THIS STARTED. I'M JUST AS TIRED AS YOU ARE, BUT--
CAP KNOWS.
HE REMEMBERED.
I SEE. AND THEN HE...
WAIT. WHAT ABOUT THE OTHERS?

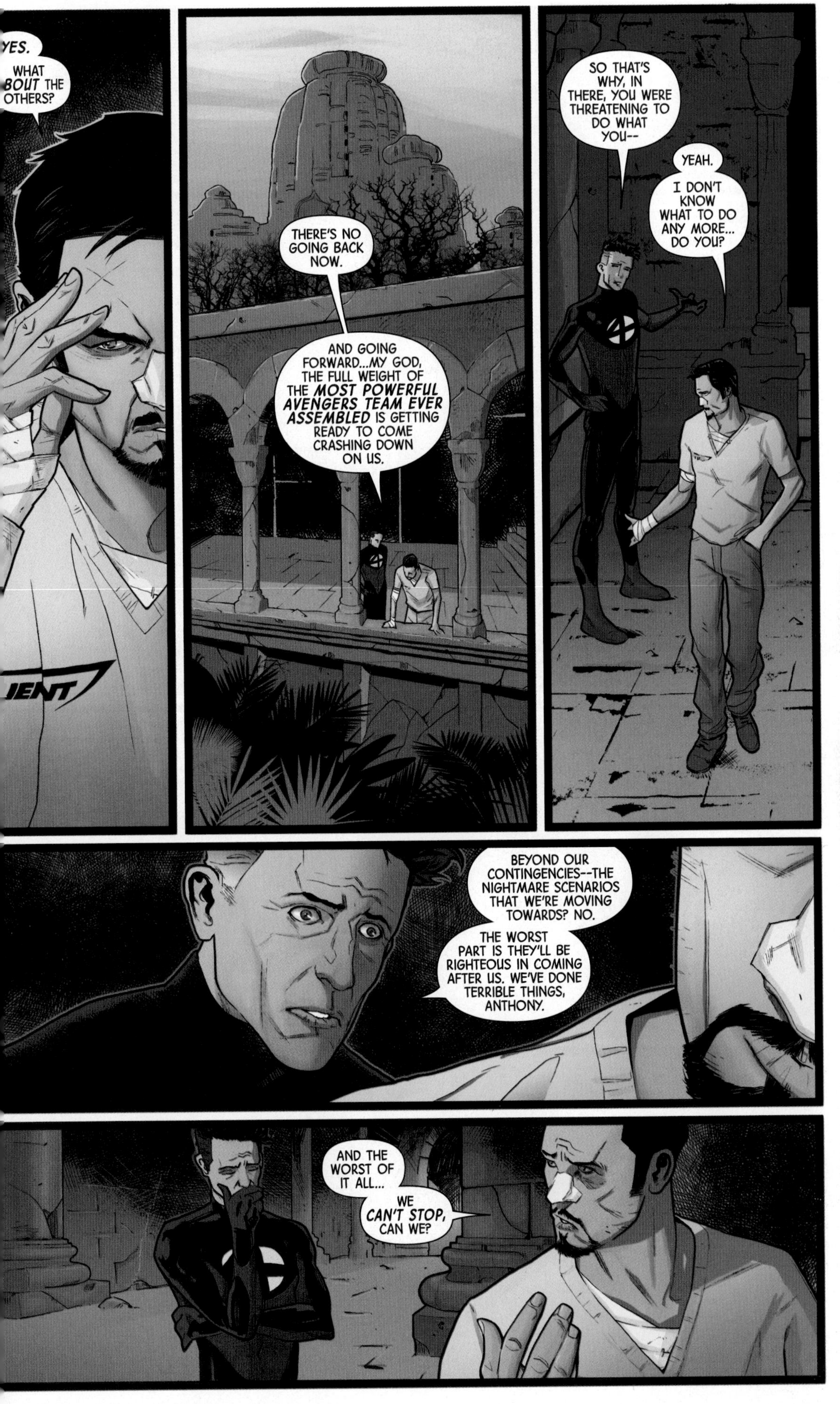
YES.
WHAT BOUT THE OTHERS?
THERE'S NO GOING BACK NOW.
AND GOING FORWARD...MY GOD, THE FULL WEIGHT OF THE MOST POWERFUL AVENGERS TEAM EVER ASSEMBLED IS GETTING READY TO COME CRASHING DOWN ON US.
SO THAT'S WHY, IN THERE, YOU WERE THREATENING TO DO WHAT YOU--
YEAH.
I DON'T KNOW WHAT TO DO ANY MORE... DO YOU?
BEYOND OUR CONTINGENCIES--THE NIGHTMARE SCENARIOS THAT WE'RE MOVING TOWARDS? NO.
THE WORST PART IS THEY'LL BE RIGHTEOUS IN COMING AFTER US. WE'VE DONE TERRIBLE THINGS, ANTHONY.
AND THE WORST OF IT ALL...
WE CAN'T STOP, CAN WE?

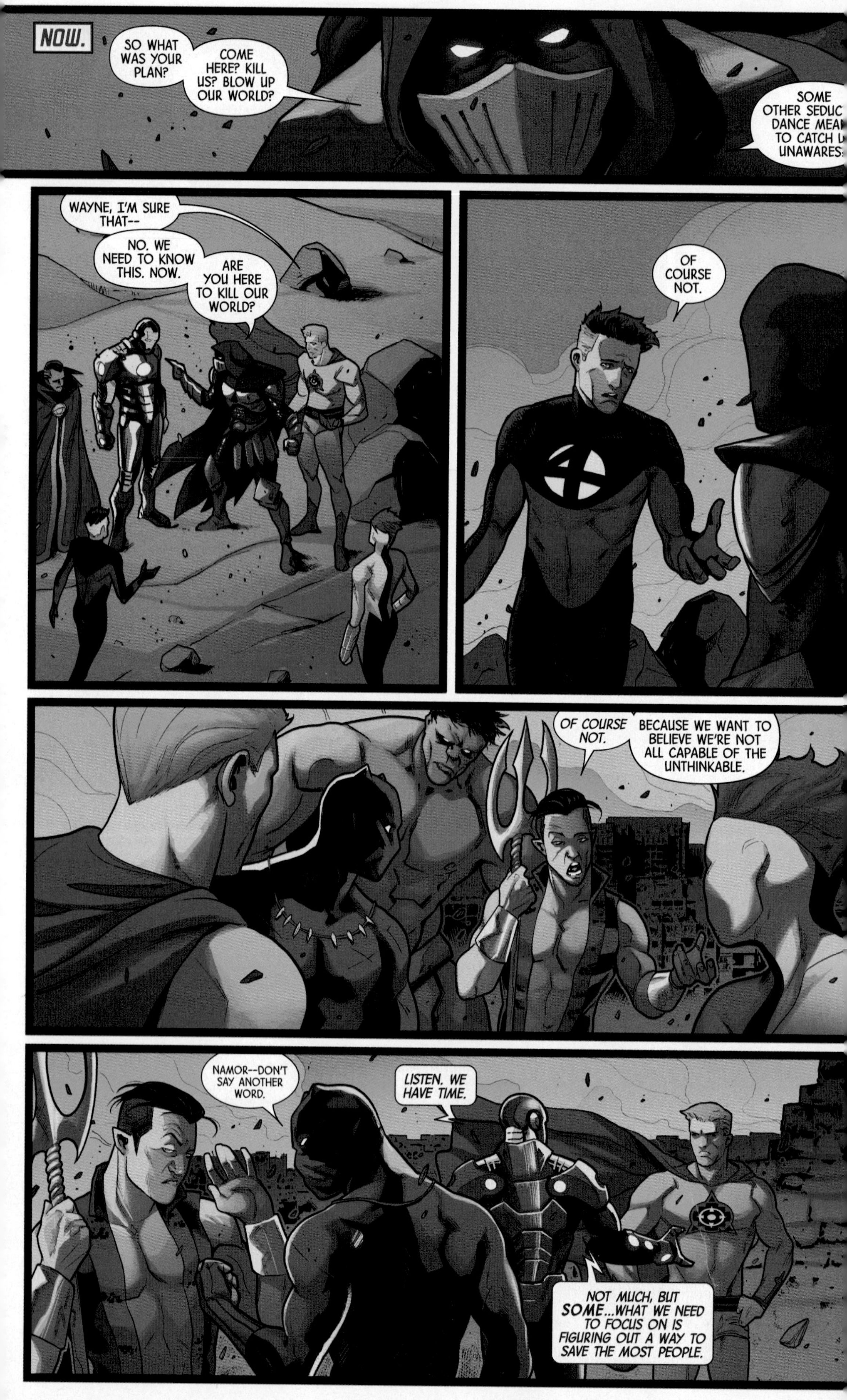
NOW.
SO WHAT WAS YOUR PLAN?
COME HERE? KILL US? BLOW UP OUR WORLD?
SOME OTHER SEDUC DANCE MEA TO CATCH UNAWARES
WAYNE, I'M SURE THAT--
NO. WE NEED TO KNOW THIS. NOW.
ARE YOU HERE TO KILL OUR WORLD?
OF COURSE NOT.
OF COURSE NOT.
BECAUSE WE WANT TO BELIEVE WE'RE NOT ALL CAPABLE OF THE UNTHINKABLE.
NAMOR--DON'T SAY ANOTHER WORD.
LISTEN. WE HAVE TIME.
NOT MUCH, BUT SOME...WHAT WE NEED TO FOCUS ON IS FIGURING OUT A WAY TO SAVE THE MOST PEOPLE.

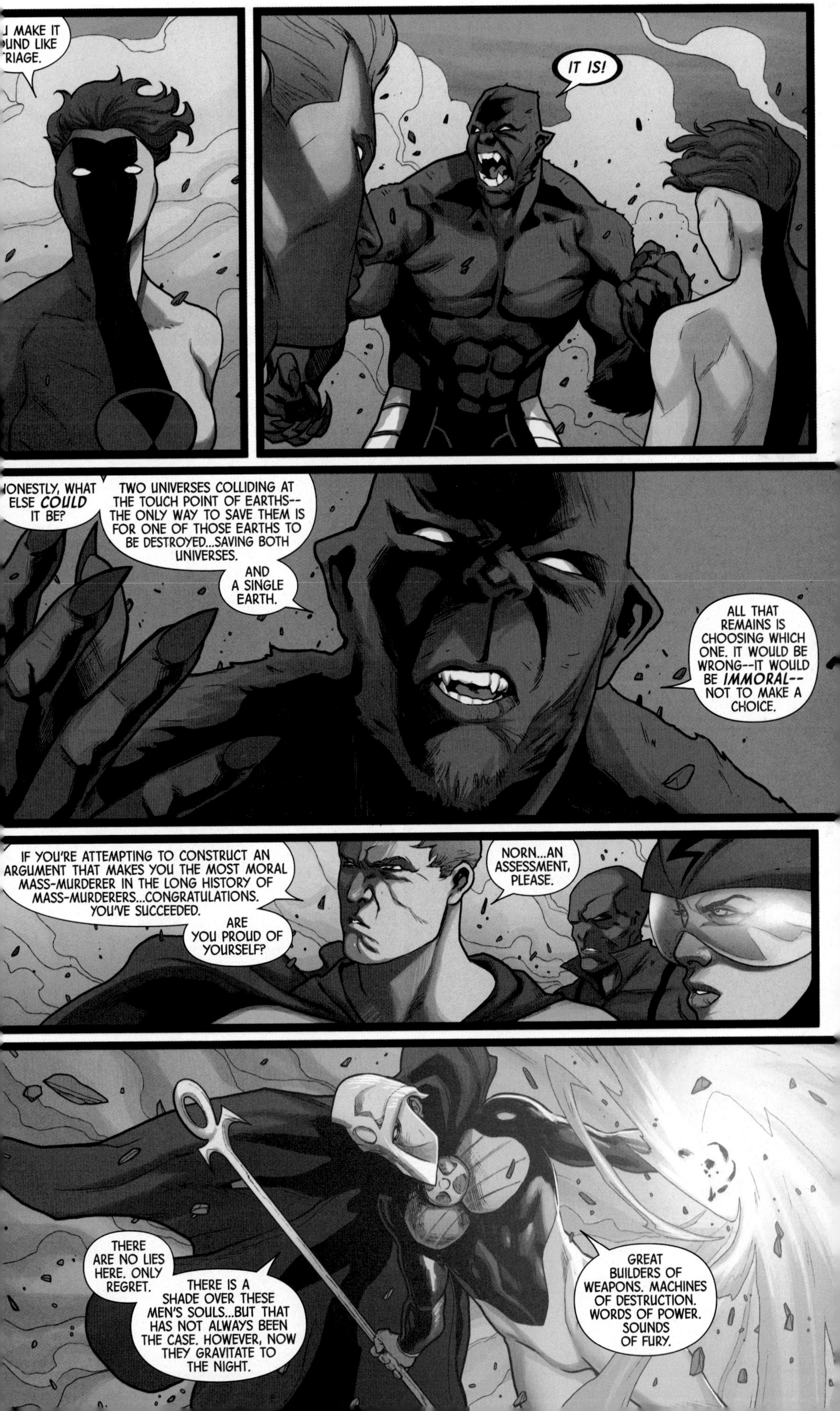

…U MAKE IT …UND LIKE …RIAGE.
IT IS!
…ONESTLY, WHAT ELSE COULD IT BE?
TWO UNIVERSES COLLIDING AT THE TOUCH POINT OF EARTHS-- THE ONLY WAY TO SAVE THEM IS FOR ONE OF THOSE EARTHS TO BE DESTROYED...SAVING BOTH UNIVERSES.
AND A SINGLE EARTH.
ALL THAT REMAINS IS CHOOSING WHICH ONE. IT WOULD BE WRONG--IT WOULD BE IMMORAL-- NOT TO MAKE A CHOICE.
IF YOU'RE ATTEMPTING TO CONSTRUCT AN ARGUMENT THAT MAKES YOU THE MOST MORAL MASS-MURDERER IN THE LONG HISTORY OF MASS-MURDERERS...CONGRATULATIONS. YOU'VE SUCCEEDED.
ARE YOU PROUD OF YOURSELF?
NORN...AN ASSESSMENT, PLEASE.
THERE ARE NO LIES HERE. ONLY REGRET.
THERE IS A SHADE OVER THESE MEN'S SOULS...BUT THAT HAS NOT ALWAYS BEEN THE CASE. HOWEVER, NOW THEY GRAVITATE TO THE NIGHT.
GREAT BUILDERS OF WEAPONS. MACHINES OF DESTRUCTION. WORDS OF POWER. SOUNDS OF FURY.

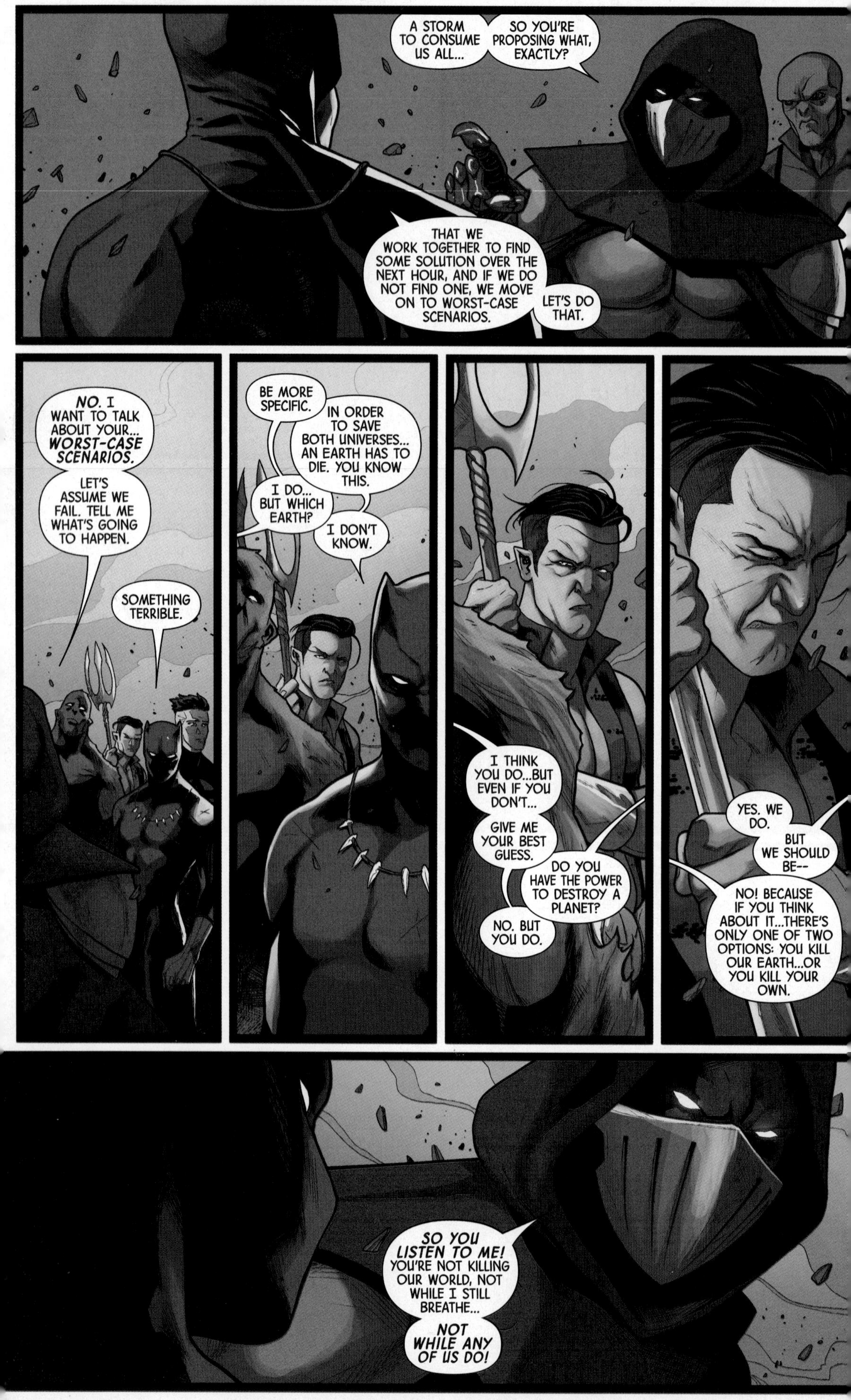
A STORM TO CONSUME US ALL...
SO YOU'RE PROPOSING WHAT, EXACTLY?
THAT WE WORK TOGETHER TO FIND SOME SOLUTION OVER THE NEXT HOUR, AND IF WE DO NOT FIND ONE, WE MOVE ON TO WORST-CASE SCENARIOS.
LET'S DO THAT.
NO. I WANT TO TALK ABOUT YOUR... WORST-CASE SCENARIOS.
LET'S ASSUME WE FAIL. TELL ME WHAT'S GOING TO HAPPEN.
SOMETHING TERRIBLE.
BE MORE SPECIFIC.
IN ORDER TO SAVE BOTH UNIVERSES... AN EARTH HAS TO DIE. YOU KNOW THIS.
I DO... BUT WHICH EARTH?
I DON'T KNOW.
I THINK YOU DO...BUT EVEN IF YOU DON'T...
GIVE ME YOUR BEST GUESS.
DO YOU HAVE THE POWER TO DESTROY A PLANET?
NO. BUT YOU DO.
YES. WE DO.
BUT WE SHOULD BE--
NO! BECAUSE IF YOU THINK ABOUT IT...THERE'S ONLY ONE OF TWO OPTIONS: YOU KILL OUR EARTH...OR YOU KILL YOUR OWN.
SO YOU LISTEN TO ME! YOU'RE NOT KILLING OUR WORLD, NOT WHILE I STILL BREATHE...
NOT WHILE ANY OF US DO!

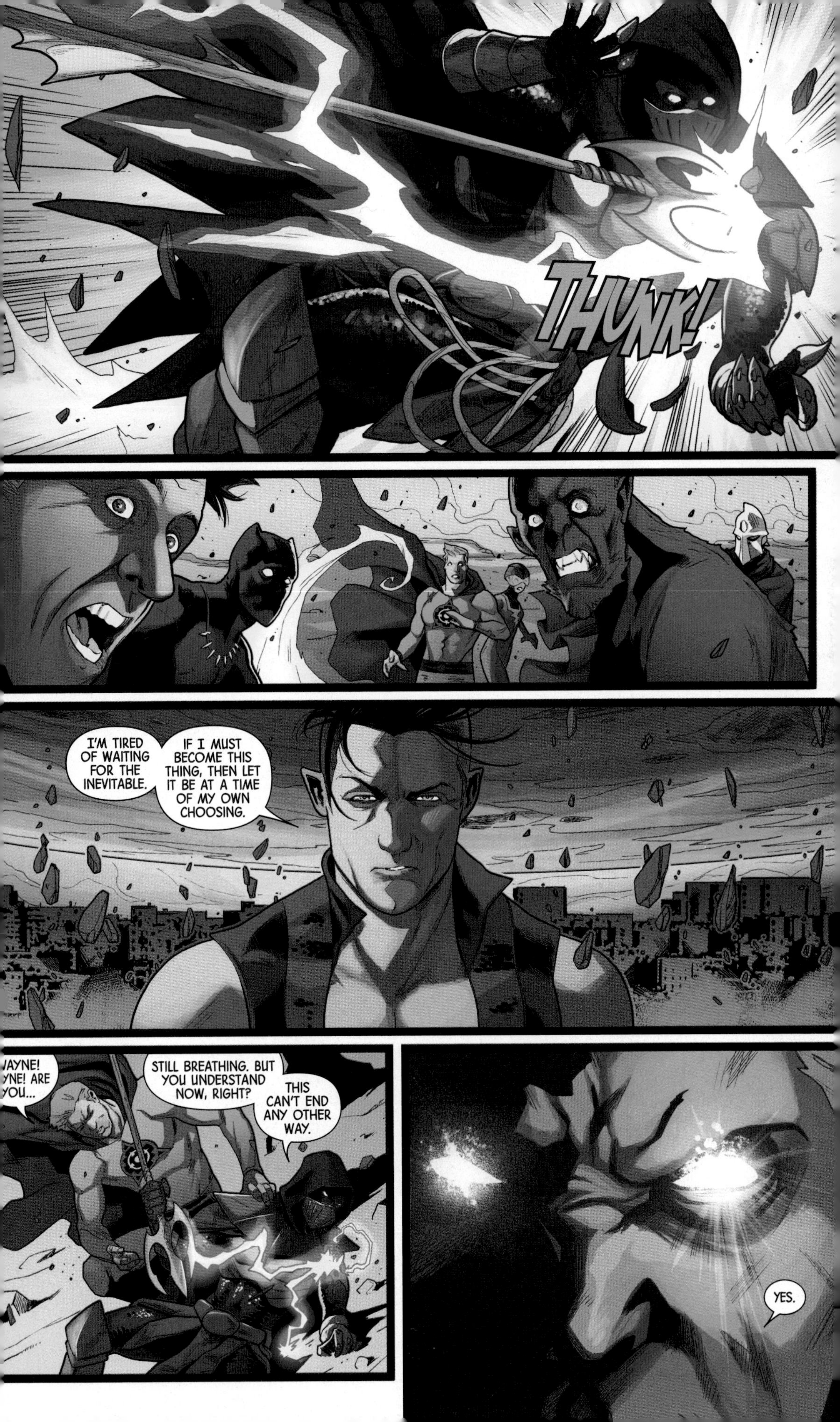
THUNK!
I'M TIRED OF WAITING FOR THE INEVITABLE.
IF I MUST BECOME THIS THING, THEN LET IT BE AT A TIME OF MY OWN CHOOSING.
AYNE! YNE! ARE YOU...
STILL BREATHING. BUT YOU UNDERSTAND NOW, RIGHT?
THIS CAN'T END ANY OTHER WAY.
YES.

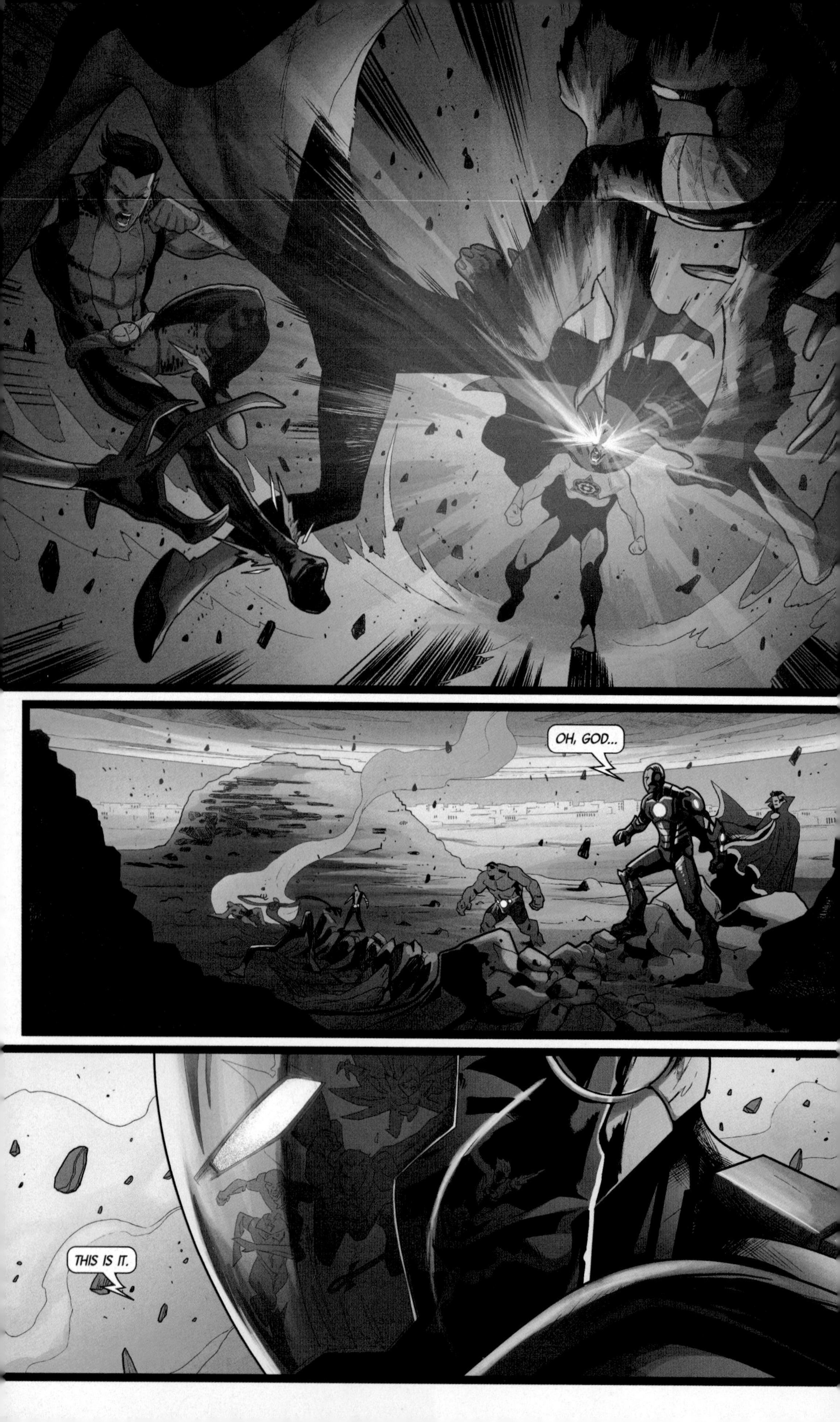
OH, GOD...
THIS IS IT.

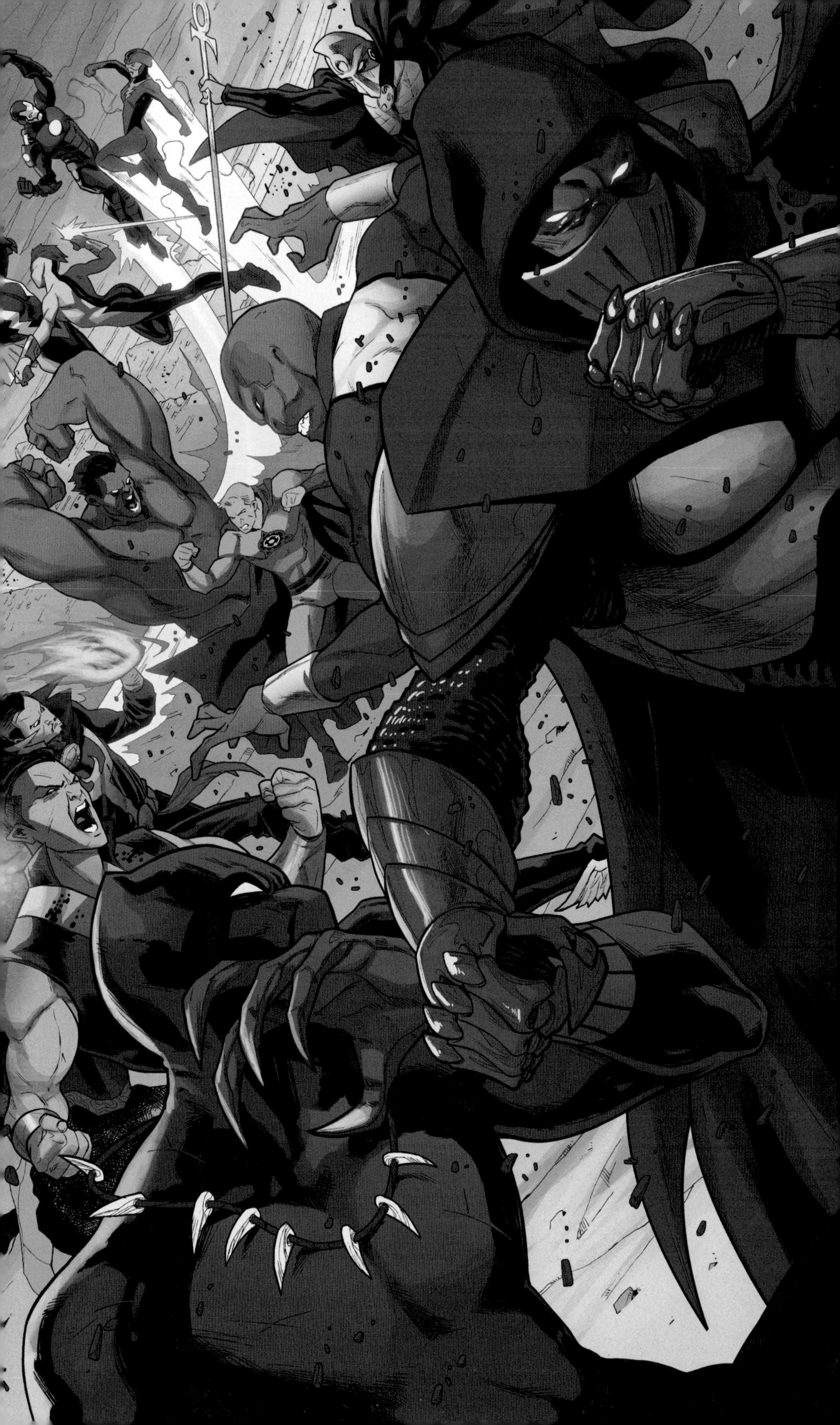

"BLU'DAKORR"

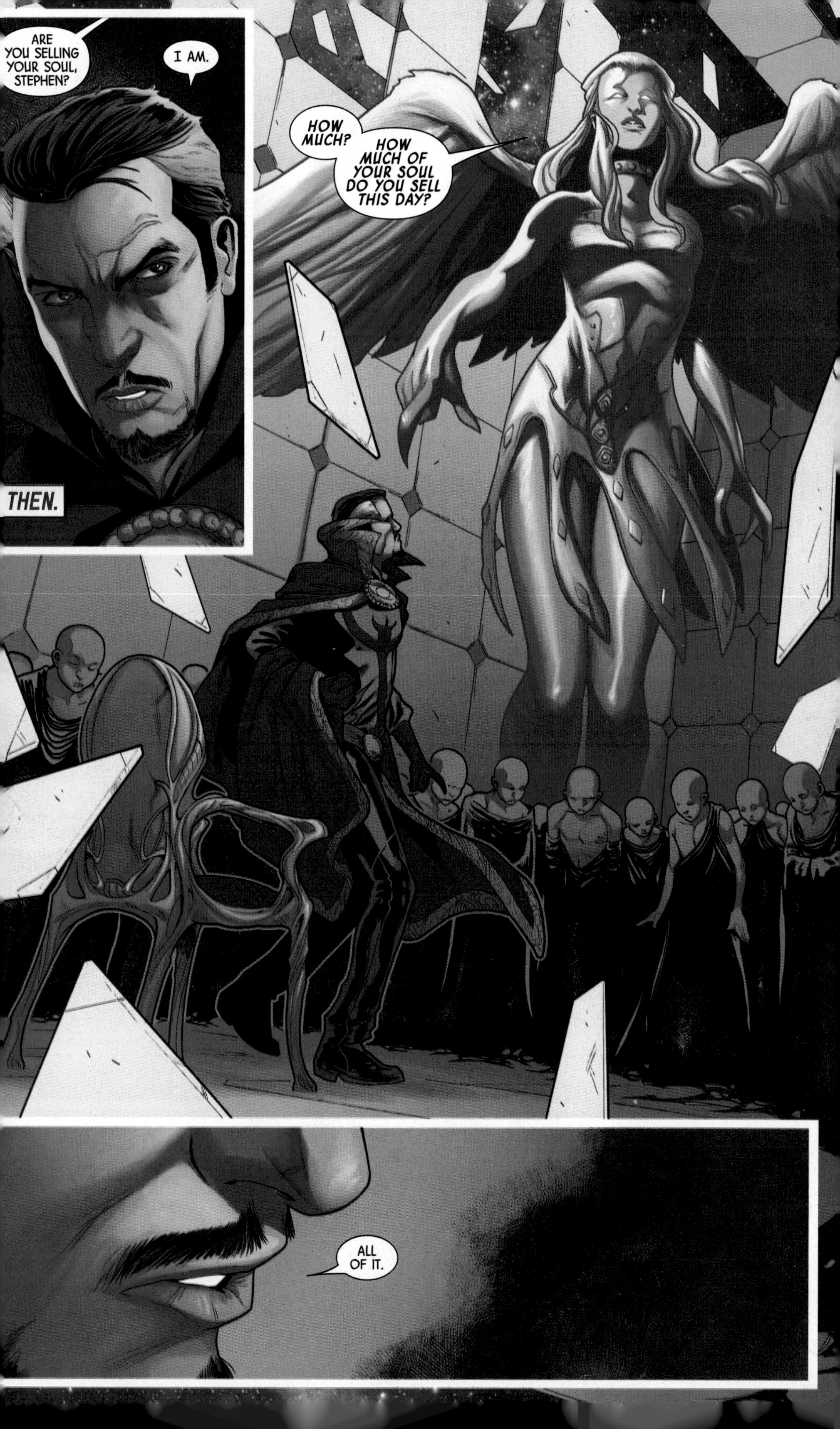
ARE YOU SELLING YOUR SOUL, STEPHEN?
I AM.
THEN.
HOW MUCH?
HOW MUCH OF YOUR SOUL DO YOU SELL THIS DAY?
ALL OF IT.

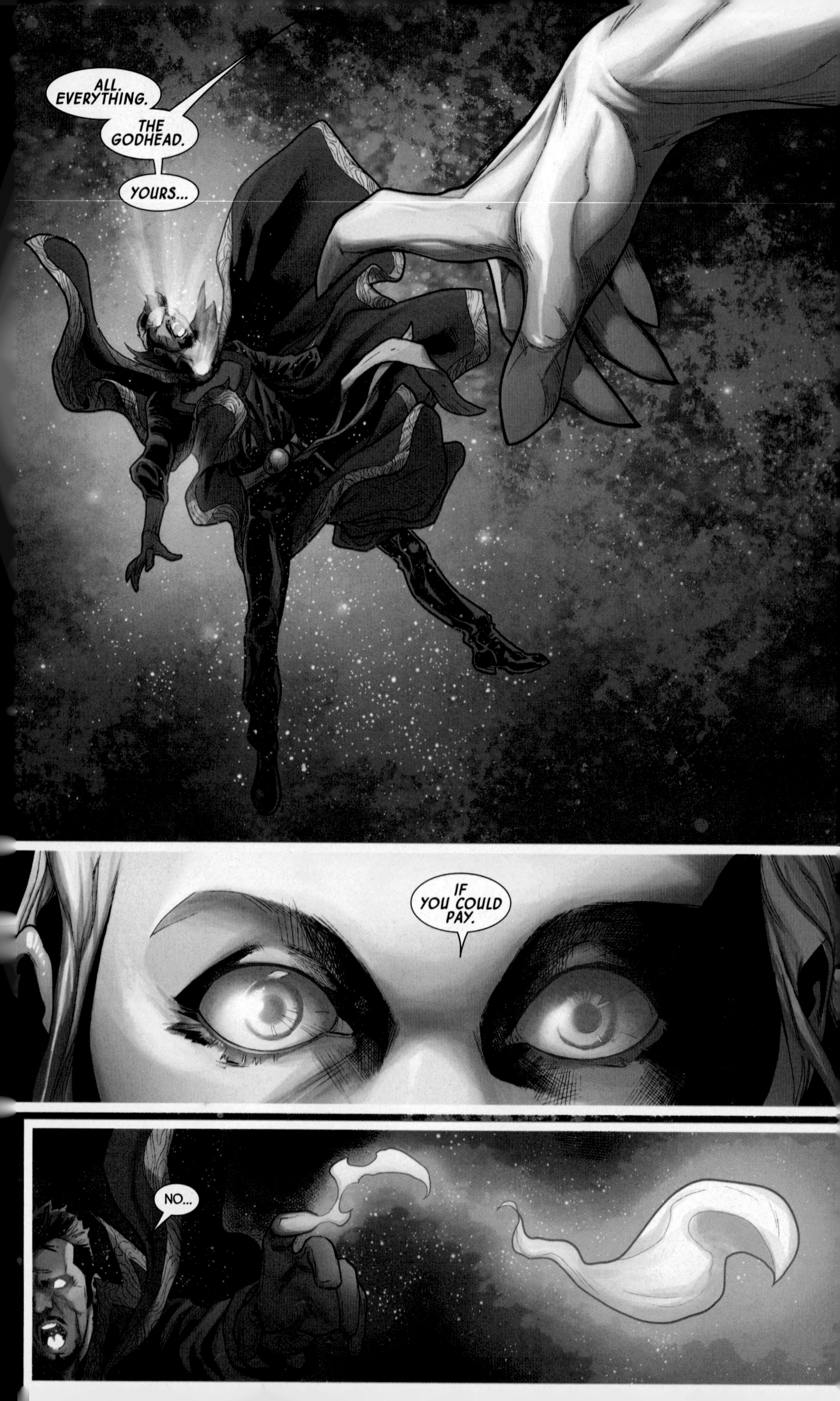
ALL. EVERYTHING.
THE GODHEAD.
YOURS...
IF YOU COULD PAY.
NO...

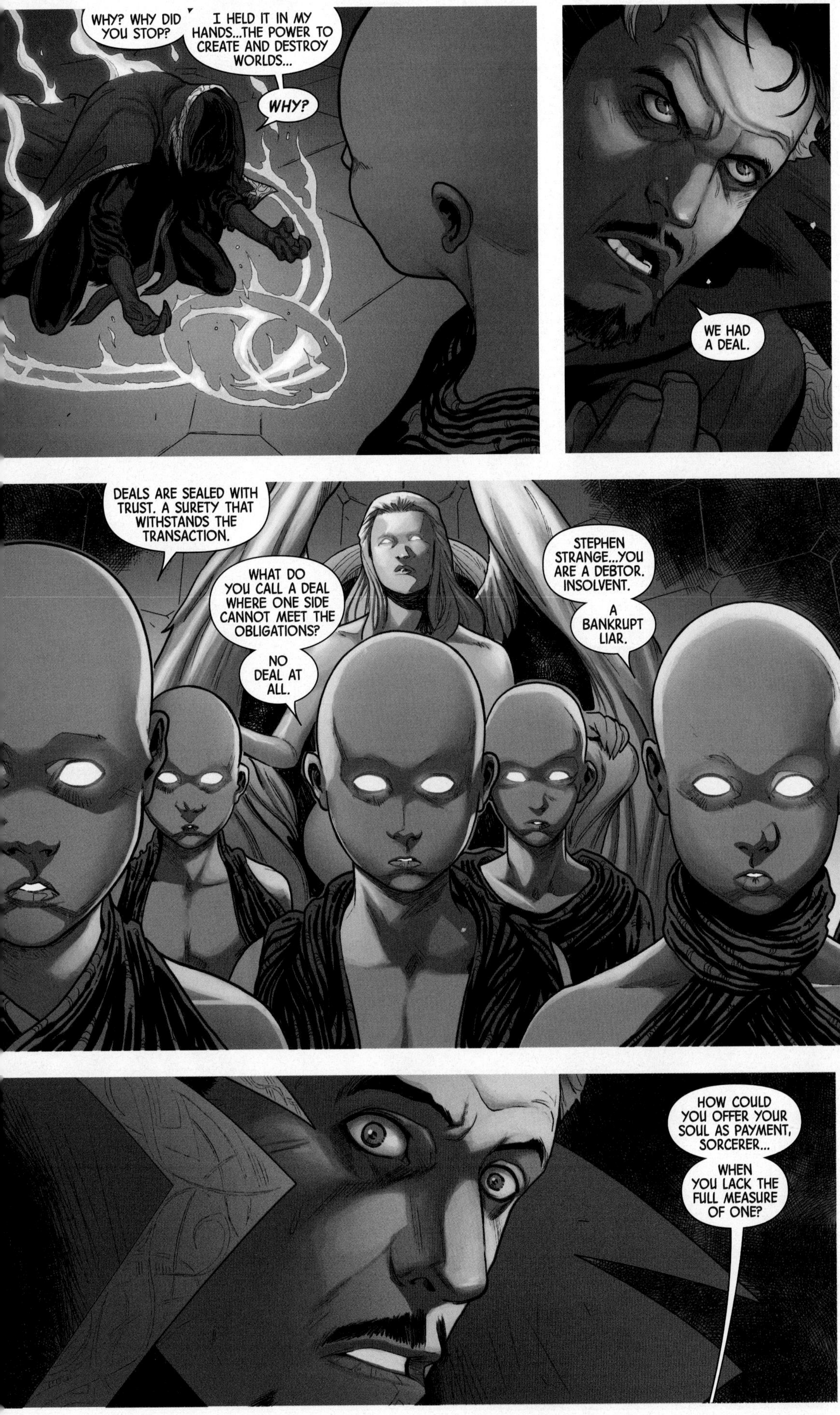
WHY? WHY DID YOU STOP?
I HELD IT IN MY HANDS...THE POWER TO CREATE AND DESTROY WORLDS...
WHY?
WE HAD A DEAL.
DEALS ARE SEALED WITH TRUST. A SURETY THAT WITHSTANDS THE TRANSACTION.
WHAT DO YOU CALL A DEAL WHERE ONE SIDE CANNOT MEET THE OBLIGATIONS?
NO DEAL AT ALL.
STEPHEN STRANGE...YOU ARE A DEBTOR. INSOLVENT.
A BANKRUPT LIAR.
HOW COULD YOU OFFER YOUR SOUL AS PAYMENT, SORCERER...
WHEN YOU LACK THE FULL MEASURE OF ONE?

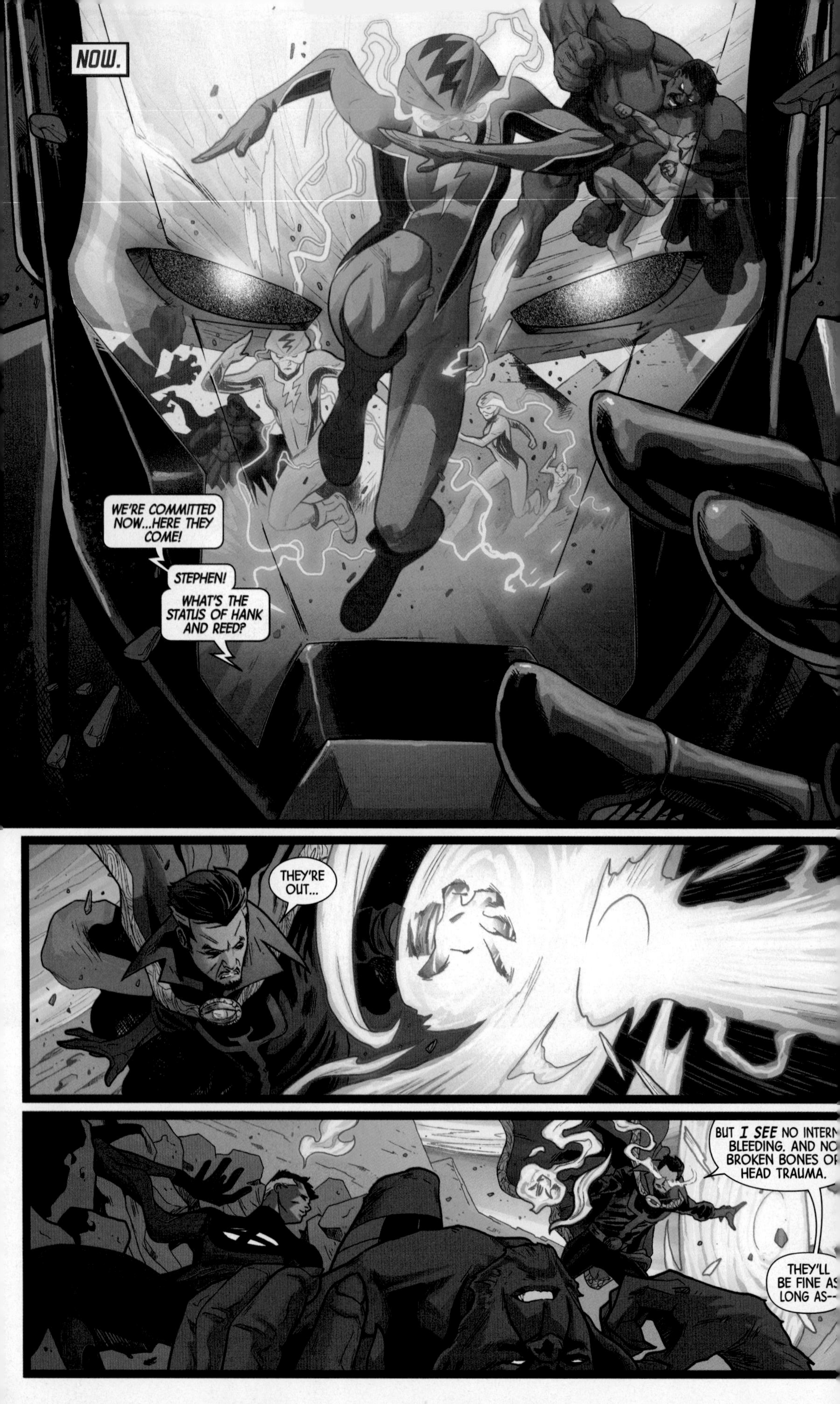
NOW.
WE'RE COMMITTED NOW...HERE THEY COME!
STEPHEN!
WHAT'S THE STATUS OF HANK AND REED?
THEY'RE OUT...
BUT I SEE NO INTERN
BLEEDING. AND NO
BROKEN BONES OR
HEAD TRAUMA.
THEY'LL BE FINE AS LONG AS--

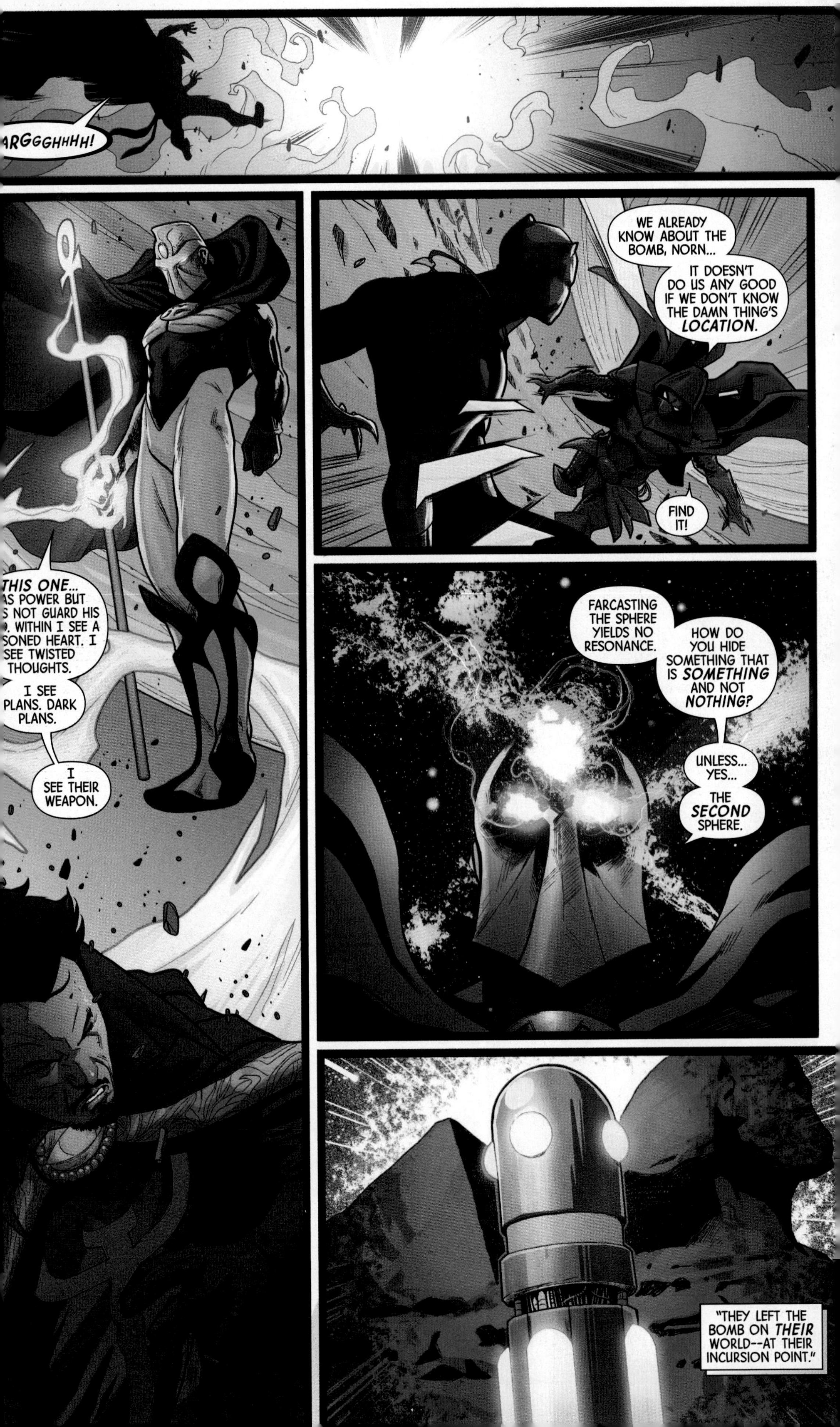
ARGGGHHHH!
THIS ONE... AS POWER BUT S NOT GUARD HIS . WITHIN I SEE A SONED HEART. I SEE TWISTED THOUGHTS.
I SEE PLANS. DARK PLANS.
I SEE THEIR WEAPON.
WE ALREADY KNOW ABOUT THE BOMB, NORN...
IT DOESN'T DO US ANY GOOD IF WE DON'T KNOW THE DAMN THING'S LOCATION.
FIND IT!
FARCASTING THE SPHERE YIELDS NO RESONANCE.
HOW DO YOU HIDE SOMETHING THAT IS SOMETHING AND NOT NOTHING?
UNLESS... YES...
THE SECOND SPHERE.
"THEY LEFT THE BOMB ON THEIR WORLD--AT THEIR INCURSION POINT."

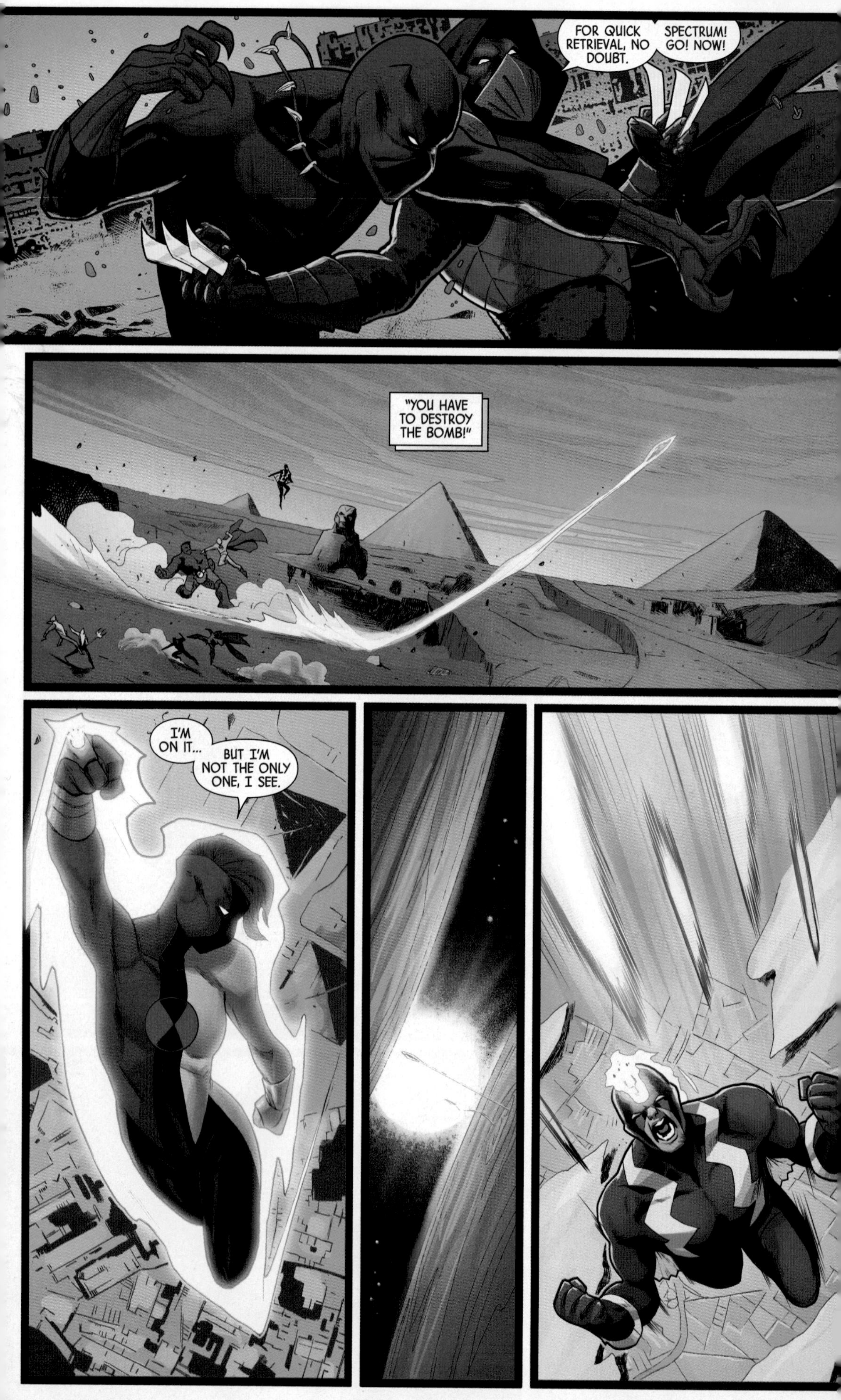
FOR QUICK RETRIEVAL, NO DOUBT.
SPECTRUM! GO! NOW!
"YOU HAVE TO DESTROY THE BOMB!"
I'M ON IT...
BUT I'M NOT THE ONLY ONE, I SEE.

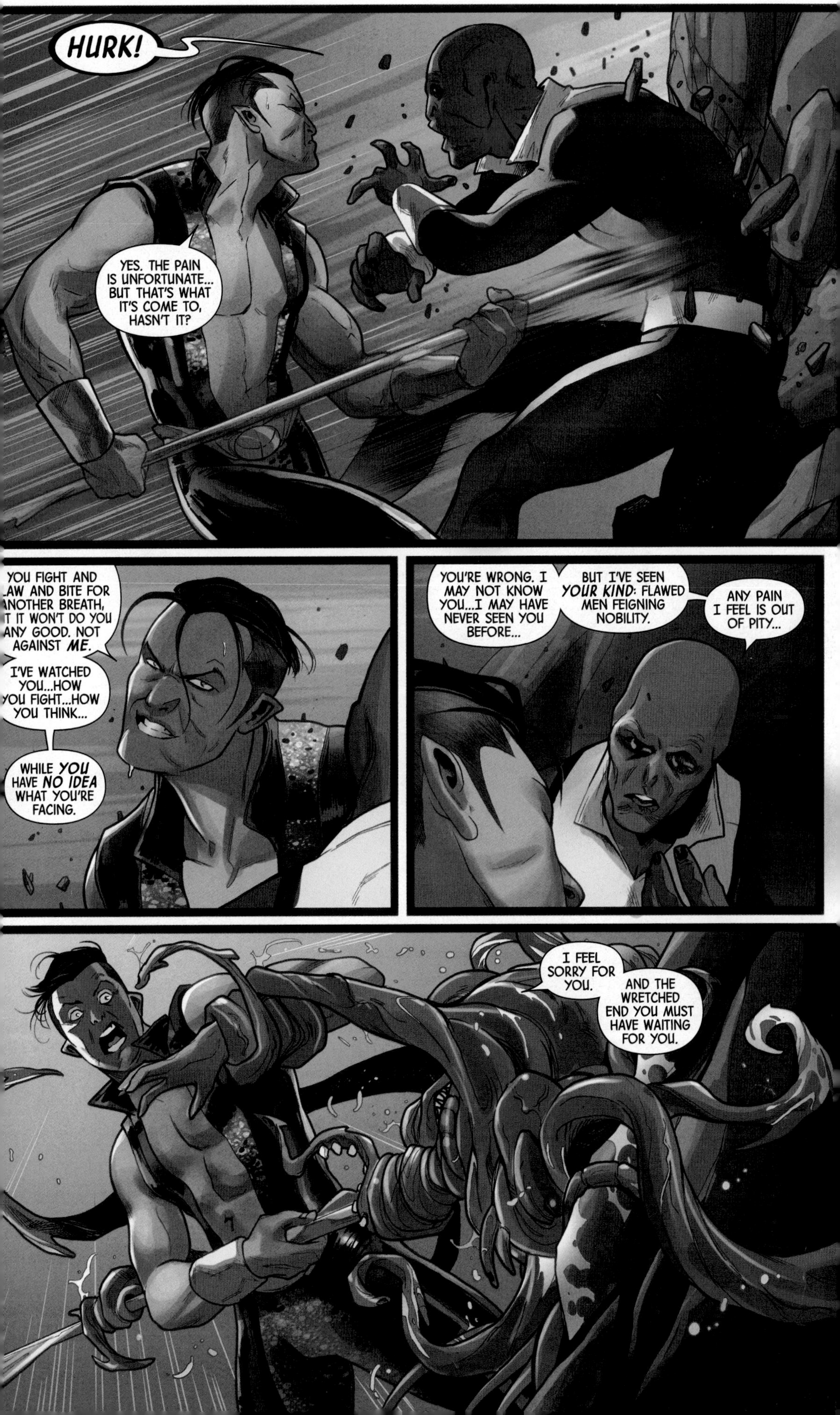
HURK!
YES. THE PAIN IS UNFORTUNATE... BUT THAT'S WHAT IT'S COME TO, HASN'T IT?
YOU FIGHT AND LAW AND BITE FOR ANOTHER BREATH, T IT WON'T DO YOU ANY GOOD. NOT AGAINST ME.
I'VE WATCHED YOU...HOW YOU FIGHT...HOW YOU THINK...
WHILE YOU HAVE NO IDEA WHAT YOU'RE FACING.
YOU'RE WRONG. I MAY NOT KNOW YOU...I MAY HAVE NEVER SEEN YOU BEFORE...
BUT I'VE SEEN YOUR KIND: FLAWED MEN FEIGNING NOBILITY.
ANY PAIN I FEEL IS OUT OF PITY...
I FEEL SORRY FOR YOU.
AND THE WRETCHED END YOU MUST HAVE WAITING FOR YOU.

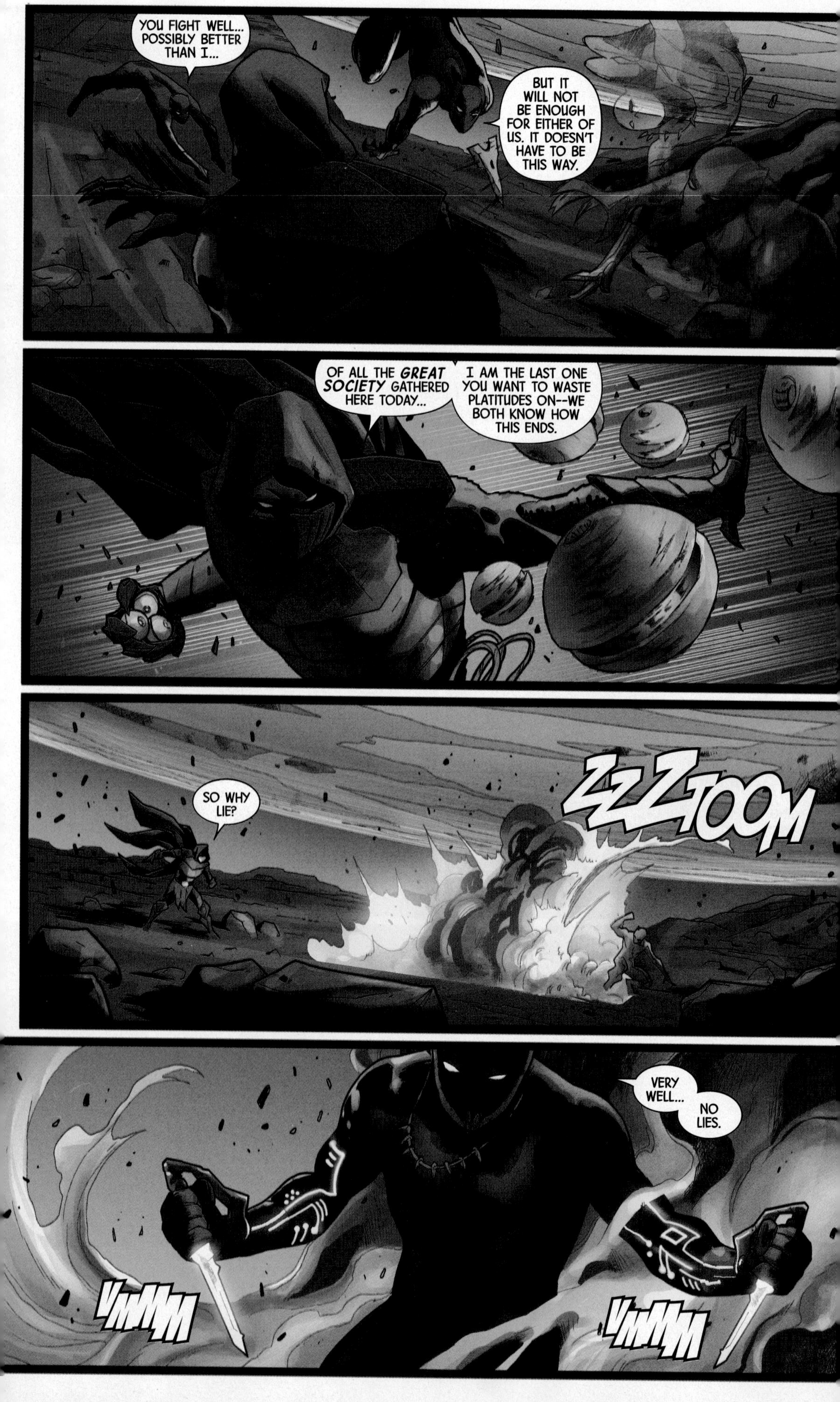
YOU FIGHT WELL... POSSIBLY BETTER THAN I...
BUT IT WILL NOT BE ENOUGH FOR EITHER OF US. IT DOESN'T HAVE TO BE THIS WAY.
OF ALL THE *GREAT SOCIETY* GATHERED HERE TODAY...
I AM THE LAST ONE YOU WANT TO WASTE PLATITUDES ON--WE BOTH KNOW HOW THIS ENDS.
SO WHY LIE?
ZZZTOOM
VERY WELL...
NO LIES.
VMMM
VMMM

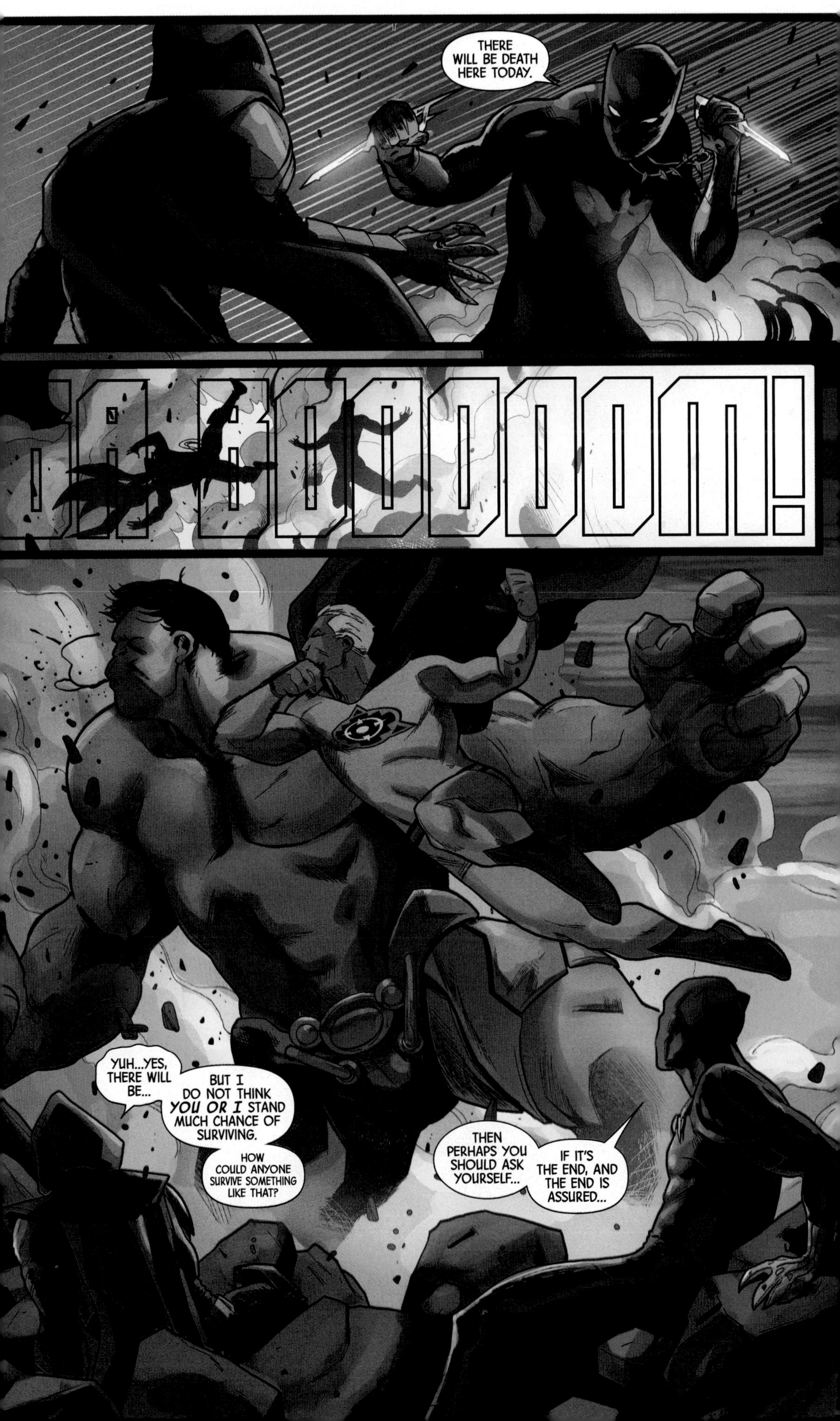
THERE WILL BE DEATH HERE TODAY.
ABOOOOOM!
YUH...YES, THERE WILL BE...
BUT I DO NOT THINK *YOU OR I* STAND MUCH CHANCE OF SURVIVING.
HOW COULD ANYONE SURVIVE SOMETHING LIKE THAT?
THEN PERHAPS YOU SHOULD ASK YOURSELF...
IF IT'S THE END, AND THE END IS ASSURED...

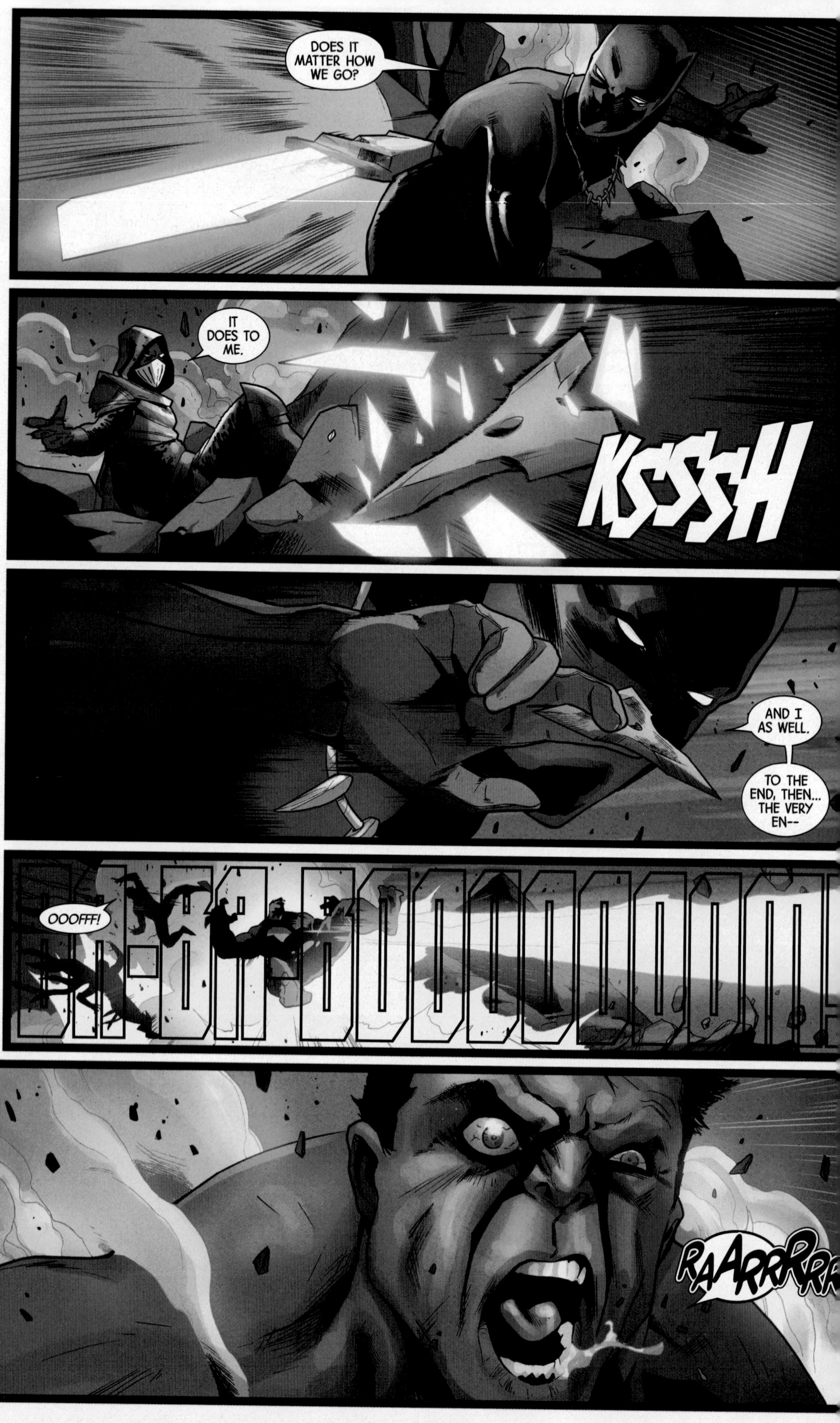
DOES IT MATTER HOW WE GO?
IT DOES TO ME.
KSSSH
AND I AS WELL.
TO THE END, THEN... THE VERY EN--
OOOFFF!
RAARRRR

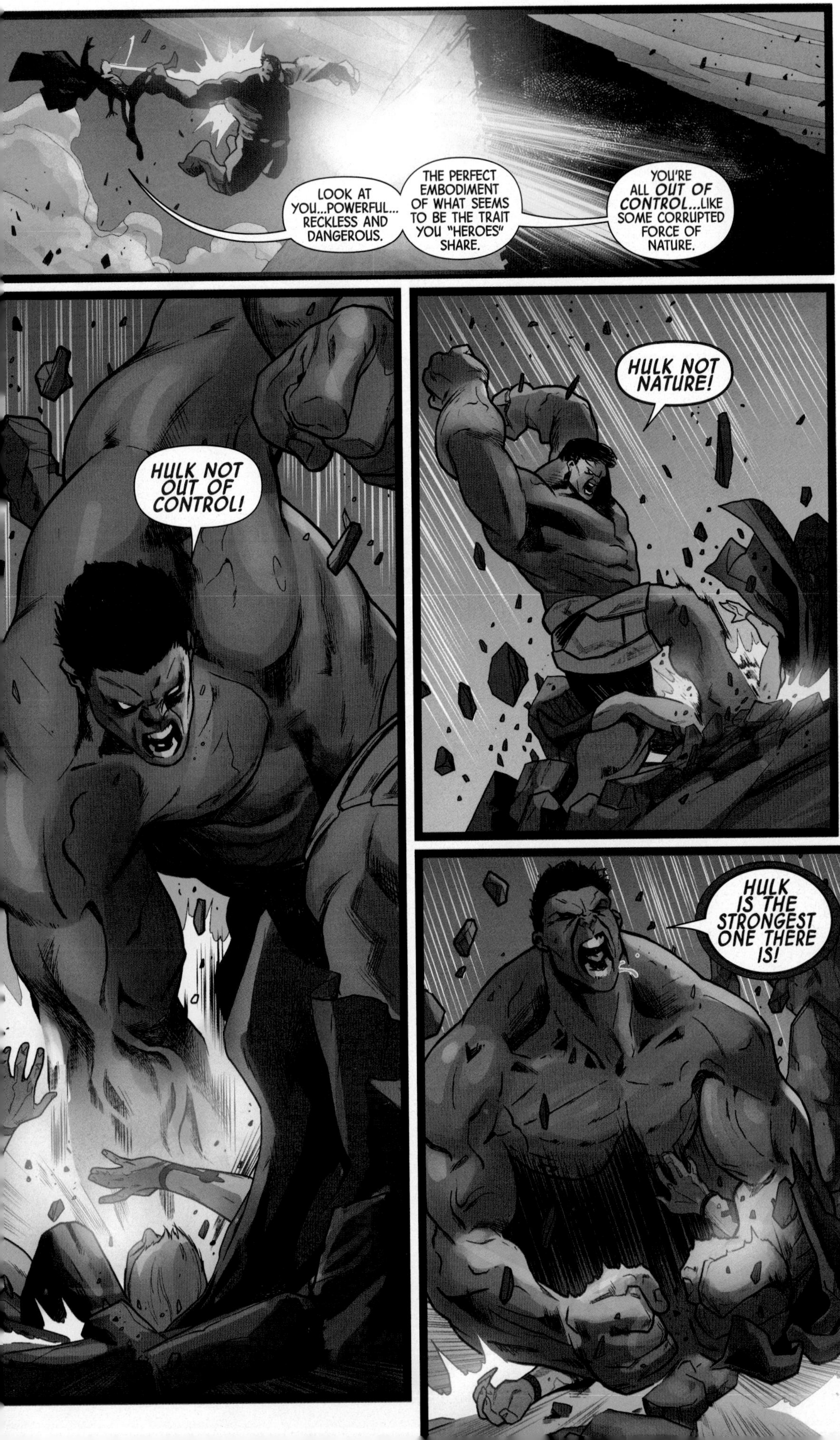
LOOK AT YOU...POWERFUL... RECKLESS AND DANGEROUS.
THE PERFECT EMBODIMENT OF WHAT SEEMS TO BE THE TRAIT YOU "HEROES" SHARE.
YOU'RE ALL OUT OF CONTROL...LIKE SOME CORRUPTED FORCE OF NATURE.
HULK NOT OUT OF CONTROL!
HULK NOT NATURE!
HULK IS THE STRONGEST ONE THERE IS!

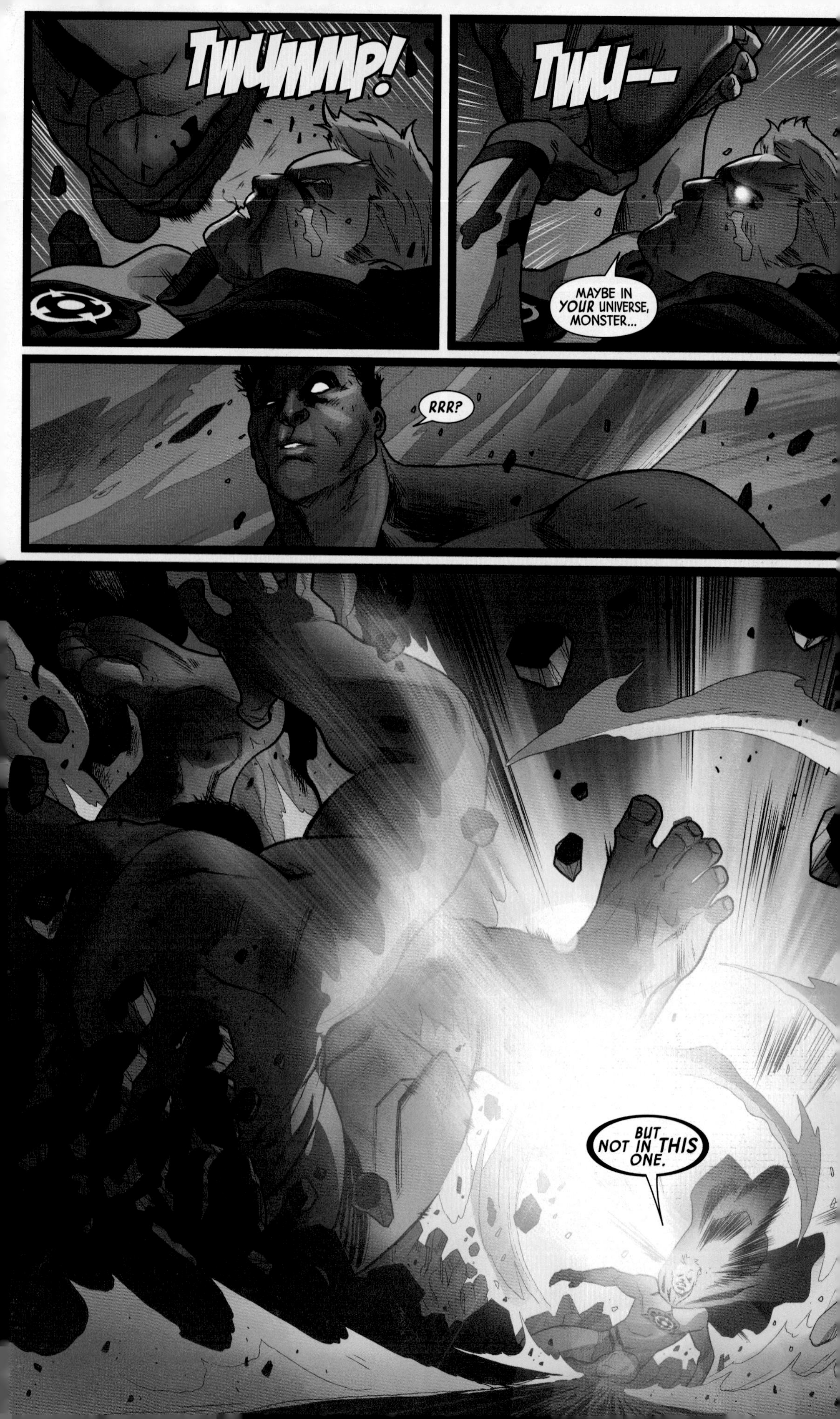
TWUMMP!
TWU--
MAYBE IN YOUR UNIVERSE, MONSTER...
RRR?
BUT NOT IN THIS ONE.

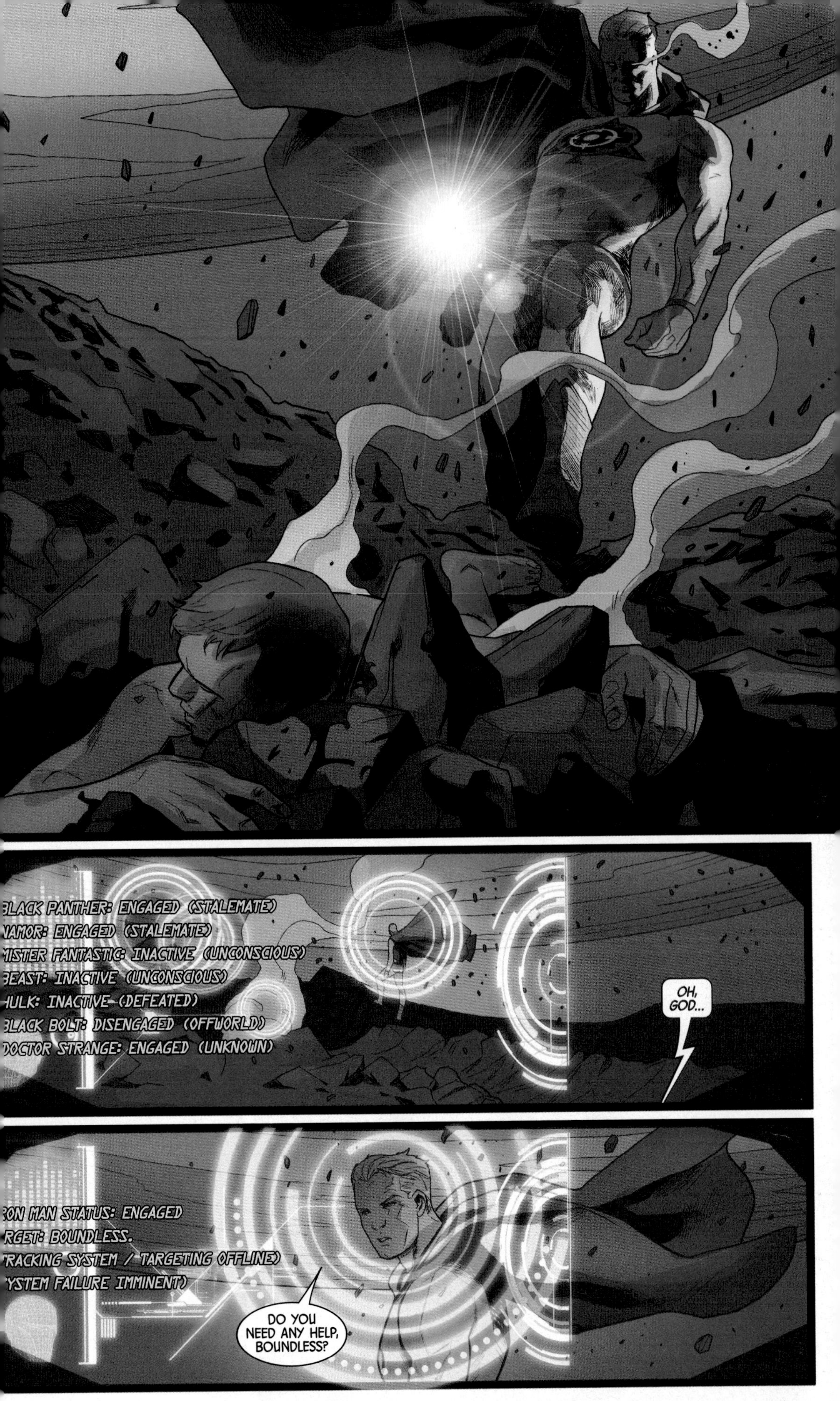
BLACK PANTHER: ENGAGED (STALEMATE)
NAMOR: ENGAGED (STALEMATE)
MISTER FANTASTIC: INACTIVE (UNCONSCIOUS)
BEAST: INACTIVE (UNCONSCIOUS)
HULK: INACTIVE (DEFEATED)
BLACK BOLT: DISENGAGED (OFFWORLD)
DOCTOR STRANGE: ENGAGED (UNKNOWN)
OH, GOD...
RON MAN STATUS: ENGAGED
RGET: BOUNDLESS.
TRACKING SYSTEM / TARGETING OFFLINE)
YSTEM FAILURE IMMINENT)
DO YOU NEED ANY HELP, BOUNDLESS?

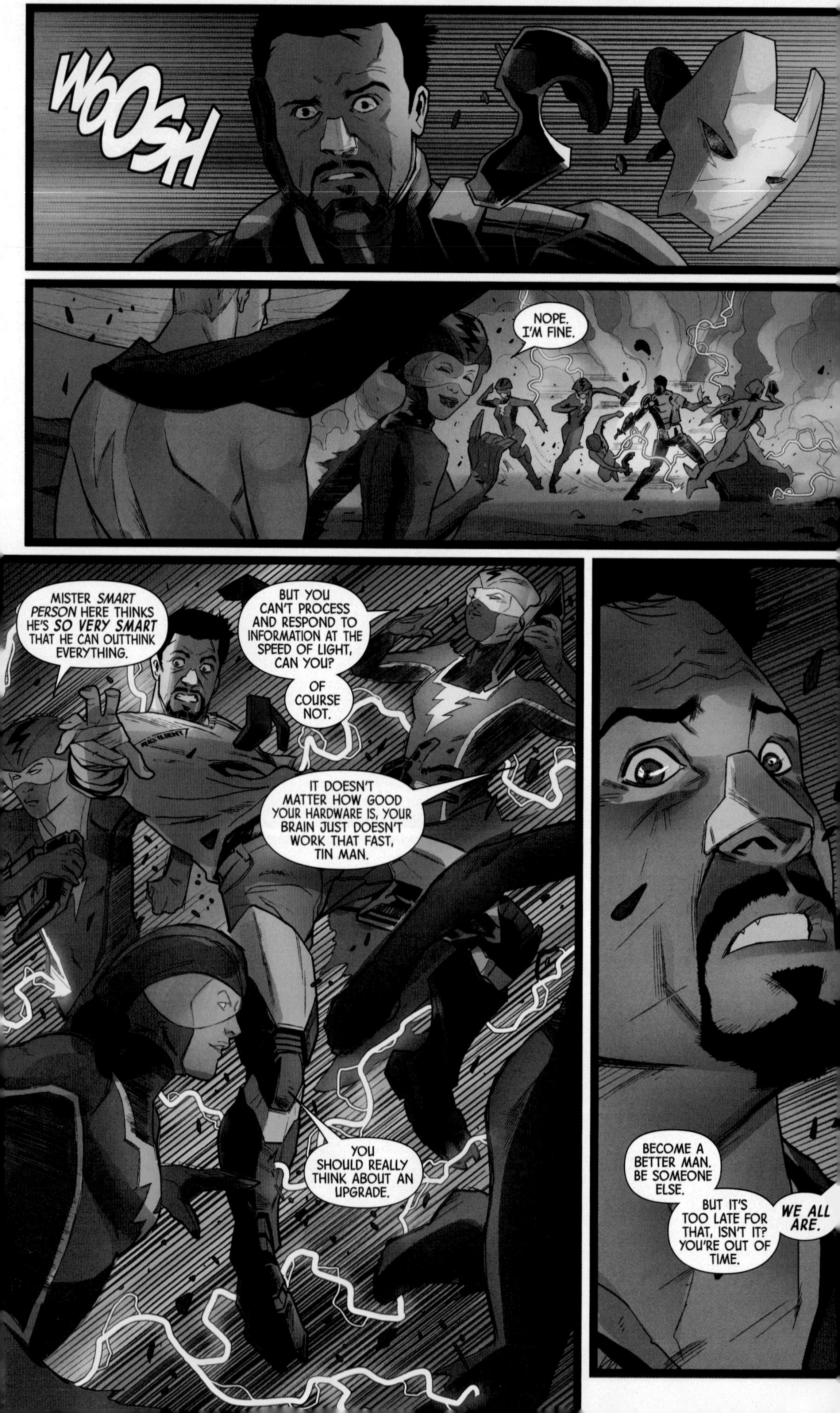
WOOSH
NOPE. I'M FINE.
MISTER SMART PERSON HERE THINKS HE'S SO VERY SMART THAT HE CAN OUTTHINK EVERYTHING.
BUT YOU CAN'T PROCESS AND RESPOND TO INFORMATION AT THE SPEED OF LIGHT, CAN YOU?
OF COURSE NOT.
IT DOESN'T MATTER HOW GOOD YOUR HARDWARE IS, YOUR BRAIN JUST DOESN'T WORK THAT FAST, TIN MAN.
YOU SHOULD REALLY THINK ABOUT AN UPGRADE.
BECOME A BETTER MAN. BE SOMEONE ELSE.
BUT IT'S TOO LATE FOR THAT, ISN'T IT? YOU'RE OUT OF TIME.
WE ALL ARE.

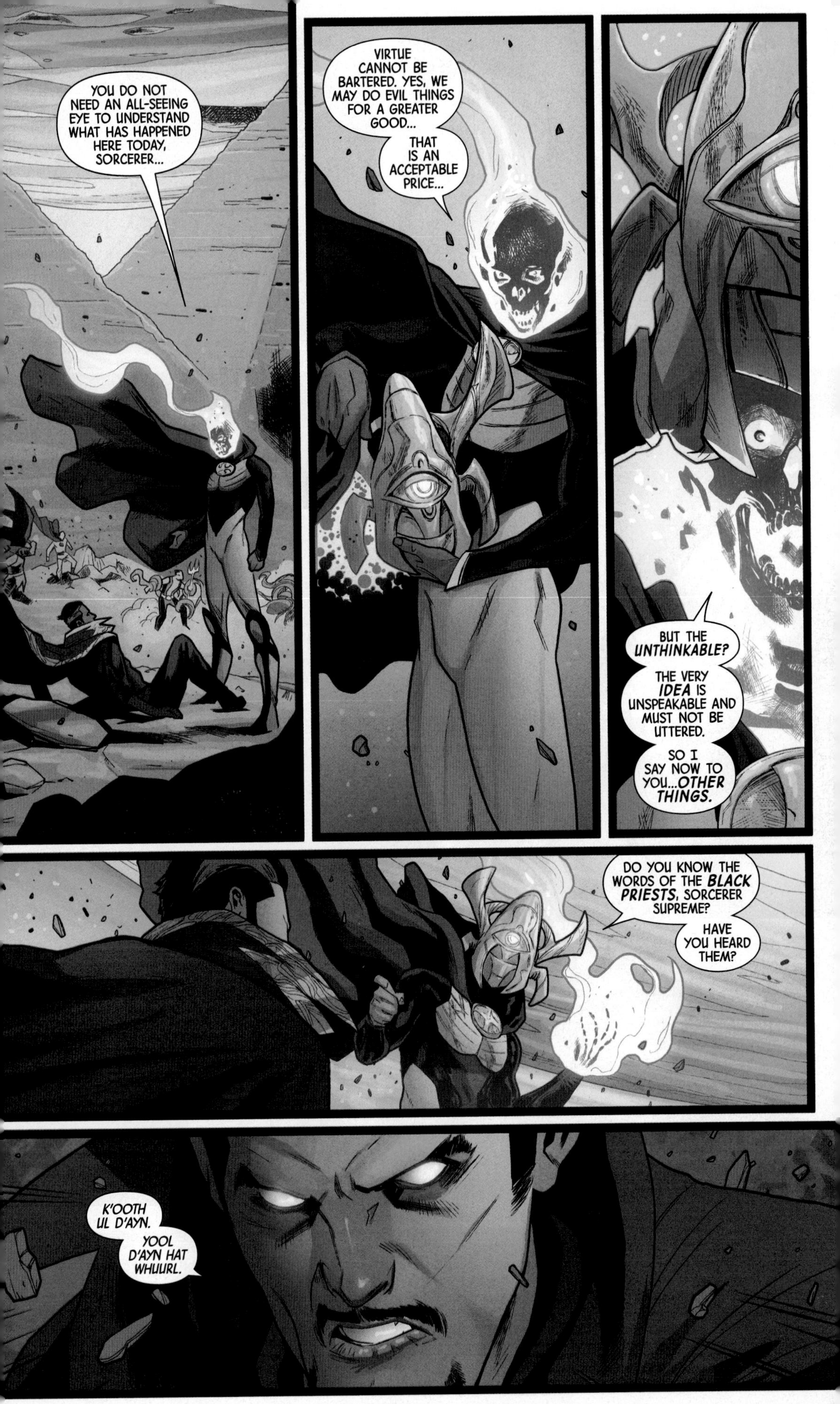
YOU DO NOT NEED AN ALL-SEEING EYE TO UNDERSTAND WHAT HAS HAPPENED HERE TODAY, SORCERER...
VIRTUE CANNOT BE BARTERED. YES, WE MAY DO EVIL THINGS FOR A GREATER GOOD...
THAT IS AN ACCEPTABLE PRICE...
BUT THE UNTHINKABLE?
THE VERY IDEA IS UNSPEAKABLE AND MUST NOT BE UTTERED.
SO I SAY NOW TO YOU...OTHER THINGS.
DO YOU KNOW THE WORDS OF THE BLACK PRIESTS, SORCERER SUPREME?
HAVE YOU HEARD THEM?
K'OOTH UL D'AYN.
YOOL D'AYN HAT WHUURL.

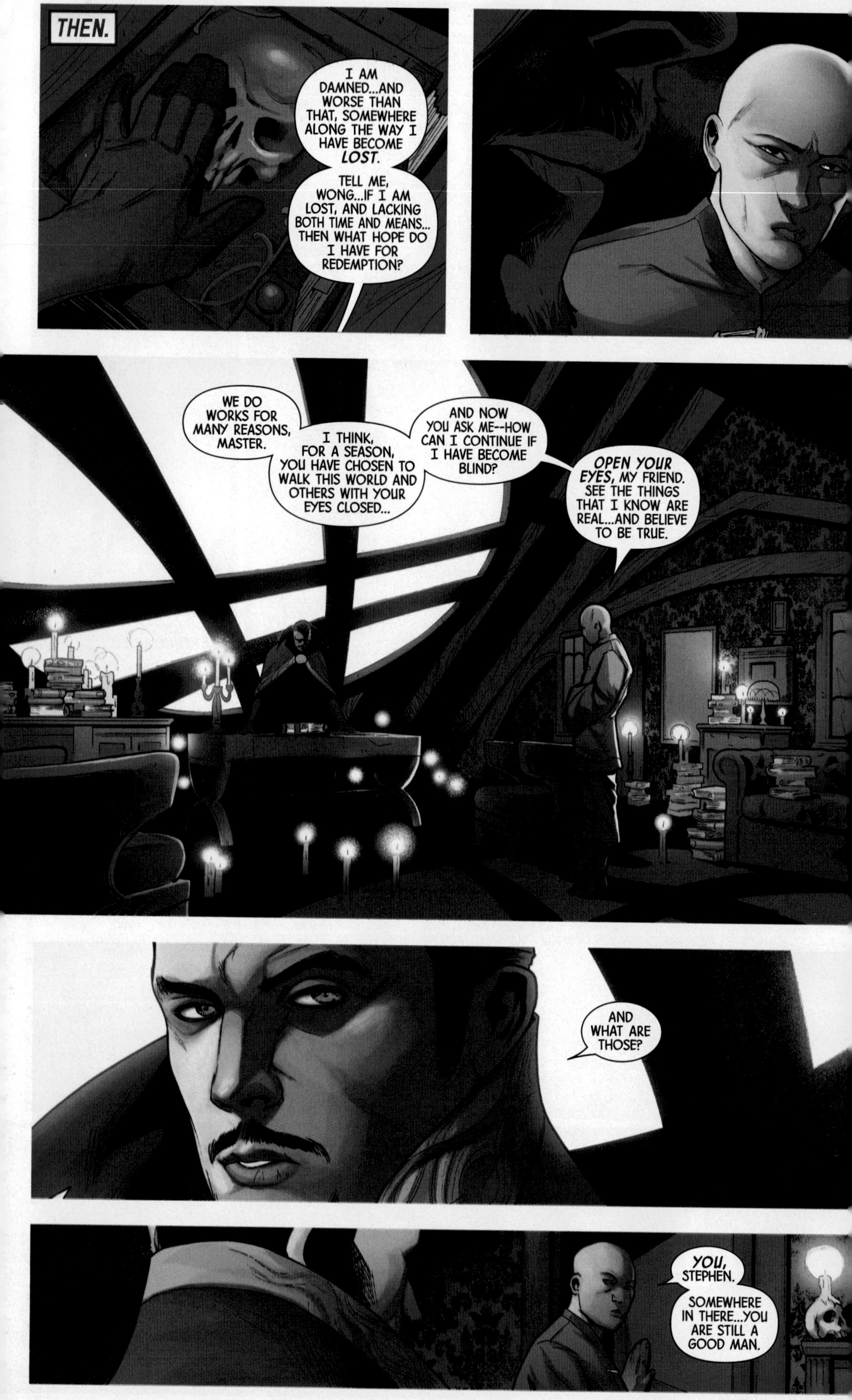

THEN.
I AM DAMNED...AND WORSE THAN THAT, SOMEWHERE ALONG THE WAY I HAVE BECOME LOST.
TELL ME, WONG...IF I AM LOST, AND LACKING BOTH TIME AND MEANS... THEN WHAT HOPE DO I HAVE FOR REDEMPTION?
WE DO WORKS FOR MANY REASONS, MASTER.
I THINK, FOR A SEASON, YOU HAVE CHOSEN TO WALK THIS WORLD AND OTHERS WITH YOUR EYES CLOSED...
AND NOW YOU ASK ME--HOW CAN I CONTINUE IF I HAVE BECOME BLIND?
OPEN YOUR EYES, MY FRIEND. SEE THE THINGS THAT I KNOW ARE REAL...AND BELIEVE TO BE TRUE.
AND WHAT ARE THOSE?
YOU, STEPHEN.
SOMEWHERE IN THERE...YOU ARE STILL A GOOD MAN.

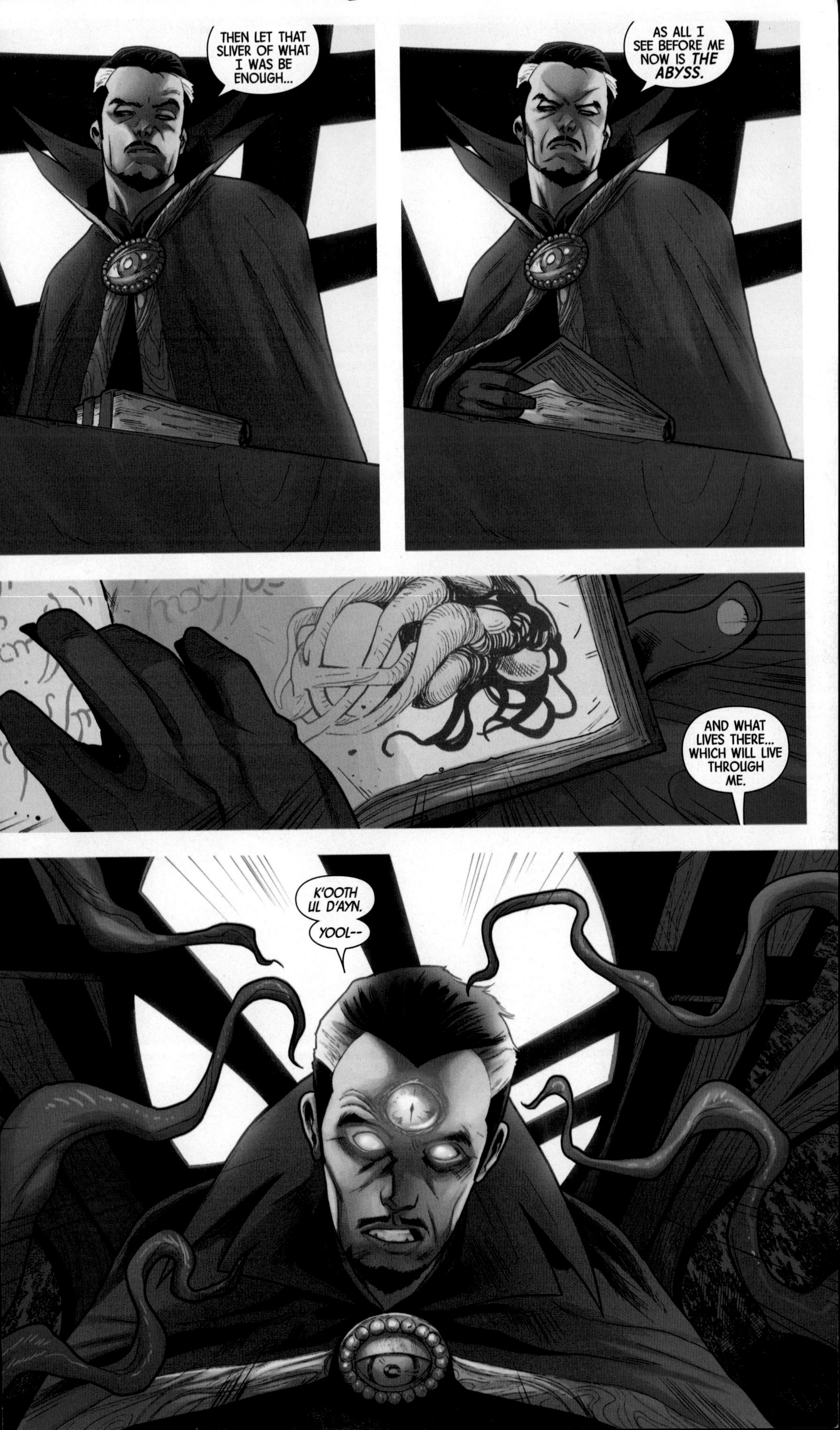
THEN LET THAT SLIVER OF WHAT I WAS BE ENOUGH...
AS ALL I SEE BEFORE ME NOW IS *THE ABYSS.*
AND WHAT LIVES THERE... WHICH WILL LIVE THROUGH ME.
K'OOTH UL D'AYN.
YOOL--

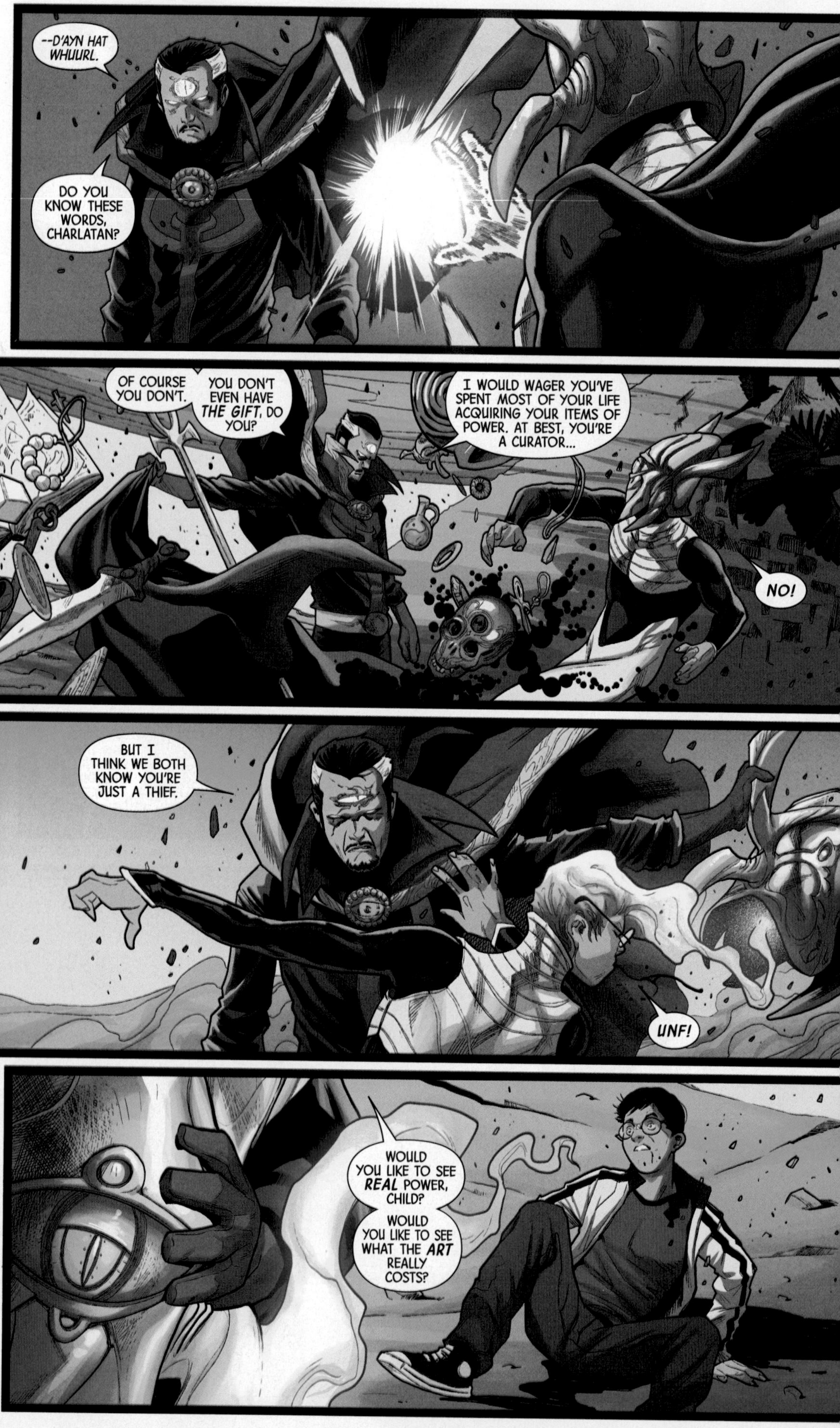
--D'AYN HAT WHUURL.
DO YOU KNOW THESE WORDS, CHARLATAN?
OF COURSE YOU DON'T.
YOU DON'T EVEN HAVE THE GIFT, DO YOU?
I WOULD WAGER YOU'VE SPENT MOST OF YOUR LIFE ACQUIRING YOUR ITEMS OF POWER. AT BEST, YOU'RE A CURATOR...
NO!
BUT I THINK WE BOTH KNOW YOU'RE JUST A THIEF.
UNF!
WOULD YOU LIKE TO SEE REAL POWER, CHILD?
WOULD YOU LIKE TO SEE WHAT THE ART REALLY COSTS?

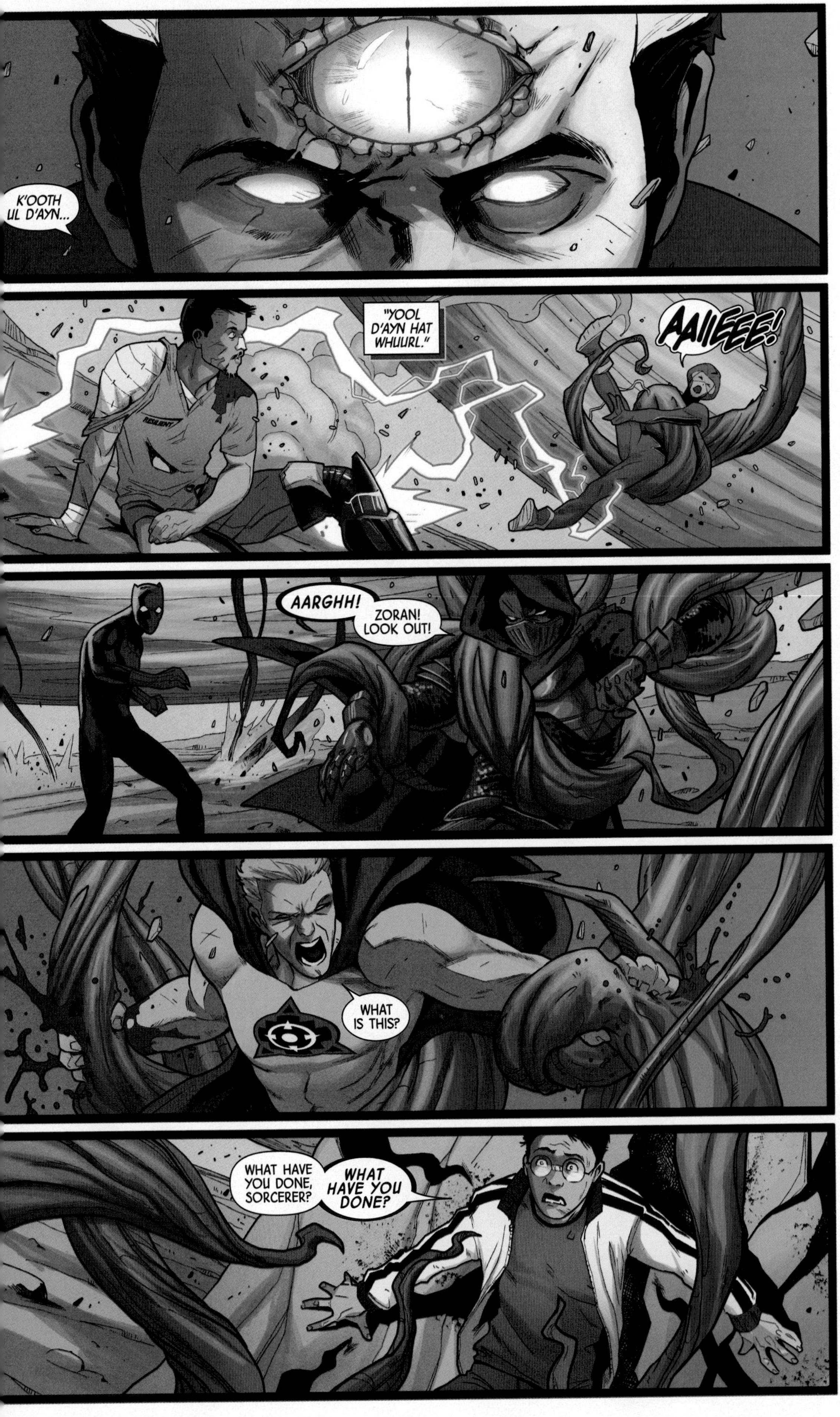
K'OOTH UL D'AYN...
"YOOL D'AYN HAT WHUURL."
AAIIEEE!
AARGHH!
ZORAN! LOOK OUT!
WHAT IS THIS?
WHAT HAVE YOU DONE, SORCERER?
WHAT HAVE YOU DONE?

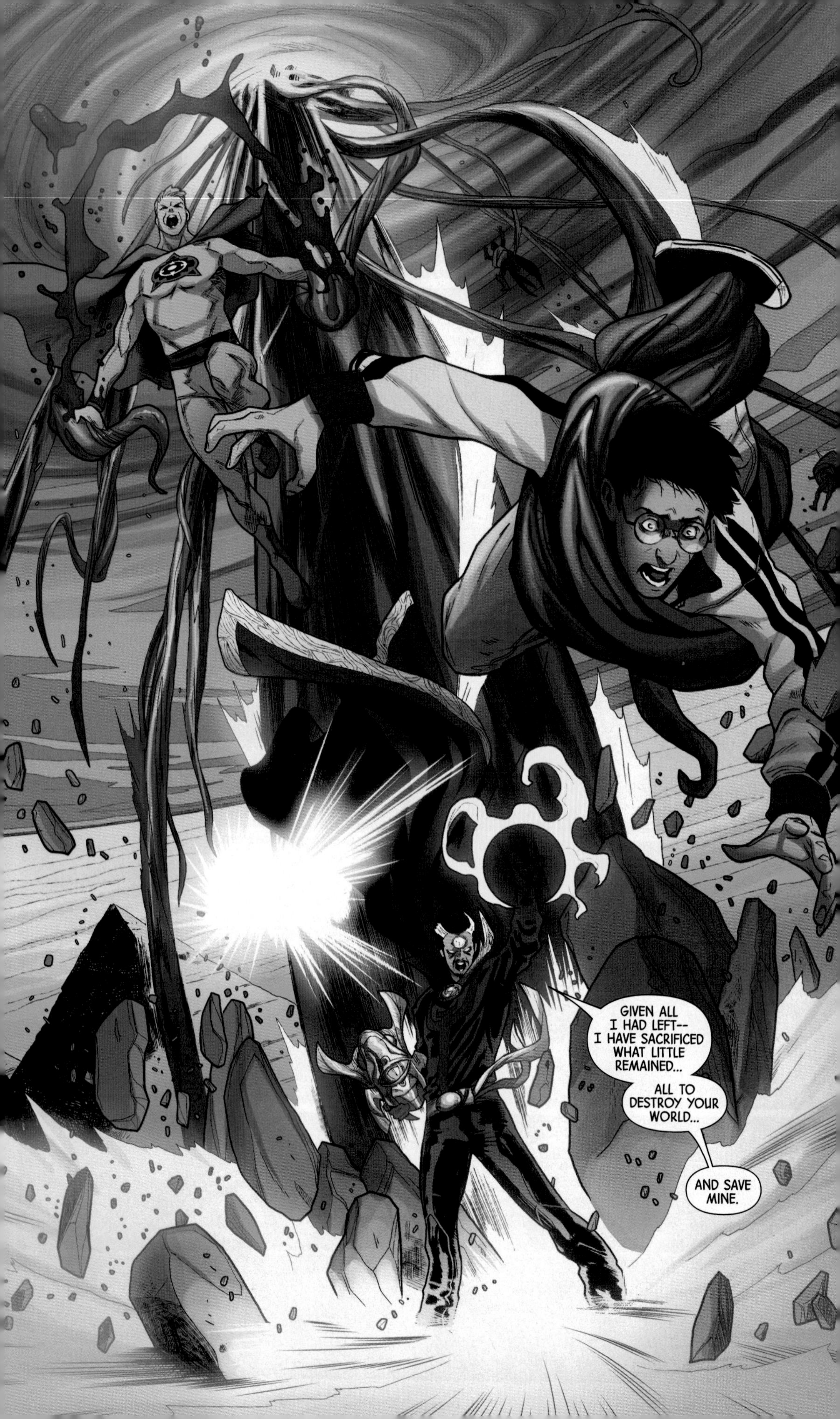
GIVEN ALL I HAD LEFT-- I HAVE SACRIFICED WHAT LITTLE REMAINED...
ALL TO DESTROY YOUR WORLD...
AND SAVE MINE.

"THE BOMB"

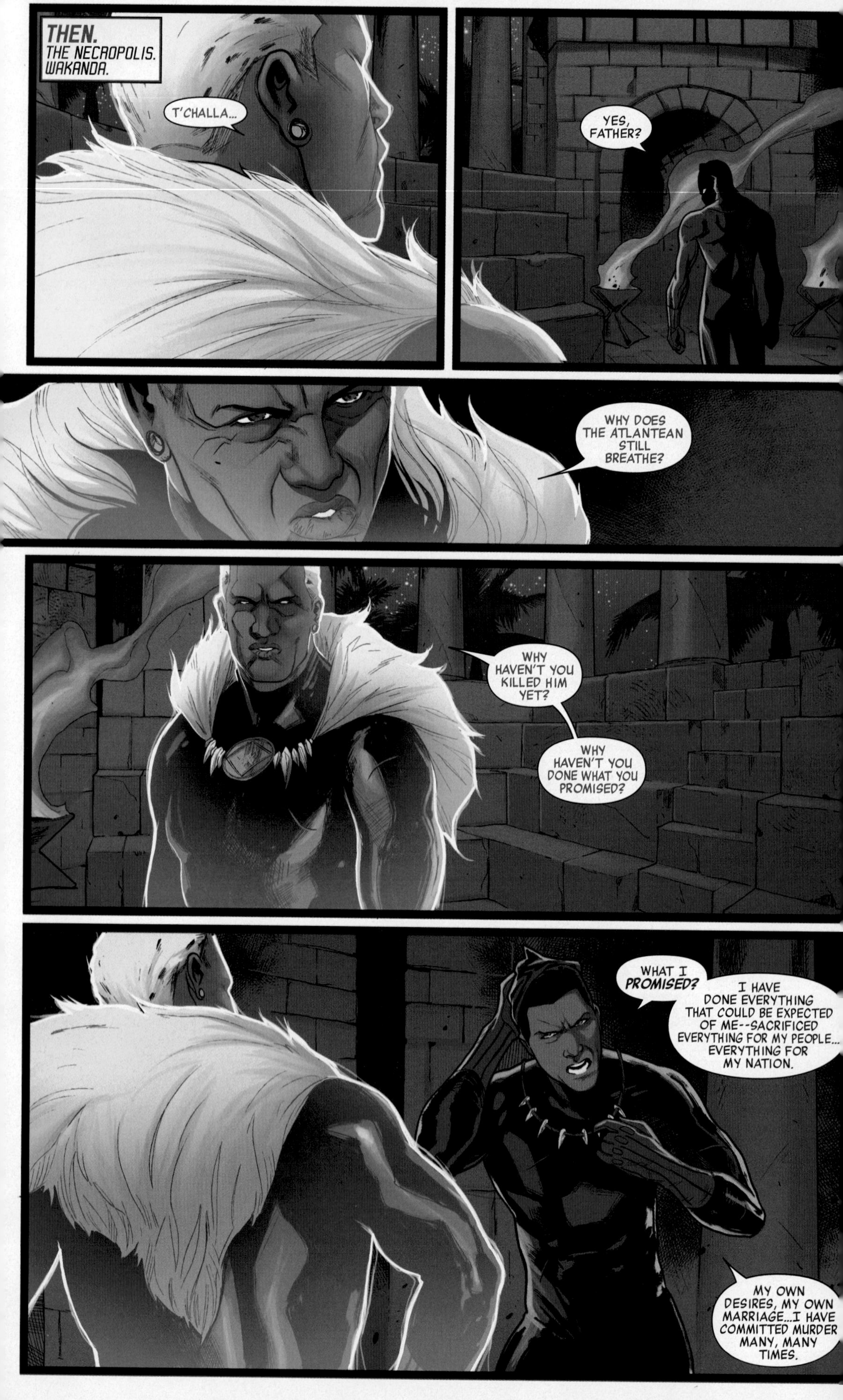
THEN.
THE NECROPOLIS.
WAKANDA.
T'CHALLA...
YES, FATHER?
WHY DOES THE ATLANTEAN STILL BREATHE?
WHY HAVEN'T YOU KILLED HIM YET?
WHY HAVEN'T YOU DONE WHAT YOU PROMISED?
WHAT I **PROMISED?**
I HAVE DONE EVERYTHING THAT COULD BE EXPECTED OF ME--SACRIFICED EVERYTHING FOR MY PEOPLE... EVERYTHING FOR MY NATION.
MY OWN DESIRES, MY OWN MARRIAGE...I HAVE COMMITTED MURDER MANY, MANY TIMES.

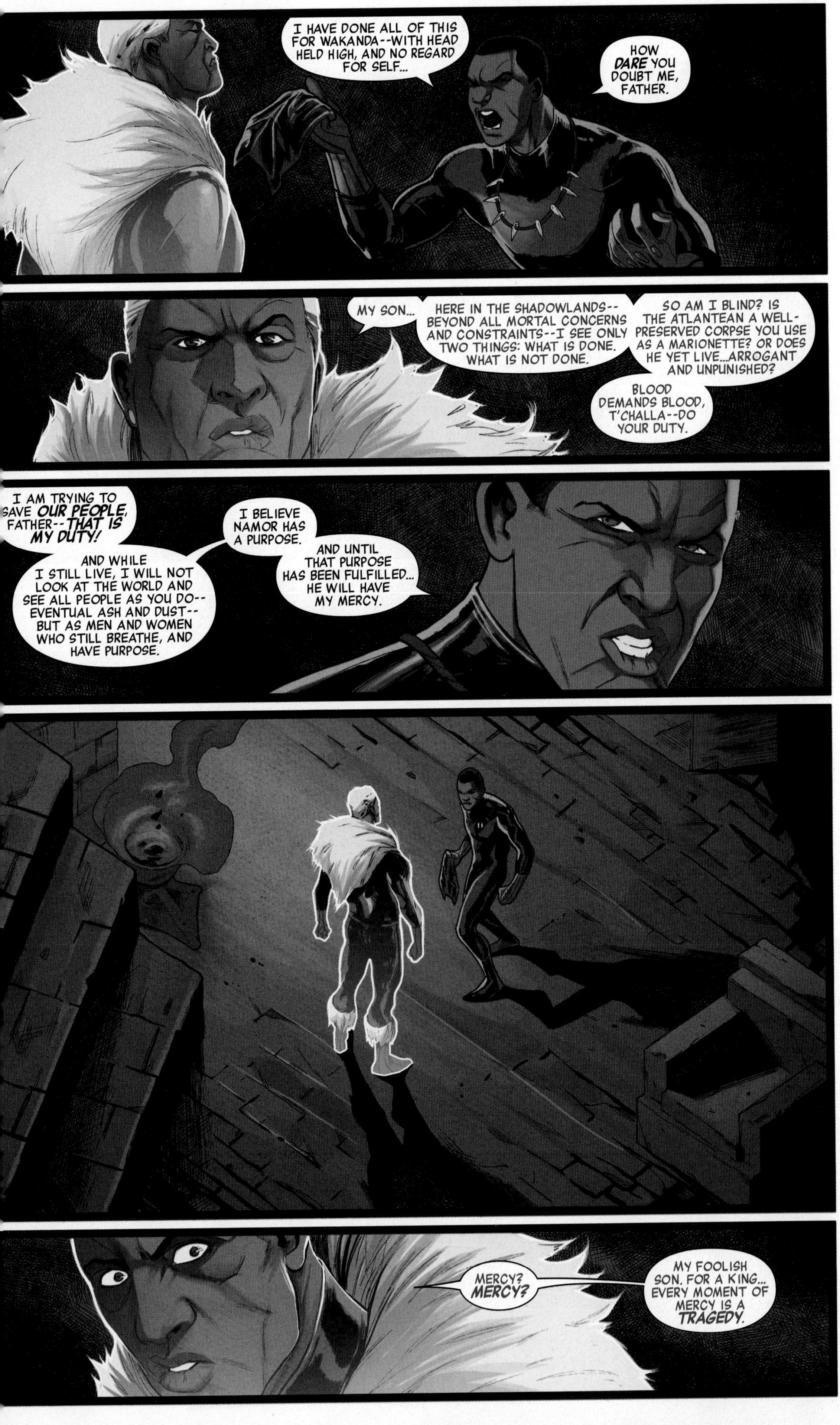
I HAVE DONE ALL OF THIS FOR WAKANDA--WITH HEAD HELD HIGH, AND NO REGARD FOR SELF...
HOW DARE YOU DOUBT ME, FATHER.
MY SON...
HERE IN THE SHADOWLANDS--BEYOND ALL MORTAL CONCERNS AND CONSTRAINTS--I SEE ONLY TWO THINGS: WHAT IS DONE. WHAT IS NOT DONE.
SO AM I BLIND? IS THE ATLANTEAN A WELL-PRESERVED CORPSE YOU USE AS A MARIONETTE? OR DOES HE YET LIVE...ARROGANT AND UNPUNISHED?
BLOOD DEMANDS BLOOD, T'CHALLA--DO YOUR DUTY.
I AM TRYING TO SAVE OUR PEOPLE, FATHER--THAT IS MY DUTY!
AND WHILE I STILL LIVE, I WILL NOT LOOK AT THE WORLD AND SEE ALL PEOPLE AS YOU DO--EVENTUAL ASH AND DUST--BUT AS MEN AND WOMEN WHO STILL BREATHE, AND HAVE PURPOSE.
I BELIEVE NAMOR HAS A PURPOSE.
AND UNTIL THAT PURPOSE HAS BEEN FULFILLED... HE WILL HAVE MY MERCY.
MERCY? MERCY?
MY FOOLISH SON. FOR A KING... EVERY MOMENT OF MERCY IS A TRAGEDY.

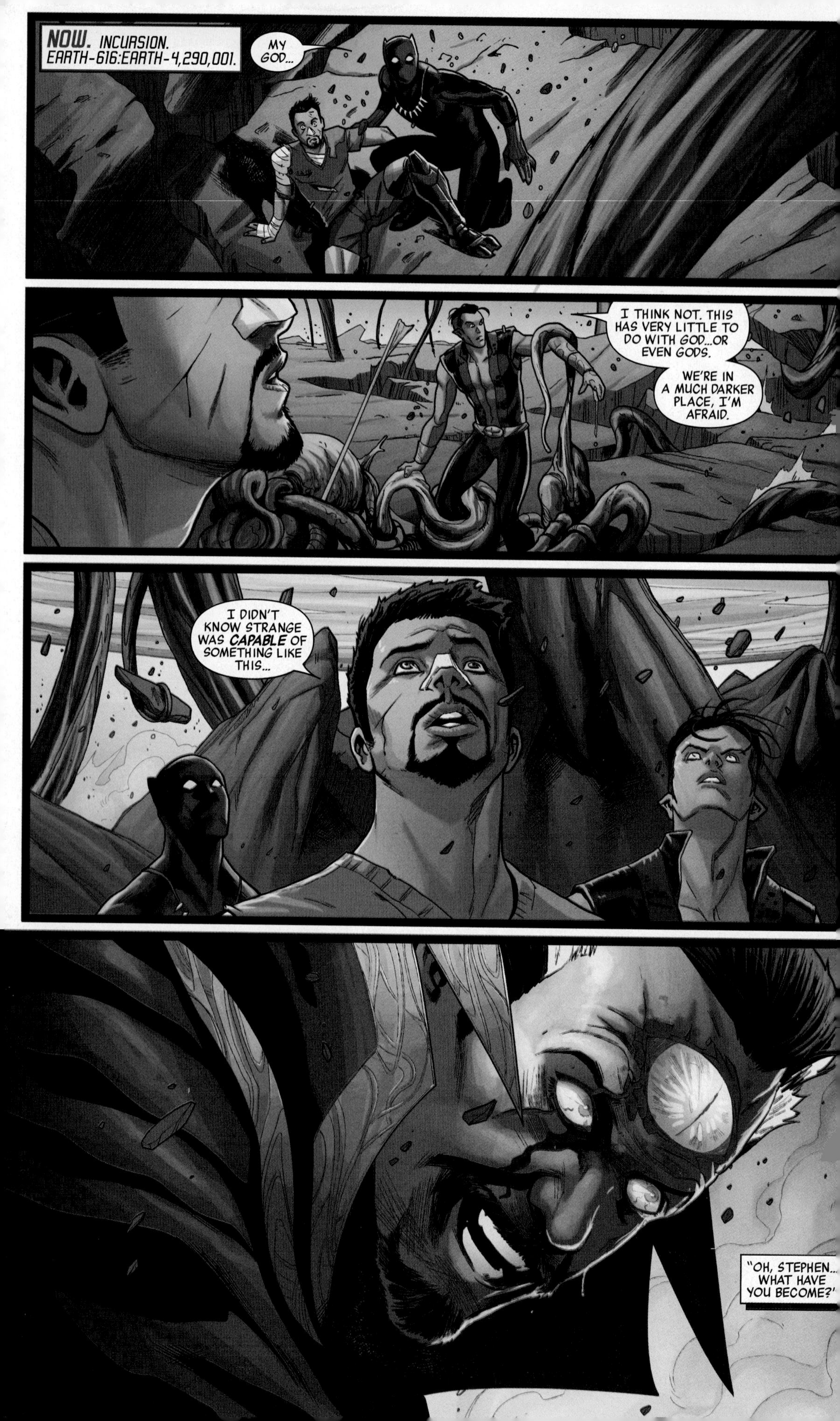
NOW. INCURSION.
EARTH-616:EARTH-4,290,001.
MY GOD...
I THINK NOT. THIS HAS VERY LITTLE TO DO WITH GOD...OR EVEN GODS.
WE'RE IN A MUCH DARKER PLACE, I'M AFRAID.
I DIDN'T KNOW STRANGE WAS CAPABLE OF SOMETHING LIKE THIS...
"OH, STEPHEN... WHAT HAVE YOU BECOME?"

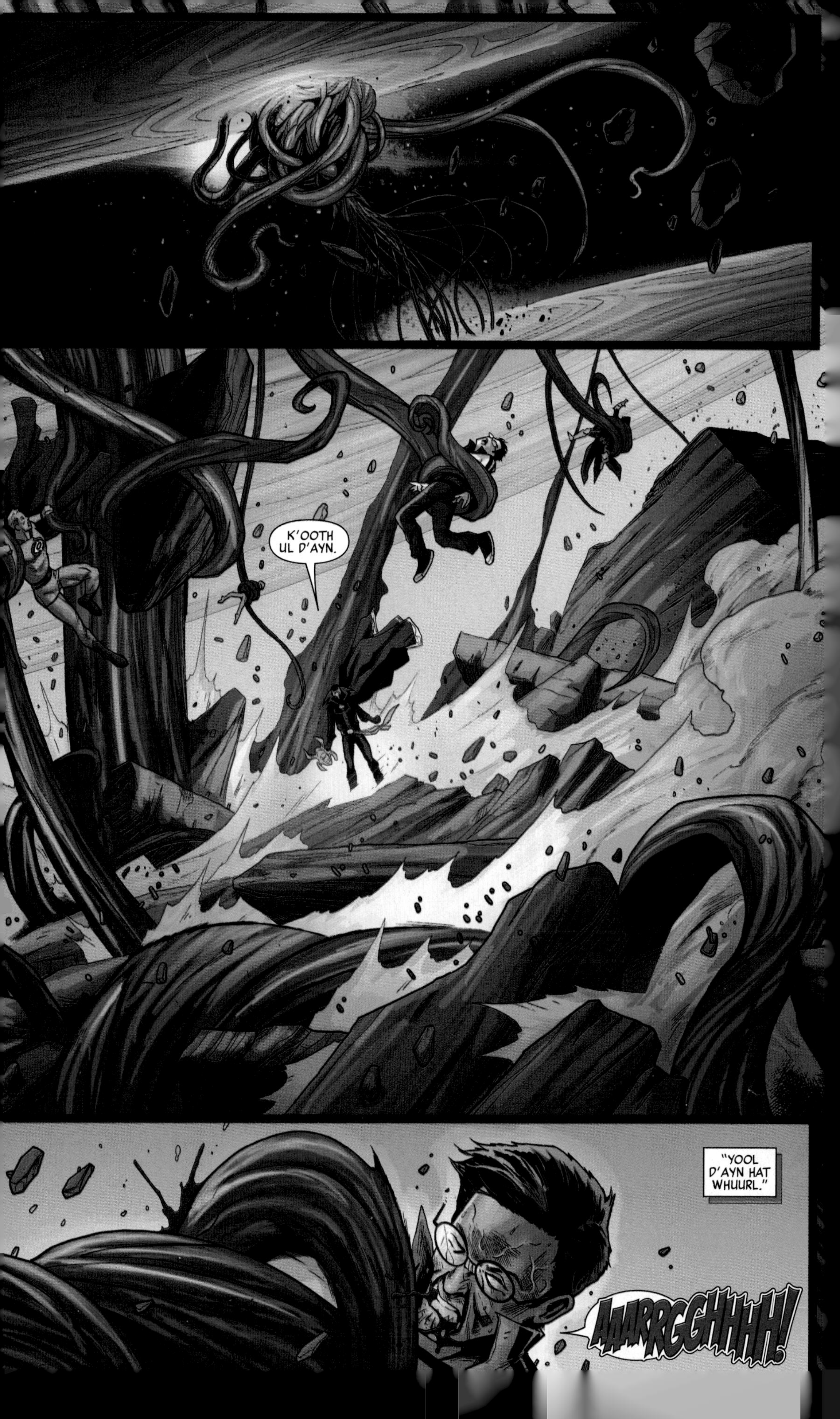
K'OOTH UL D'AYN.
"YOOL D'AYN HAT WHUURL."
AAARRGGHHHH!

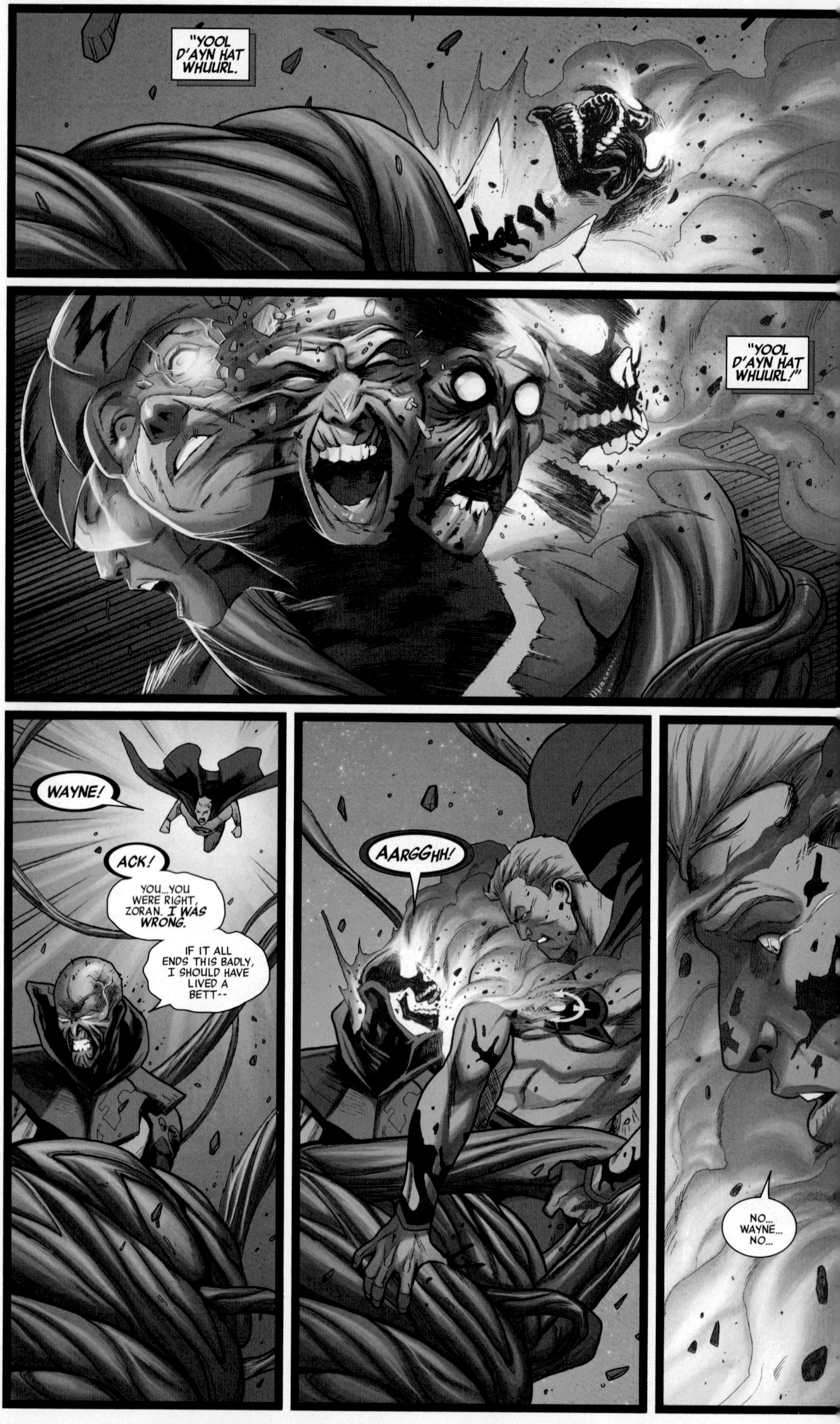
"YOOL D'AYN HAT WHUURL.
"YOOL D'AYN HAT WHUURL!"
WAYNE!
ACK!
YOU...YOU WERE RIGHT, ZORAN. I WAS WRONG.
IF IT ALL ENDS THIS BADLY, I SHOULD HAVE LIVED A BETT--
AARGGHH!
NO... WAYNE... NO...

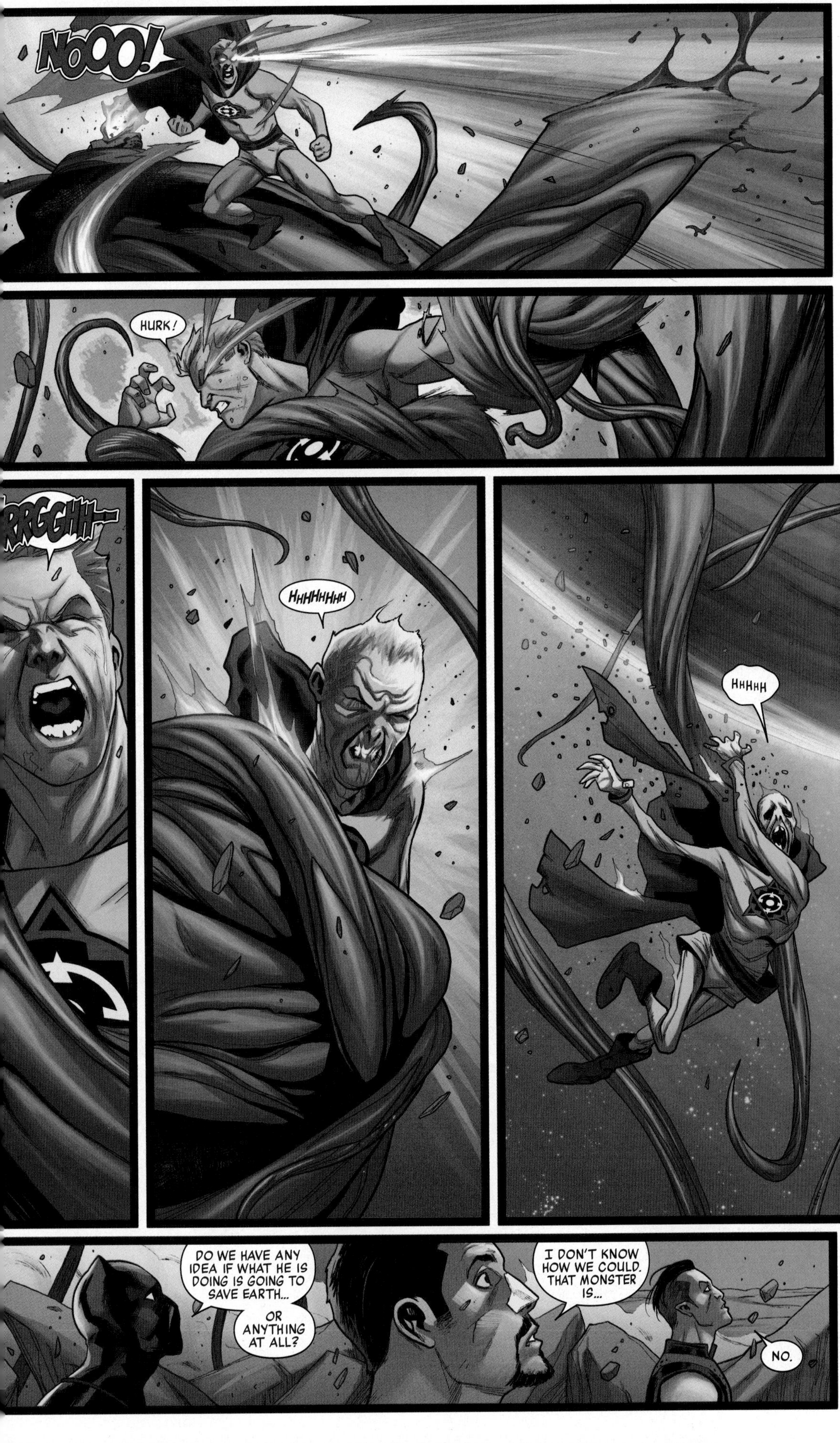
NOOO!
HURK!
RRGGHH--
HHHHHHHH
HHHHH
DO WE HAVE ANY IDEA IF WHAT HE IS DOING IS GOING TO SAVE EARTH...
OR ANYTHING AT ALL?
I DON'T KNOW HOW WE COULD. THAT MONSTER IS...
NO.

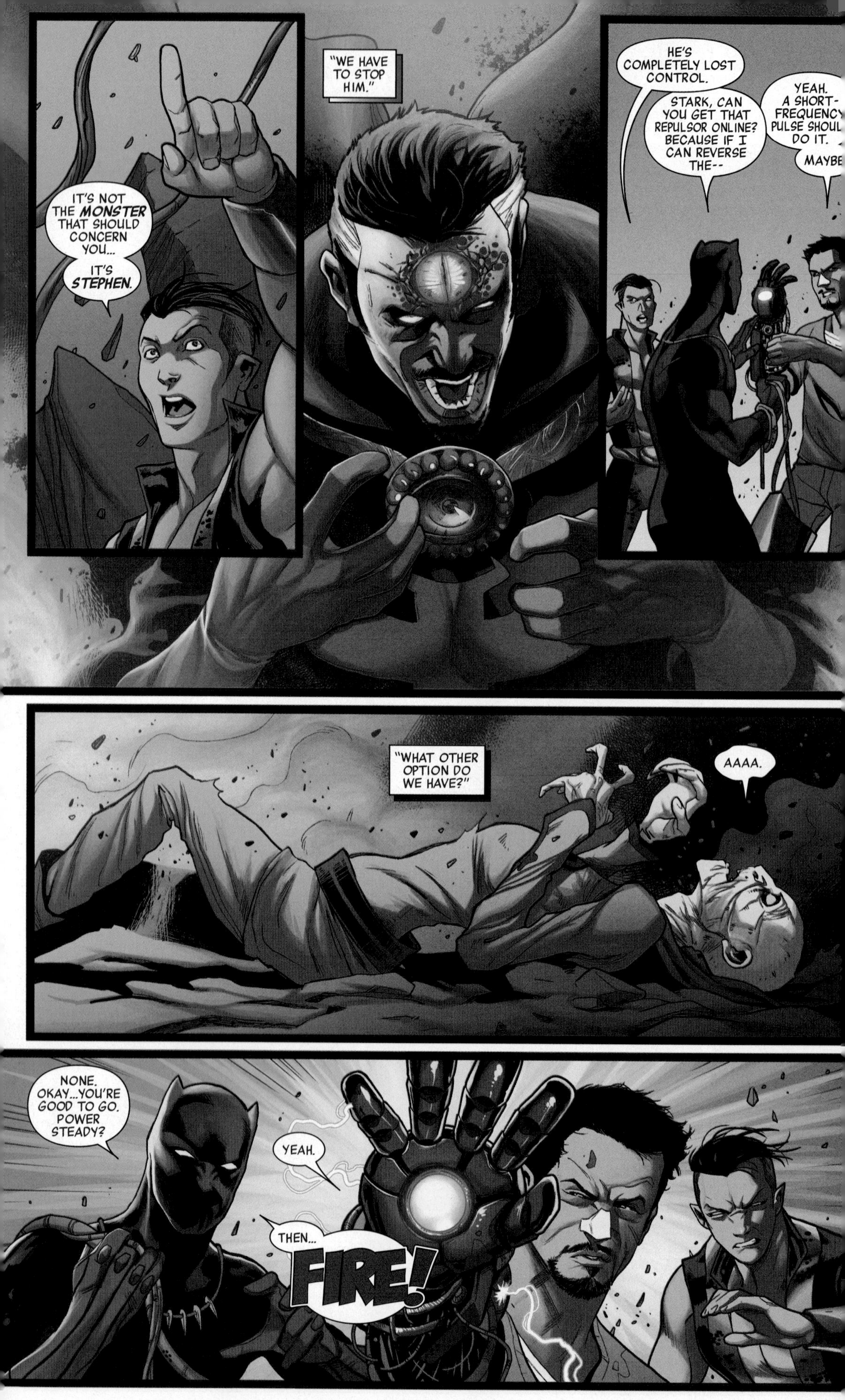
IT'S NOT THE MONSTER THAT SHOULD CONCERN YOU...
IT'S STEPHEN.
"WE HAVE TO STOP HIM."
HE'S COMPLETELY LOST CONTROL.
STARK, CAN YOU GET THAT REPULSOR ONLINE? BECAUSE IF I CAN REVERSE THE--
YEAH. A SHORT-FREQUENCY PULSE SHOULD DO IT.
MAYBE
"WHAT OTHER OPTION DO WE HAVE?"
AAAA.
NONE. OKAY...YOU'RE GOOD TO GO. POWER STEADY?
YEAH.
THEN...
FIRE!

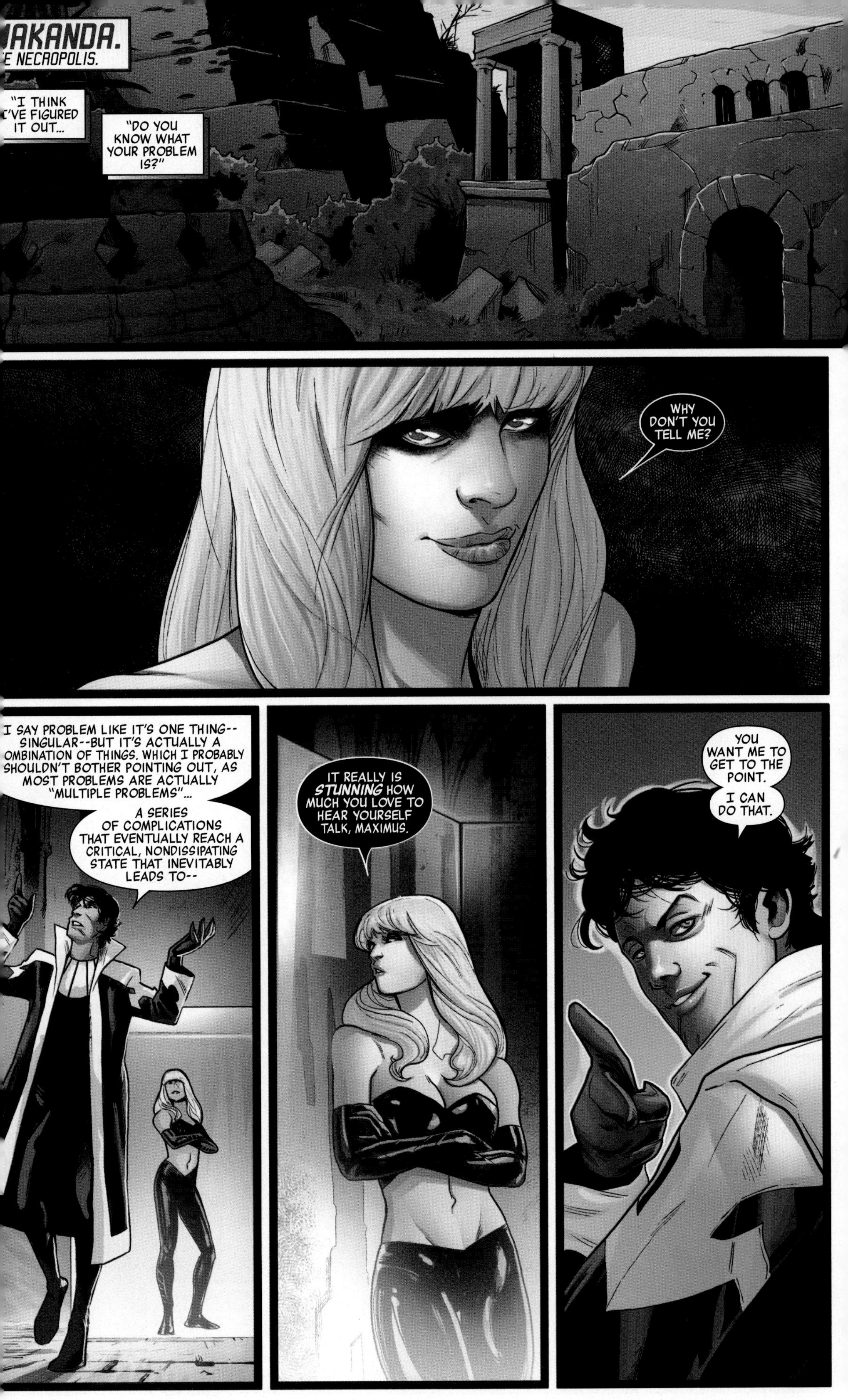

AKANDA.
E NECROPOLIS.
"I THINK I'VE FIGURED IT OUT...
"DO YOU KNOW WHAT YOUR PROBLEM IS?"
WHY DON'T YOU TELL ME?
I SAY PROBLEM LIKE IT'S ONE THING--SINGULAR--BUT IT'S ACTUALLY A OMBINATION OF THINGS. WHICH I PROBABLY SHOULDN'T BOTHER POINTING OUT, AS MOST PROBLEMS ARE ACTUALLY "MULTIPLE PROBLEMS"...
A SERIES OF COMPLICATIONS THAT EVENTUALLY REACH A CRITICAL, NONDISSIPATING STATE THAT INEVITABLY LEADS TO--
IT REALLY IS STUNNING HOW MUCH YOU LOVE TO HEAR YOURSELF TALK, MAXIMUS.
YOU WANT ME TO GET TO THE POINT.
I CAN DO THAT.

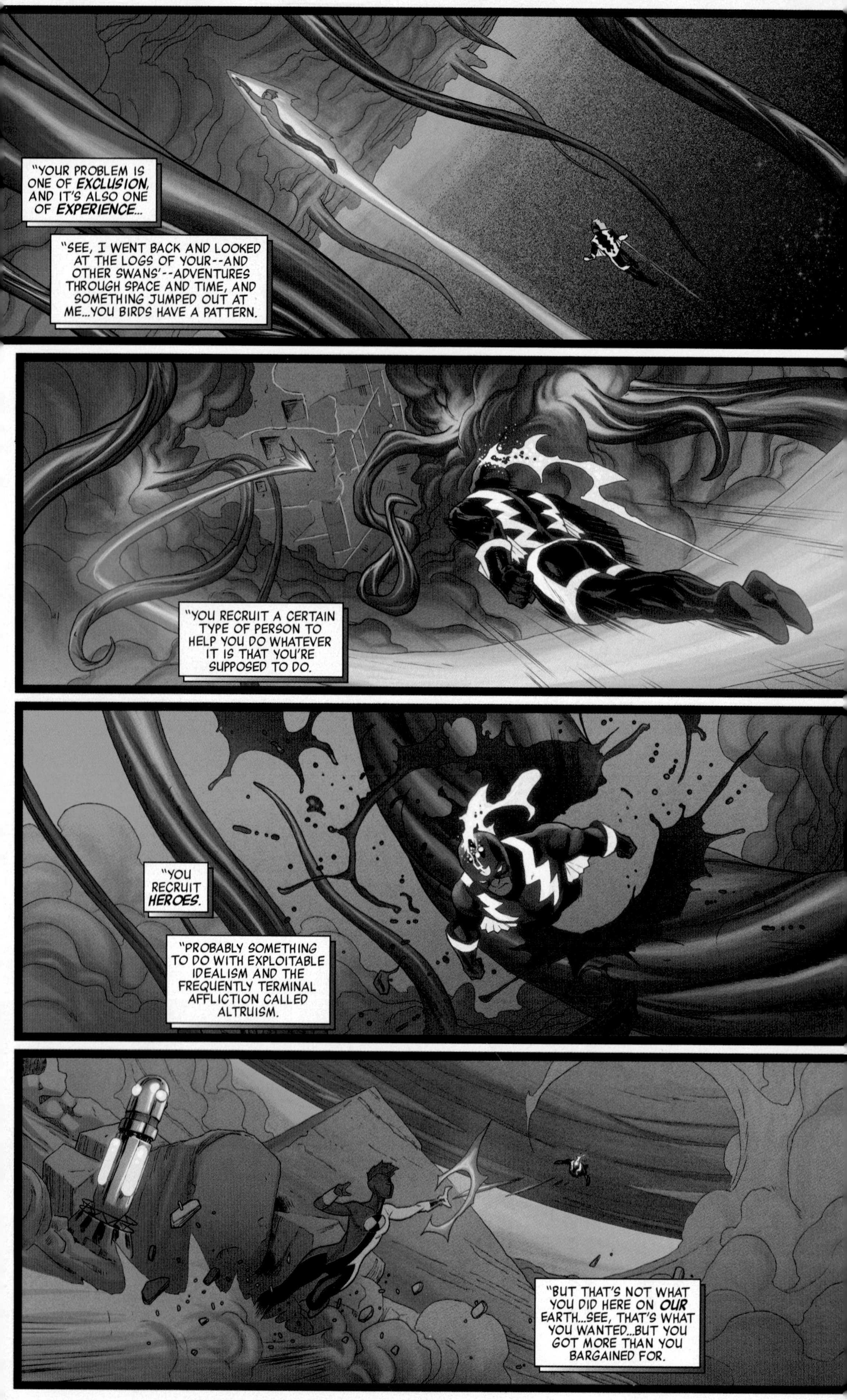
"YOUR PROBLEM IS ONE OF EXCLUSION, AND IT'S ALSO ONE OF EXPERIENCE...
"SEE, I WENT BACK AND LOOKED AT THE LOGS OF YOUR--AND OTHER SWANS'--ADVENTURES THROUGH SPACE AND TIME, AND SOMETHING JUMPED OUT AT ME...YOU BIRDS HAVE A PATTERN.
"YOU RECRUIT A CERTAIN TYPE OF PERSON TO HELP YOU DO WHATEVER IT IS THAT YOU'RE SUPPOSED TO DO.
"YOU RECRUIT HEROES.
"PROBABLY SOMETHING TO DO WITH EXPLOITABLE IDEALISM AND THE FREQUENTLY TERMINAL AFFLICTION CALLED ALTRUISM.
"BUT THAT'S NOT WHAT YOU DID HERE ON OUR EARTH...SEE, THAT'S WHAT YOU WANTED...BUT YOU GOT MORE THAN YOU BARGAINED FOR.

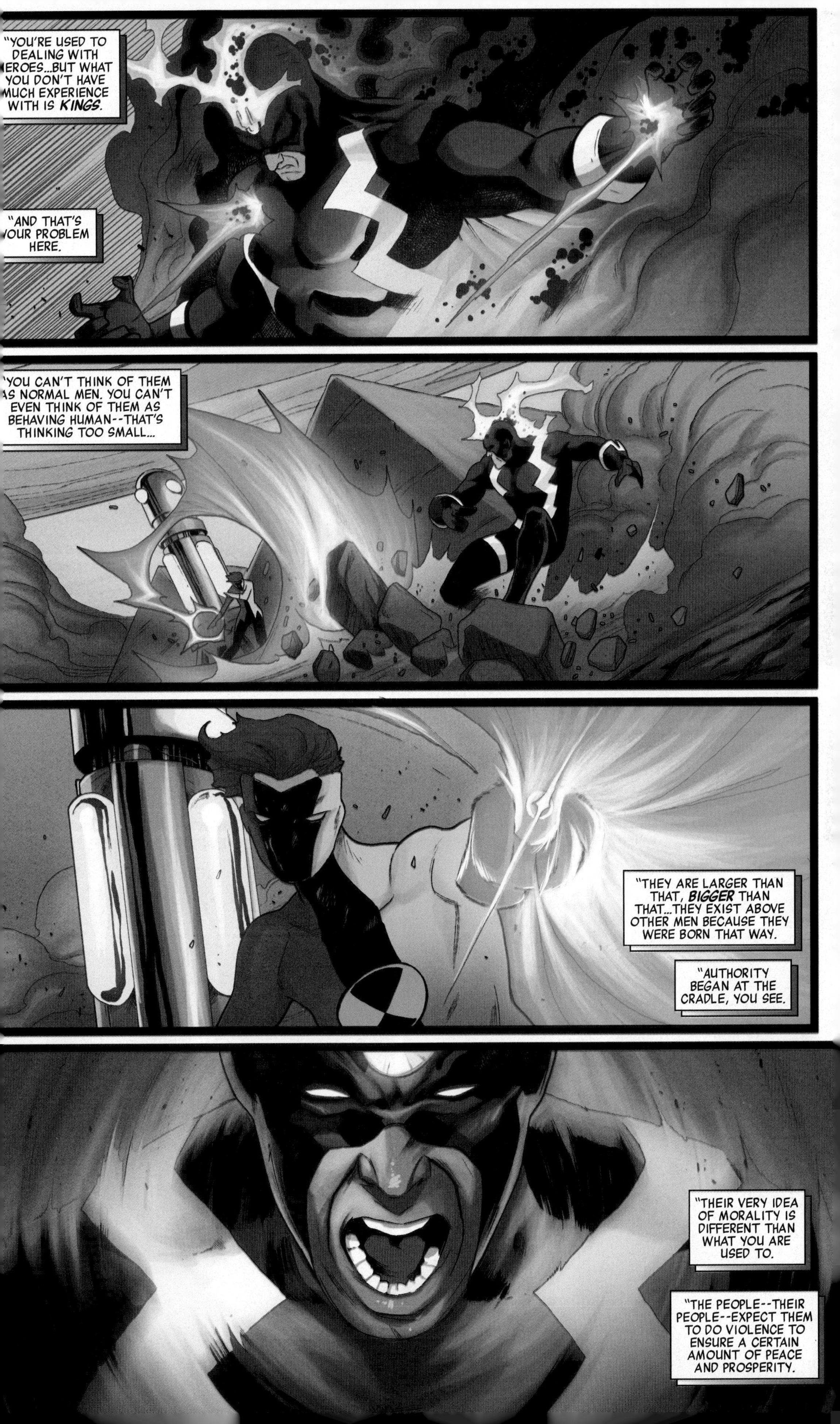
"YOU'RE USED TO DEALING WITH HEROES...BUT WHAT YOU DON'T HAVE MUCH EXPERIENCE WITH IS KINGS.
"AND THAT'S YOUR PROBLEM HERE.
"YOU CAN'T THINK OF THEM AS NORMAL MEN. YOU CAN'T EVEN THINK OF THEM AS BEHAVING HUMAN--THAT'S THINKING TOO SMALL...
"THEY ARE LARGER THAN THAT, BIGGER THAN THAT...THEY EXIST ABOVE OTHER MEN BECAUSE THEY WERE BORN THAT WAY.
"AUTHORITY BEGAN AT THE CRADLE, YOU SEE.
"THEIR VERY IDEA OF MORALITY IS DIFFERENT THAN WHAT YOU ARE USED TO.
"THE PEOPLE--THEIR PEOPLE--EXPECT THEM TO DO VIOLENCE TO ENSURE A CERTAIN AMOUNT OF PEACE AND PROSPERITY.

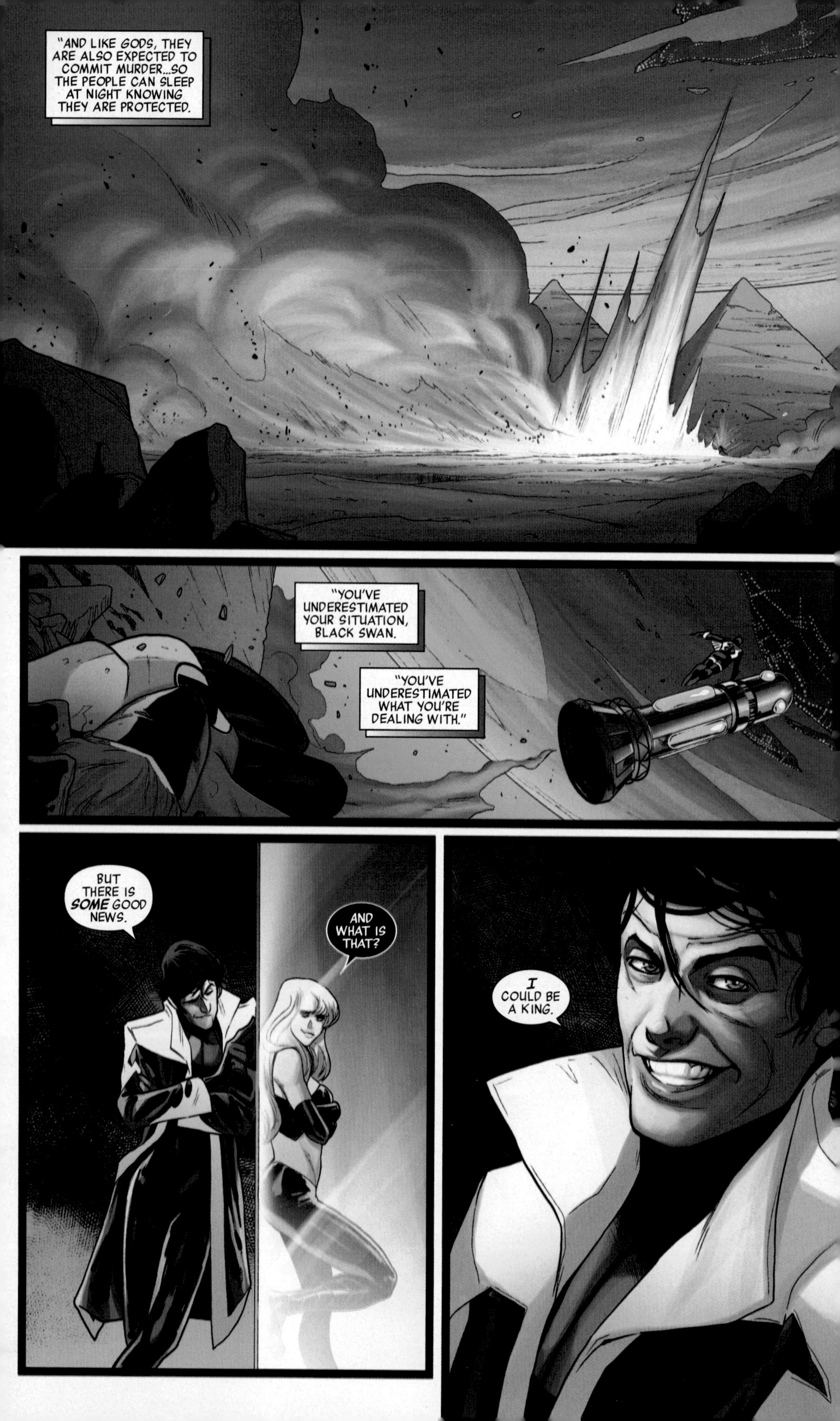
"AND LIKE GODS, THEY ARE ALSO EXPECTED TO COMMIT MURDER...SO THE PEOPLE CAN SLEEP AT NIGHT KNOWING THEY ARE PROTECTED.
"YOU'VE UNDERESTIMATED YOUR SITUATION, BLACK SWAN.
"YOU'VE UNDERESTIMATED WHAT YOU'RE DEALING WITH."
BUT THERE IS SOME GOOD NEWS.
AND WHAT IS THAT?
I COULD BE A KING.

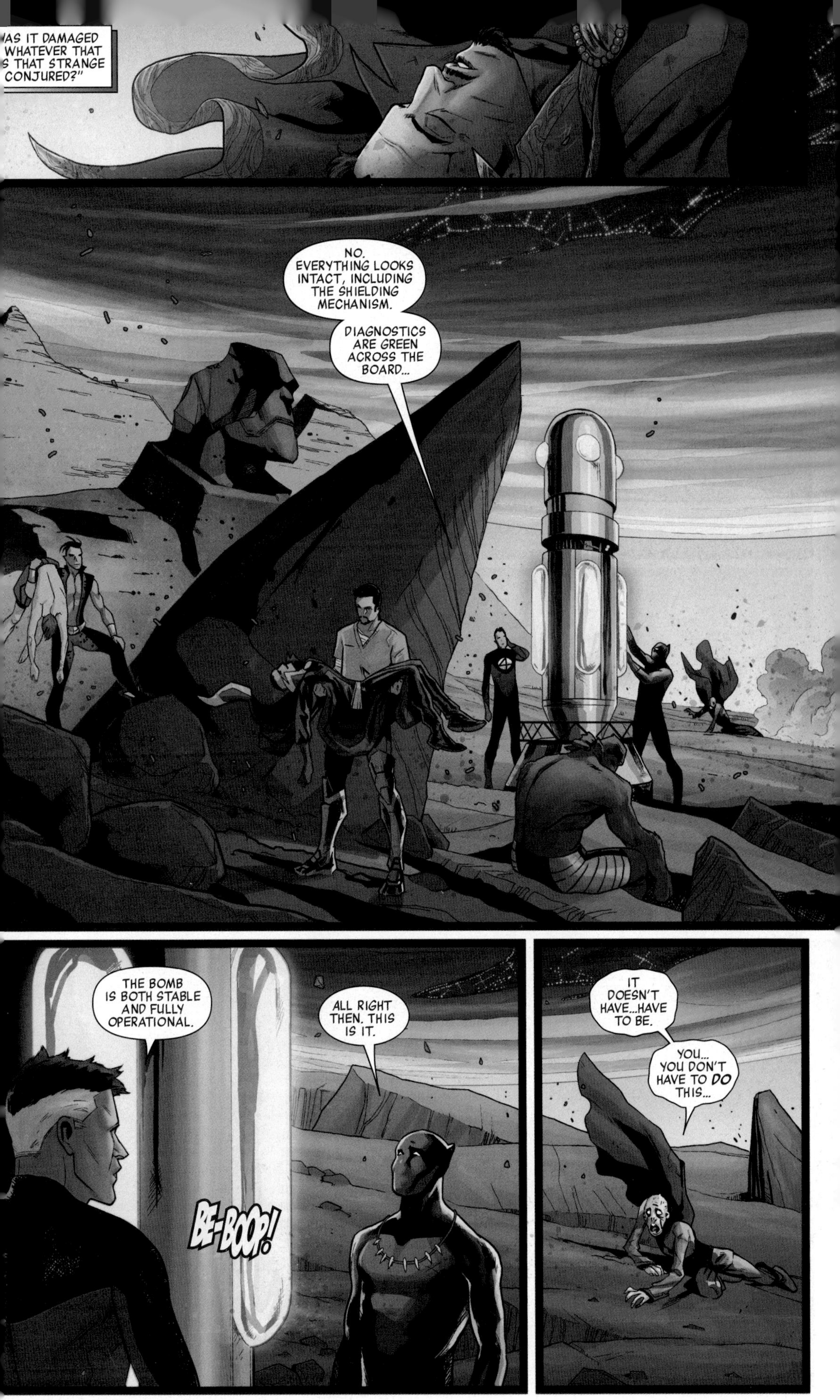

AS IT DAMAGED
WHATEVER THAT
S THAT STRANGE
CONJURED?"
NO. EVERYTHING LOOKS INTACT, INCLUDING THE SHIELDING MECHANISM.
DIAGNOSTICS ARE GREEN ACROSS THE BOARD...
THE BOMB IS BOTH STABLE AND FULLY OPERATIONAL.
ALL RIGHT THEN. THIS IS IT.
BE-BOOP!
IT DOESN'T HAVE...HAVE TO BE.
YOU... YOU DON'T HAVE TO DO THIS...

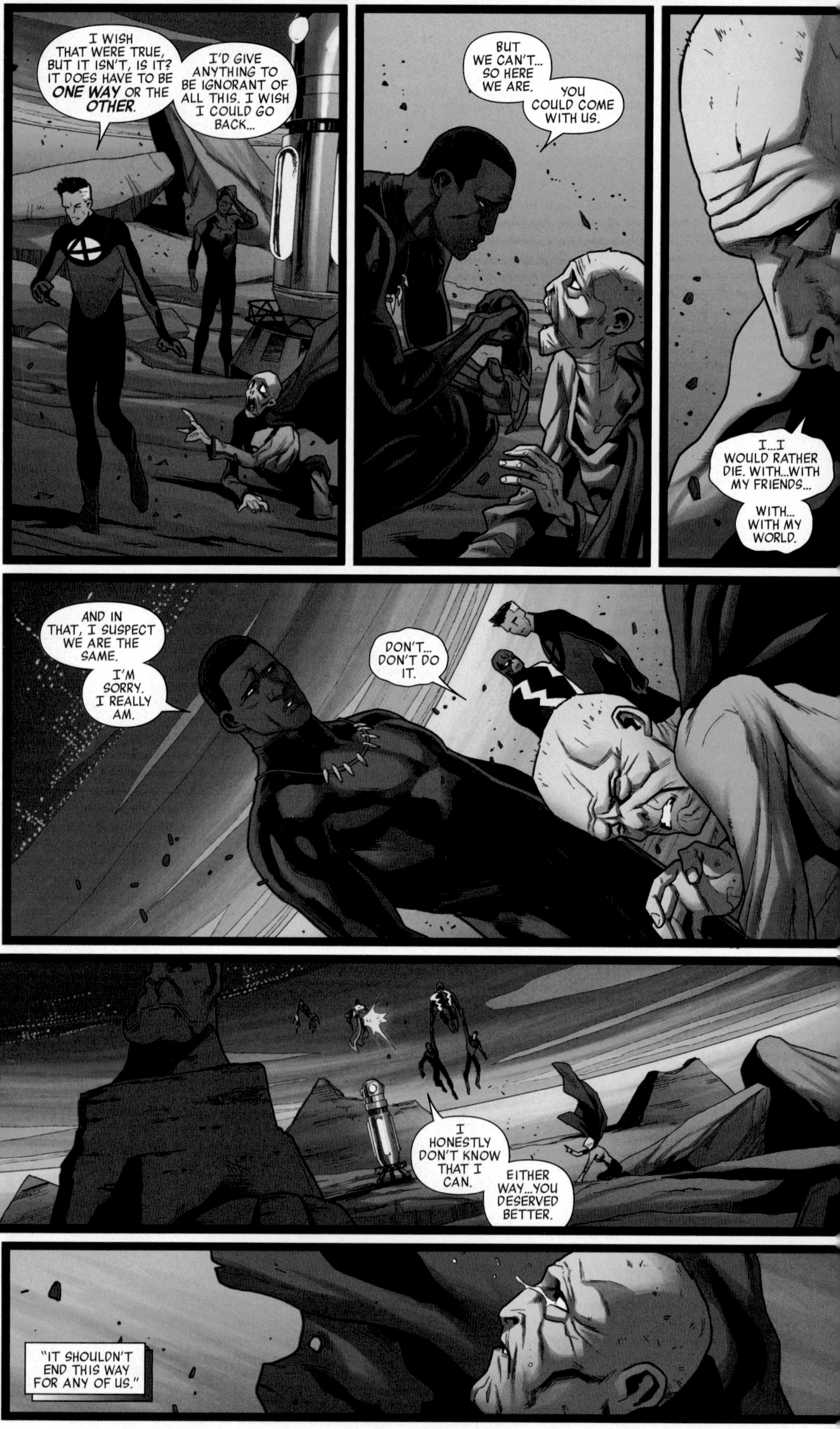
I WISH THAT WERE TRUE, BUT IT ISN'T, IS IT? IT DOES HAVE TO BE ONE WAY OR THE OTHER.
I'D GIVE ANYTHING TO BE IGNORANT OF ALL THIS. I WISH I COULD GO BACK...
BUT WE CAN'T... SO HERE WE ARE.
YOU COULD COME WITH US.
I...I WOULD RATHER DIE. WITH...WITH MY FRIENDS...
WITH... WITH MY WORLD.
AND IN THAT, I SUSPECT WE ARE THE SAME.
I'M SORRY. I REALLY AM.
DON'T... DON'T DO IT.
I HONESTLY DON'T KNOW THAT I CAN.
EITHER WAY...YOU DESERVED BETTER.
"IT SHOULDN'T END THIS WAY FOR ANY OF US."

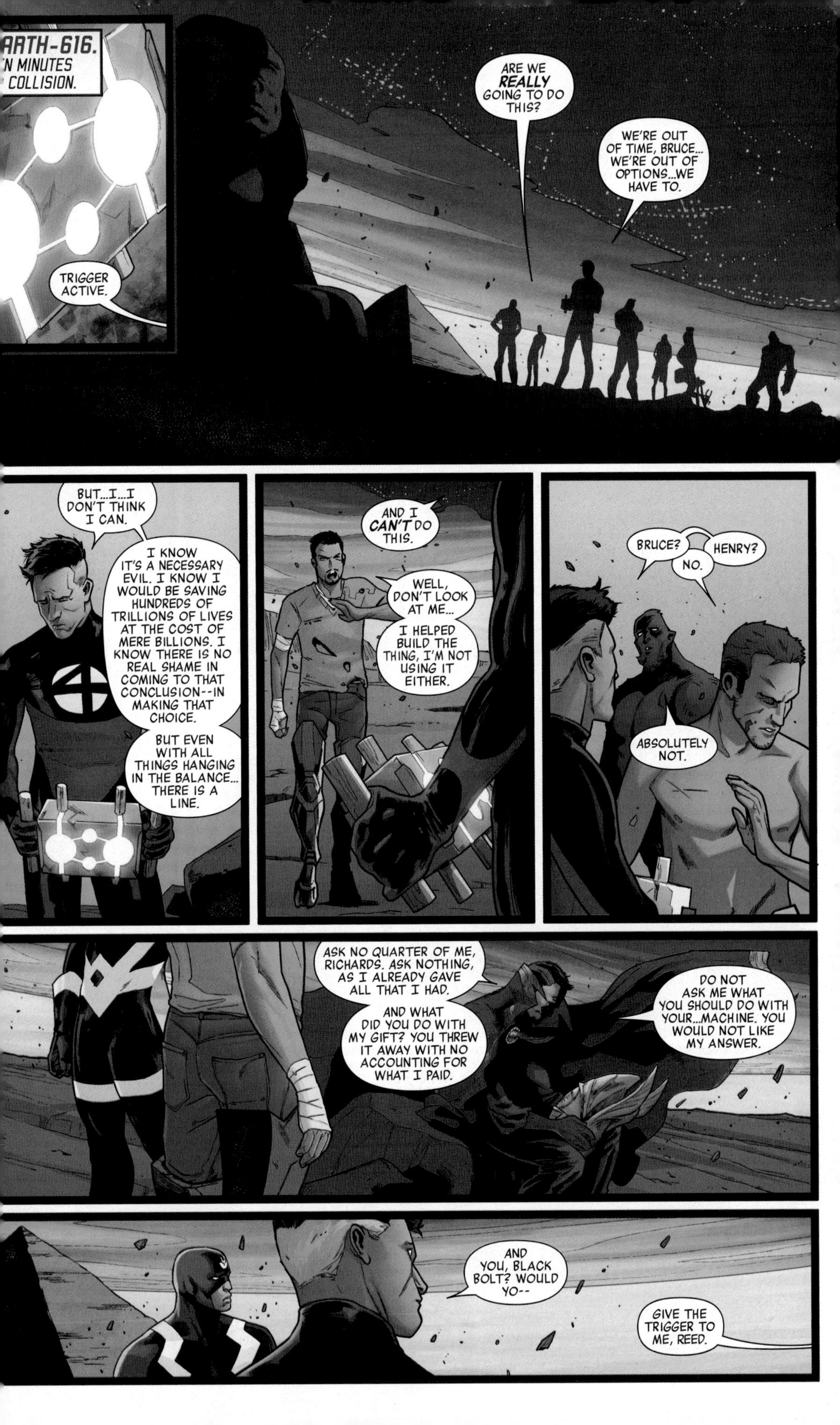

ARTH-616.
N MINUTES
COLLISION.
TRIGGER ACTIVE.
ARE WE REALLY GOING TO DO THIS?
WE'RE OUT OF TIME, BRUCE... WE'RE OUT OF OPTIONS...WE HAVE TO.
BUT...I...I DON'T THINK I CAN.
I KNOW IT'S A NECESSARY EVIL. I KNOW I WOULD BE SAVING HUNDREDS OF TRILLIONS OF LIVES AT THE COST OF MERE BILLIONS. I KNOW THERE IS NO REAL SHAME IN COMING TO THAT CONCLUSION--IN MAKING THAT CHOICE.
BUT EVEN WITH ALL THINGS HANGING IN THE BALANCE... THERE IS A LINE.
AND I CAN'T DO THIS.
WELL, DON'T LOOK AT ME...
I HELPED BUILD THE THING, I'M NOT USING IT EITHER.
BRUCE?
NO.
HENRY?
ABSOLUTELY NOT.
ASK NO QUARTER OF ME, RICHARDS. ASK NOTHING, AS I ALREADY GAVE ALL THAT I HAD.
AND WHAT DID YOU DO WITH MY GIFT? YOU THREW IT AWAY WITH NO ACCOUNTING FOR WHAT I PAID.
DO NOT ASK ME WHAT YOU SHOULD DO WITH YOUR...MACHINE. YOU WOULD NOT LIKE MY ANSWER.
AND YOU, BLACK BOLT? WOULD YO--
GIVE THE TRIGGER TO ME, REED.

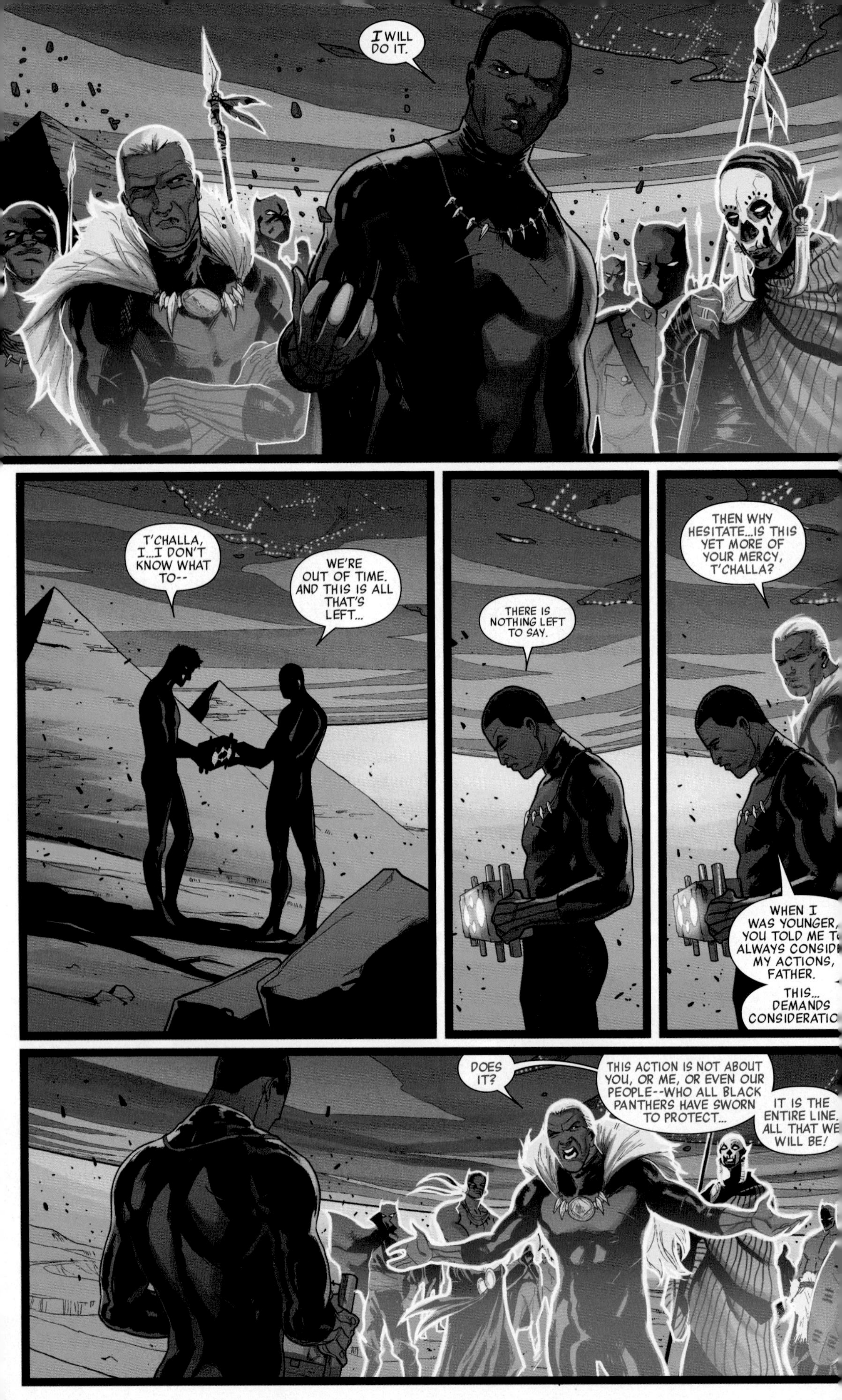
I WILL DO IT.
T'CHALLA, I...I DON'T KNOW WHAT TO--
WE'RE OUT OF TIME. AND THIS IS ALL THAT'S LEFT...
THERE IS NOTHING LEFT TO SAY.
THEN WHY HESITATE...IS THIS YET MORE OF YOUR MERCY, T'CHALLA?
WHEN I WAS YOUNGER, YOU TOLD ME T
ALWAYS CONSID
MY ACTIONS, FATHER.
THIS... DEMANDS CONSIDERATIO
DOES IT?
THIS ACTION IS NOT ABOUT YOU, OR ME, OR EVEN OUR PEOPLE--WHO ALL BLACK PANTHERS HAVE SWORN TO PROTECT...
IT IS THE ENTIRE LINE. ALL THAT WE WILL BE!

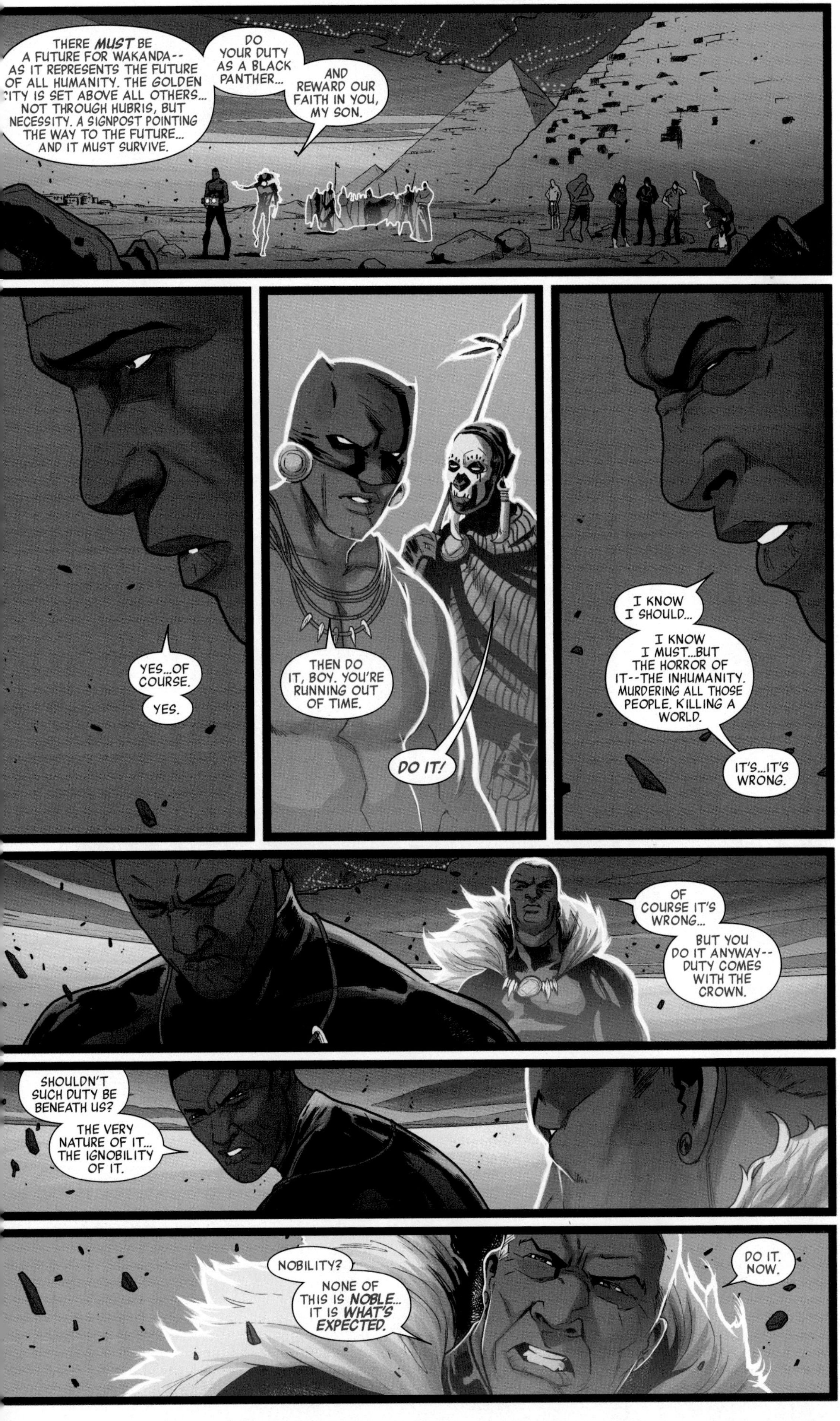
THERE MUST BE A FUTURE FOR WAKANDA-- AS IT REPRESENTS THE FUTURE OF ALL HUMANITY. THE GOLDEN CITY IS SET ABOVE ALL OTHERS... NOT THROUGH HUBRIS, BUT NECESSITY. A SIGNPOST POINTING THE WAY TO THE FUTURE... AND IT MUST SURVIVE.
DO YOUR DUTY AS A BLACK PANTHER...
AND REWARD OUR FAITH IN YOU, MY SON.
YES...OF COURSE.
YES.
THEN DO IT, BOY. YOU'RE RUNNING OUT OF TIME.
DO IT!
I KNOW I SHOULD...
I KNOW I MUST...BUT THE HORROR OF IT--THE INHUMANITY. MURDERING ALL THOSE PEOPLE. KILLING A WORLD.
IT'S...IT'S WRONG.
OF COURSE IT'S WRONG...
BUT YOU DO IT ANYWAY-- DUTY COMES WITH THE CROWN.
SHOULDN'T SUCH DUTY BE BENEATH US?
THE VERY NATURE OF IT... THE IGNOBILITY OF IT.
NOBILITY?
NONE OF THIS IS NOBLE... IT IS WHAT'S EXPECTED.
DO IT. NOW.

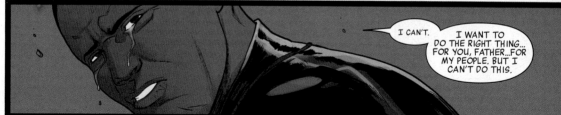

I CAN'T. I WANT TO DO THE RIGHT THING... FOR YOU, FATHER...FOR MY PEOPLE. BUT I CAN'T DO THIS.

WE WERE CURSED WHEN WE MADE THIS MACHINE...

WE WERE DAMNED THE VERY DAY WE THOUGHT IT WAS FOR MEN TO DECIDE THINGS SUCH AS THIS.

DAMNED, T'CHALLA?

PERHAPS THAT WOULD BE FITTING...

BUT YOU STILL HAVE TIME.

IT...IS WRONG...

AND I CANNOT DO IT, FATHER!

I CANNOT.

NO. YOU CHOOSE NOT TO-IT IS YOUR CHOICE.

SO HERE IS MINE: THERE IS AN ETERNITY AND IN IT, YOU ARE DEAD TO ME, AND TO US ALL.

YOU HAVE NO PEOPLE.

YOU ARE NO BLACK PANTHER.

YOU ARE NO LONGER MY SON.

I'M SORRY...I'M SORRY...

IT'S OKAY, T'CHALLA.

IT'S OKAY. I UNDERSTAND...

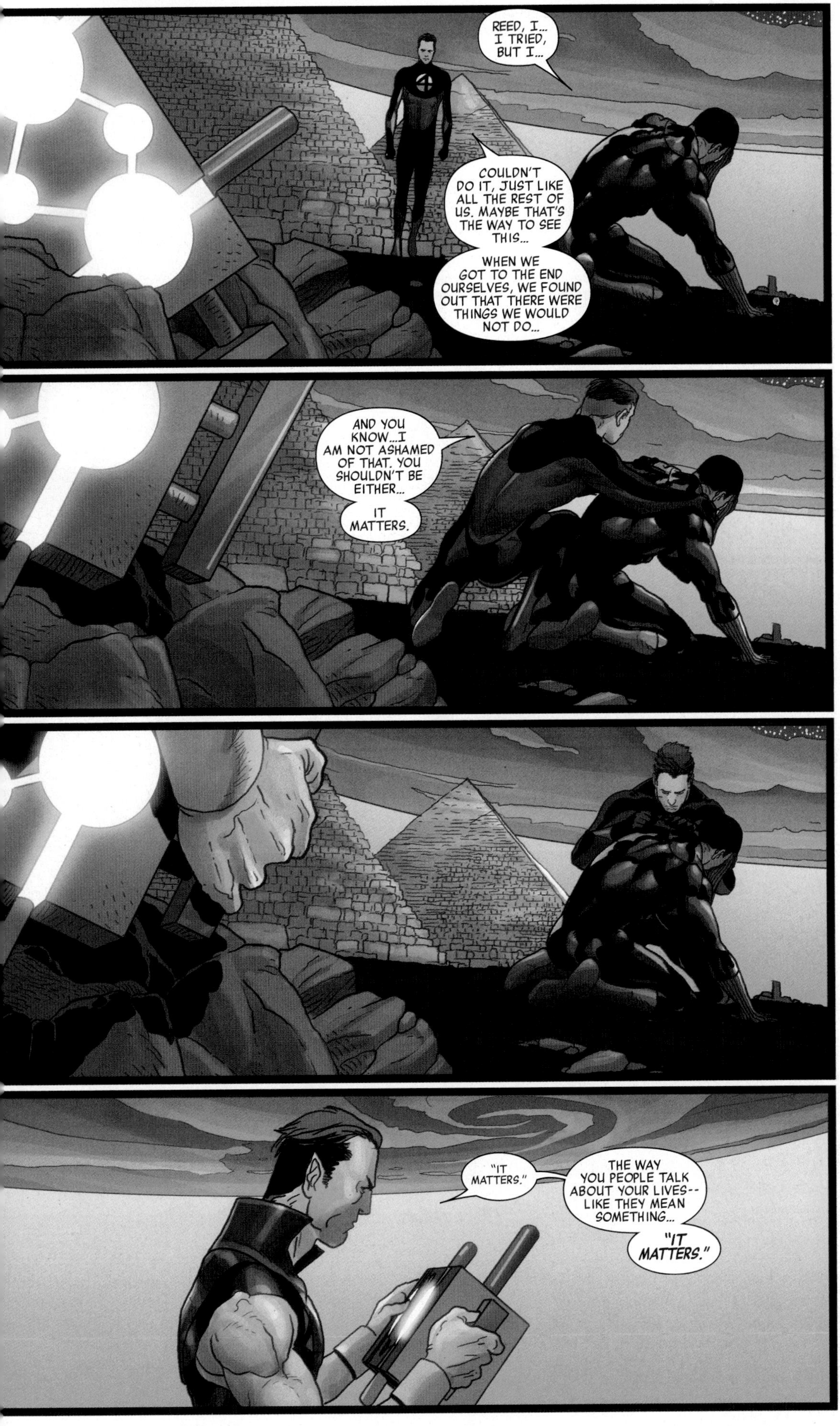
REED, I... I TRIED, BUT I...
COULDN'T DO IT, JUST LIKE ALL THE REST OF US. MAYBE THAT'S THE WAY TO SEE THIS...
WHEN WE GOT TO THE END OURSELVES, WE FOUND OUT THAT THERE WERE THINGS WE WOULD NOT DO...
AND YOU KNOW...I AM NOT ASHAMED OF THAT. YOU SHOULDN'T BE EITHER...
IT MATTERS.
"IT MATTERS."
THE WAY YOU PEOPLE TALK ABOUT YOUR LIVES-- LIKE THEY MEAN SOMETHING...
"IT MATTERS."

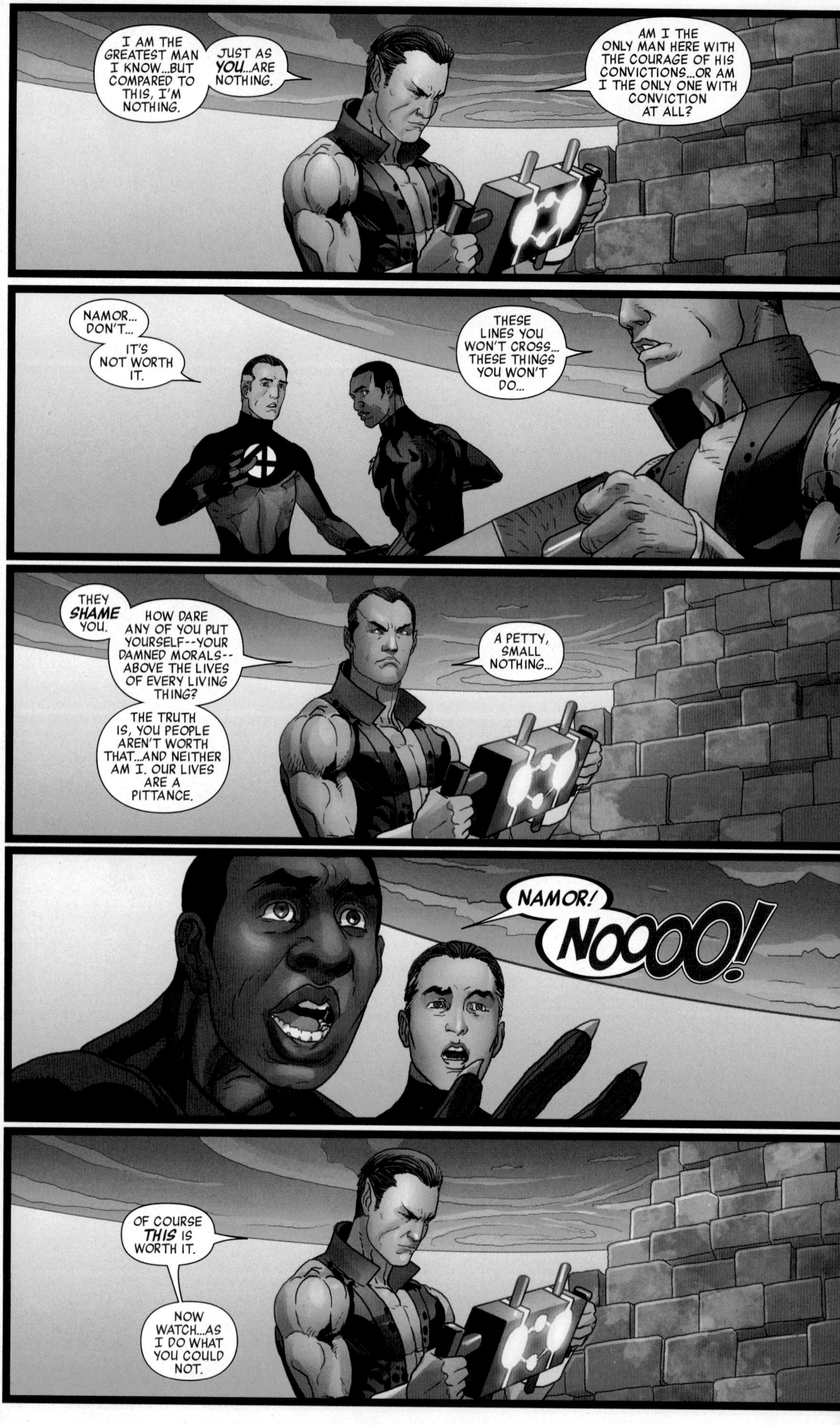
I AM THE GREATEST MAN I KNOW...BUT COMPARED TO THIS, I'M NOTHING.
JUST AS YOU...ARE NOTHING.
AM I THE ONLY MAN HERE WITH THE COURAGE OF HIS CONVICTIONS...OR AM I THE ONLY ONE WITH CONVICTION AT ALL?
NAMOR... DON'T...
IT'S NOT WORTH IT.
THESE LINES YOU WON'T CROSS... THESE THINGS YOU WON'T DO...
THEY SHAME YOU.
HOW DARE ANY OF YOU PUT YOURSELF--YOUR DAMNED MORALS--ABOVE THE LIVES OF EVERY LIVING THING?
THE TRUTH IS, YOU PEOPLE AREN'T WORTH THAT...AND NEITHER AM I. OUR LIVES ARE A PITTANCE.
A PETTY, SMALL NOTHING...
NAMOR!
NOOOOO!
OF COURSE THIS IS WORTH IT.
NOW WATCH...AS I DO WHAT YOU COULD NOT.

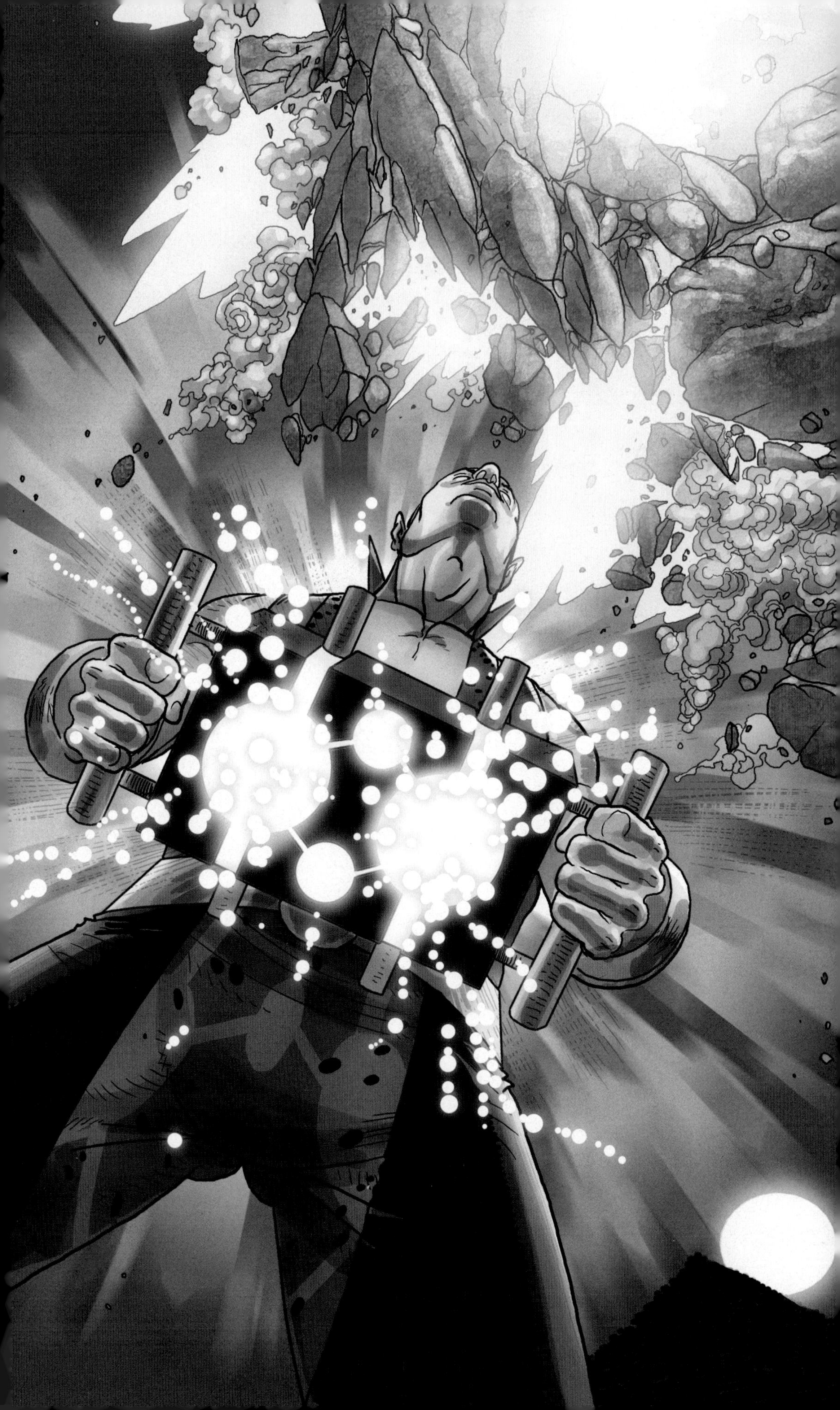

"WE ARE NOT BROTHERS"

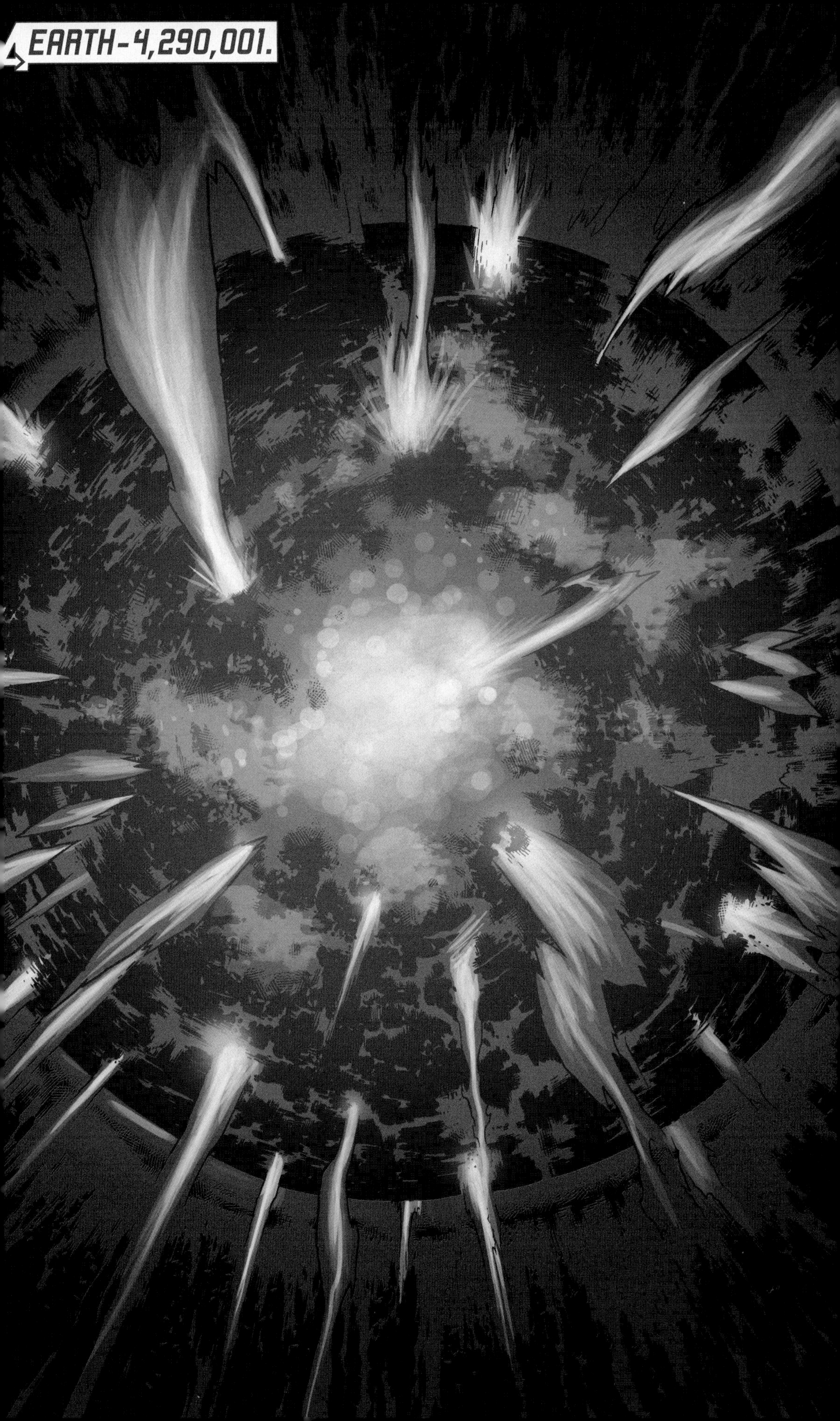
EARTH-4,290,001.

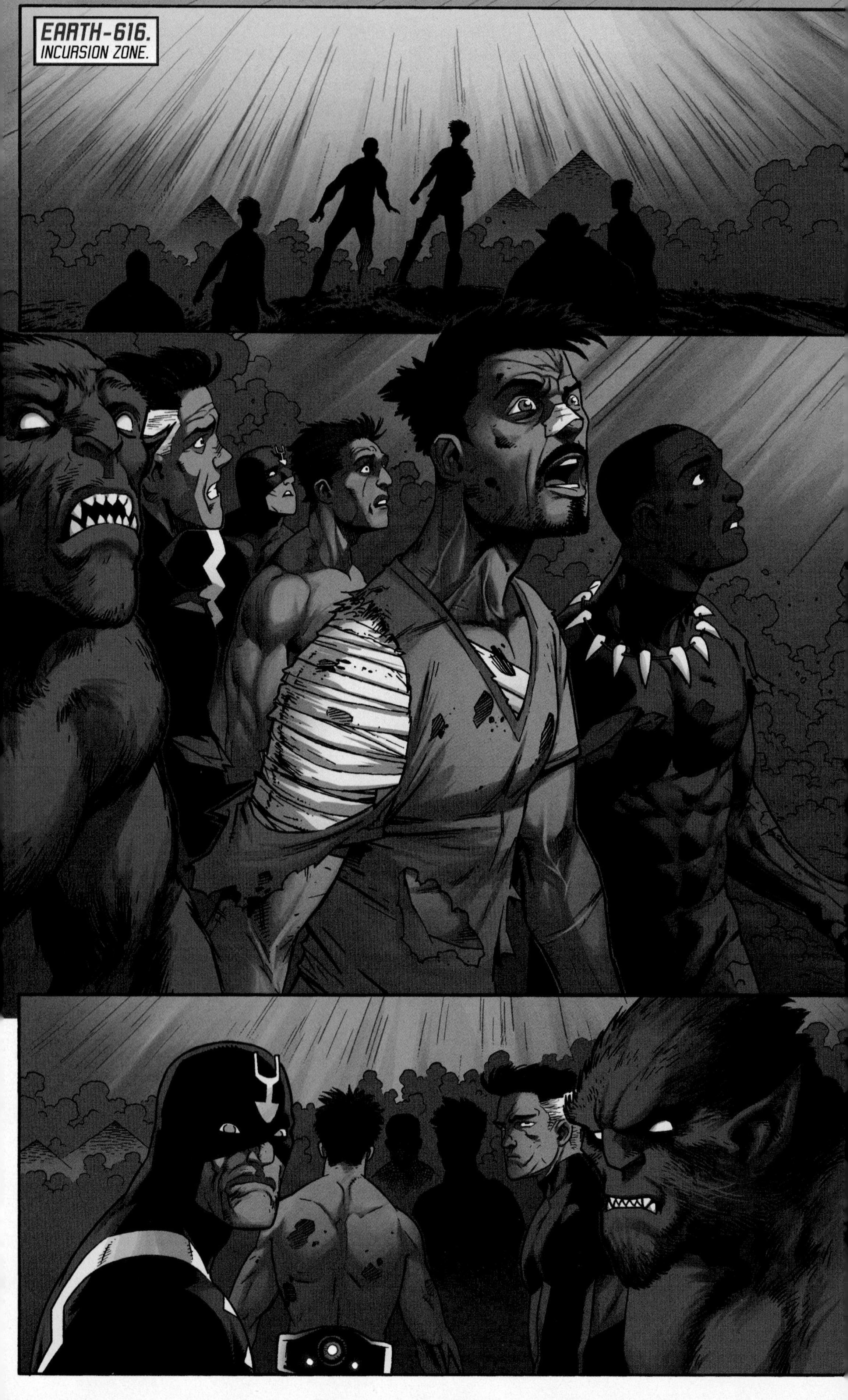
EARTH-616.
INCURSION ZONE.

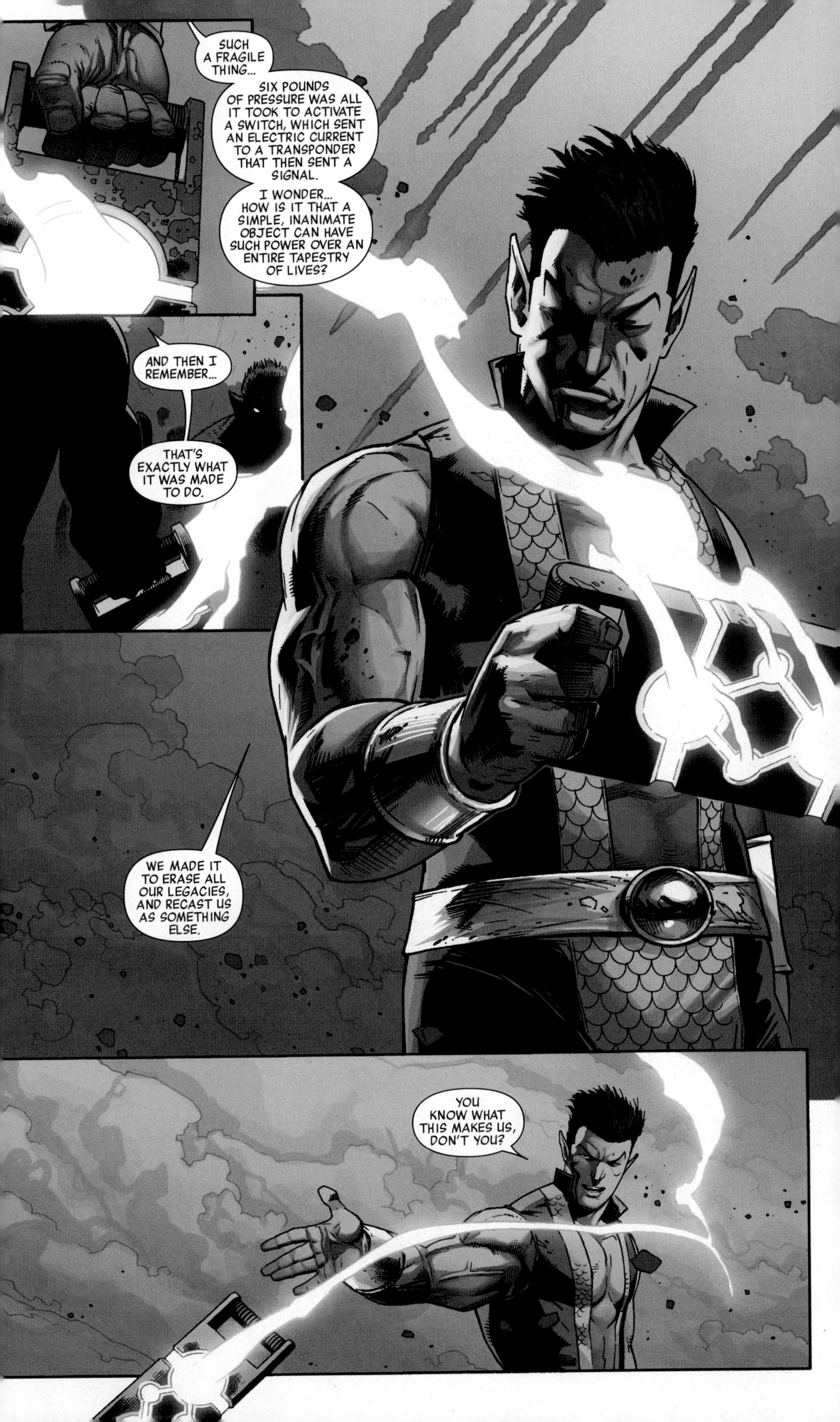

SUCH A FRAGILE THING...
SIX POUNDS OF PRESSURE WAS ALL IT TOOK TO ACTIVATE A SWITCH, WHICH SENT AN ELECTRIC CURRENT TO A TRANSPONDER THAT THEN SENT A SIGNAL.
I WONDER... HOW IS IT THAT A SIMPLE, INANIMATE OBJECT CAN HAVE SUCH POWER OVER AN ENTIRE TAPESTRY OF LIVES?
AND THEN I REMEMBER...
THAT'S EXACTLY WHAT IT WAS MADE TO DO.
WE MADE IT TO ERASE ALL OUR LEGACIES, AND RECAST US AS SOMETHING ELSE.
YOU KNOW WHAT THIS MAKES US, DON'T YOU?

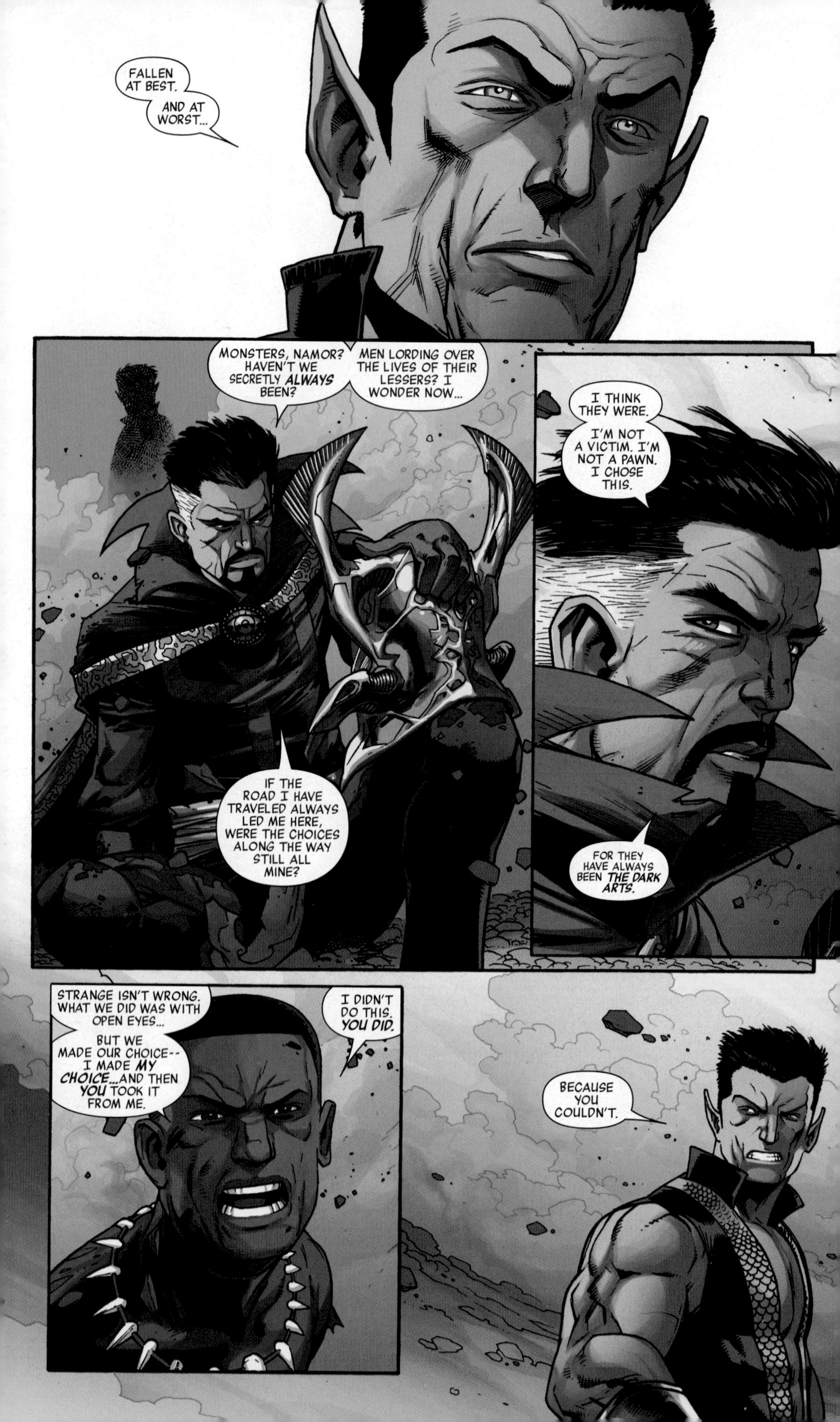
FALLEN AT BEST.
AND AT WORST...
MONSTERS, NAMOR? HAVEN'T WE SECRETLY *ALWAYS* BEEN?
MEN LORDING OVER THE LIVES OF THEIR LESSERS? I WONDER NOW...
IF THE ROAD I HAVE TRAVELED ALWAYS LED ME HERE, WERE THE CHOICES ALONG THE WAY STILL ALL MINE?
I THINK THEY WERE.
I'M NOT A VICTIM. I'M NOT A PAWN. I CHOSE THIS.
FOR THEY HAVE ALWAYS BEEN *THE DARK ARTS.*
STRANGE ISN'T WRONG. WHAT WE DID WAS WITH OPEN EYES...
BUT WE MADE OUR CHOICE-- I MADE *MY CHOICE*...AND THEN *YOU* TOOK IT FROM ME.
I DIDN'T DO THIS. *YOU DID.*
BECAUSE YOU COULDN'T.

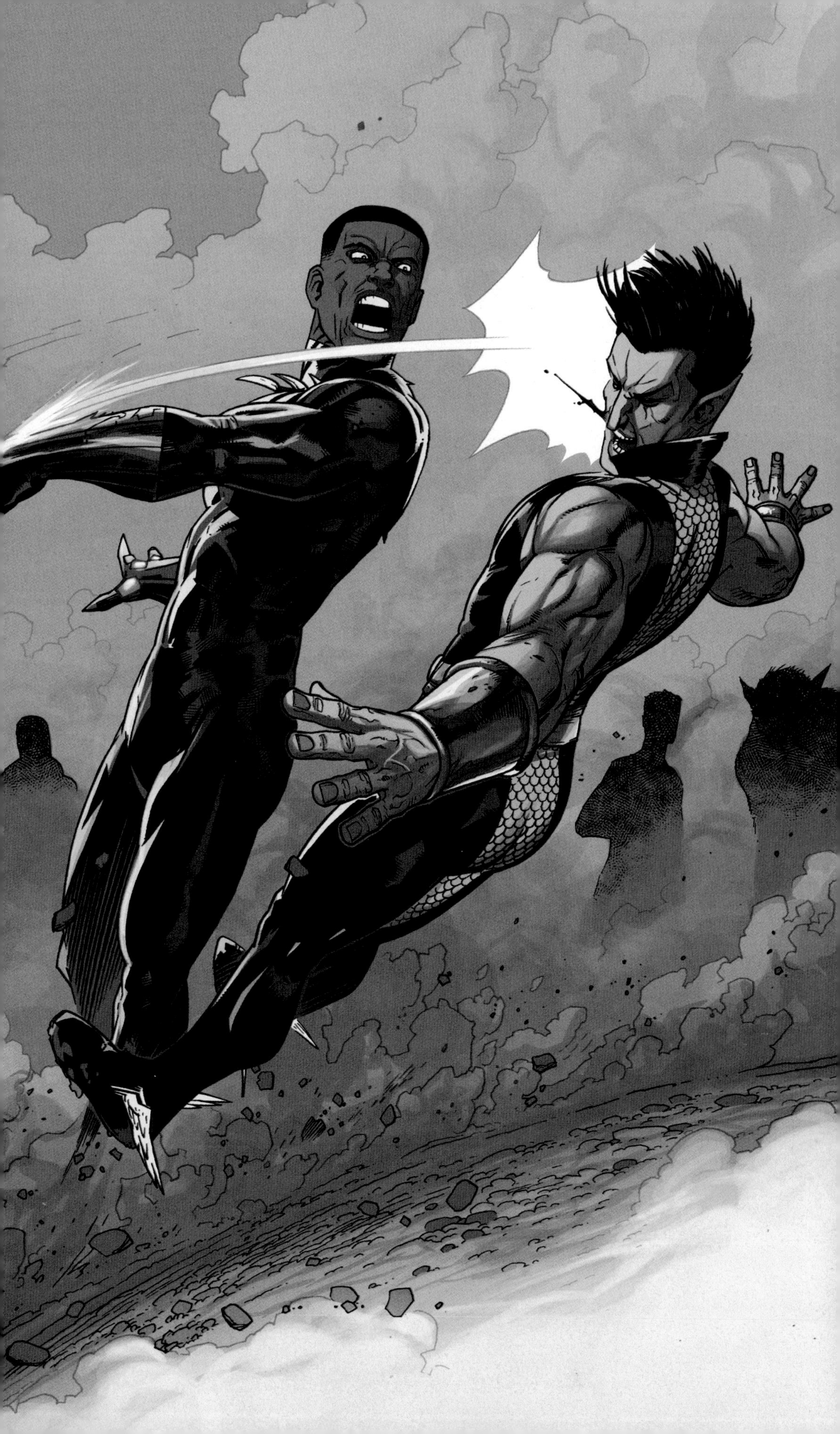

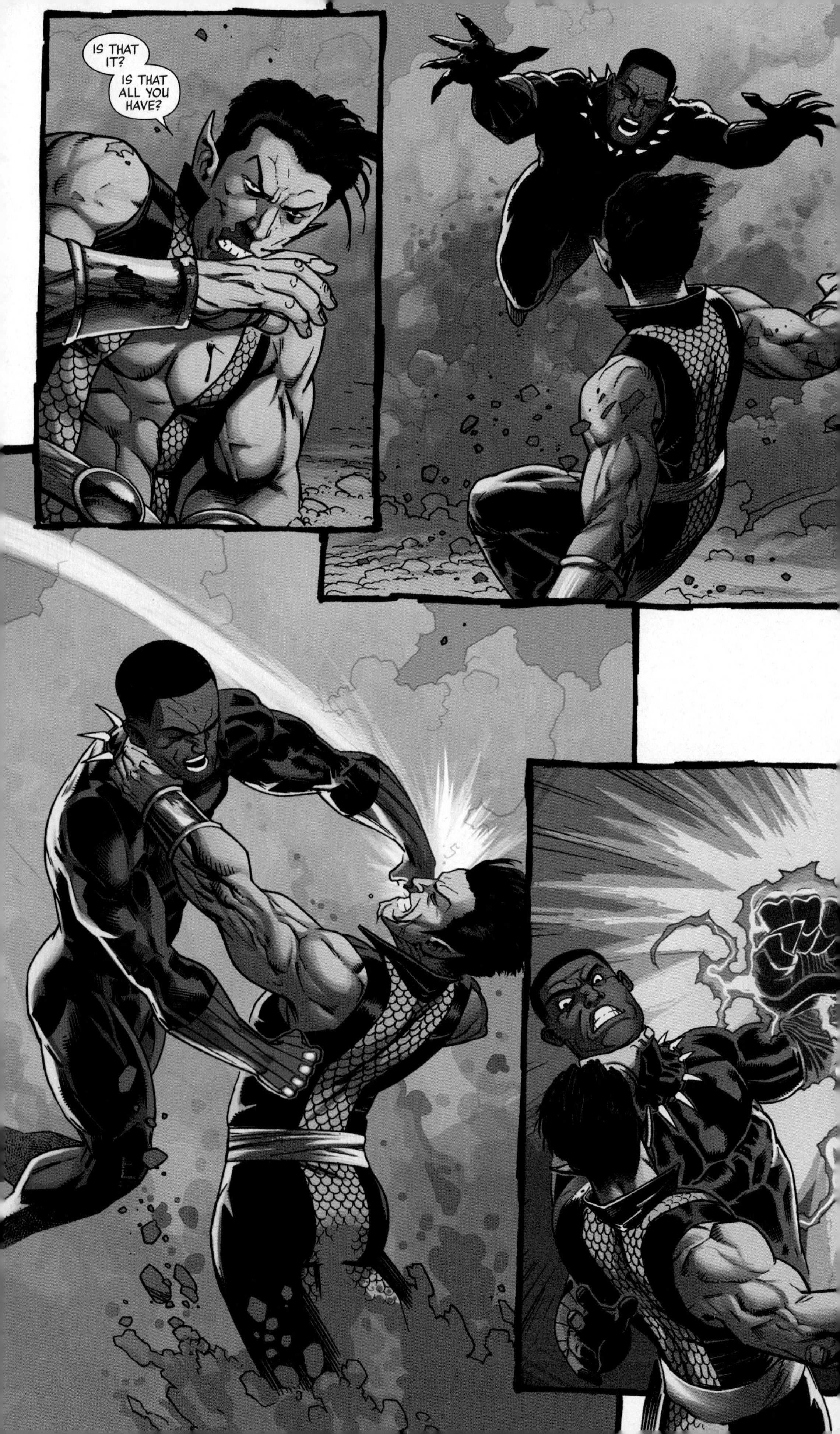
IS THAT IT? IS THAT ALL YOU HAVE?

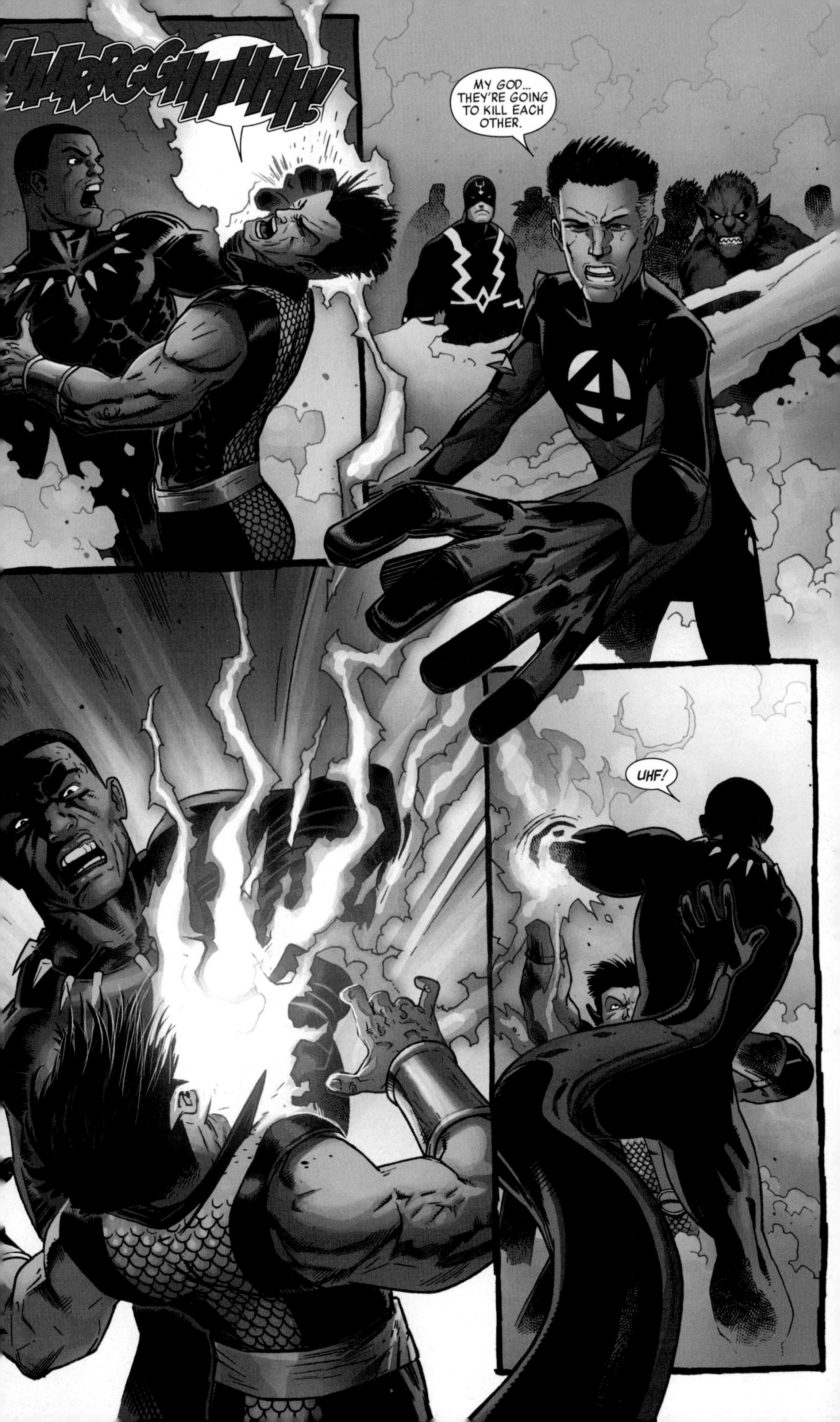
MY GOD... THEY'RE GOING TO KILL EACH OTHER.
UHF!

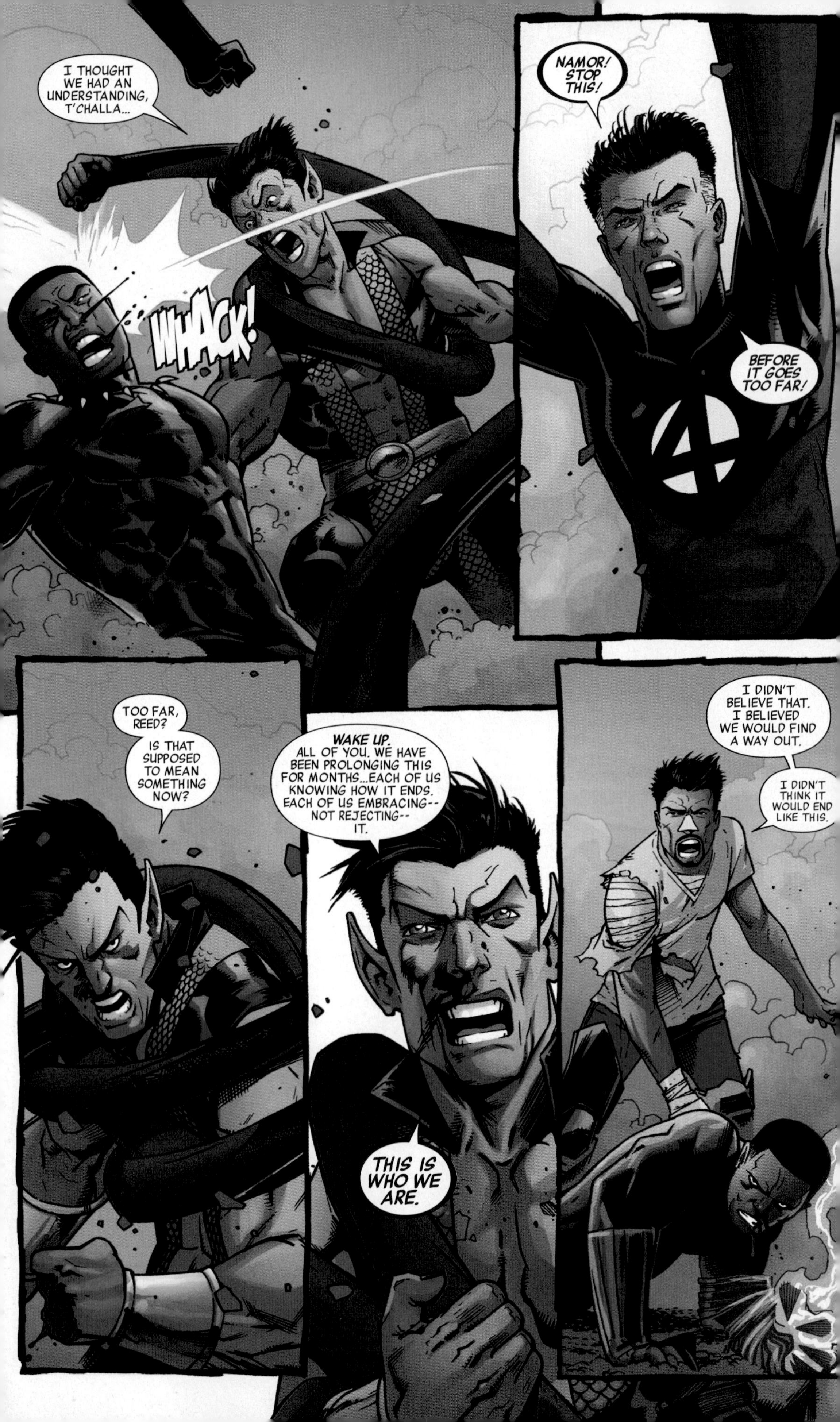
I THOUGHT WE HAD AN UNDERSTANDING, T'CHALLA...
WHACK!
NAMOR! STOP THIS!
BEFORE IT GOES TOO FAR!
TOO FAR, REED?
IS THAT SUPPOSED TO MEAN SOMETHING NOW?
WAKE UP. ALL OF YOU. WE HAVE BEEN PROLONGING THIS FOR MONTHS...EACH OF US KNOWING HOW IT ENDS. EACH OF US EMBRACING-- NOT REJECTING-- IT.
THIS IS WHO WE ARE.
I DIDN'T BELIEVE THAT. I BELIEVED WE WOULD FIND A WAY OUT.
I DIDN'T THINK IT WOULD END LIKE THIS.

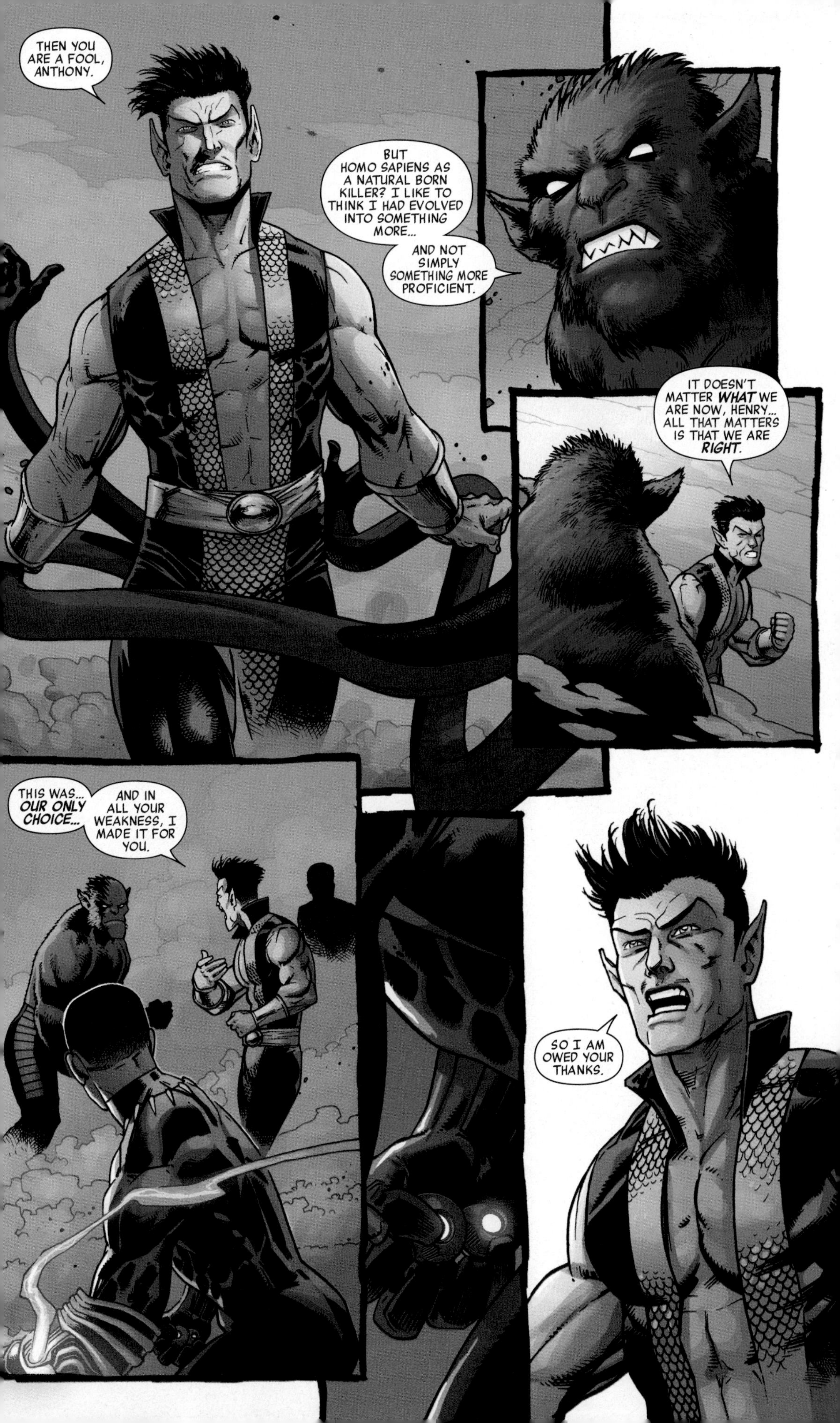
THEN YOU ARE A FOOL, ANTHONY.
BUT HOMO SAPIENS AS A NATURAL BORN KILLER? I LIKE TO THINK I HAD EVOLVED INTO SOMETHING MORE...
AND NOT SIMPLY SOMETHING MORE PROFICIENT.
IT DOESN'T MATTER WHAT WE ARE NOW, HENRY... ALL THAT MATTERS IS THAT WE ARE RIGHT.
THIS WAS... OUR ONLY CHOICE...
AND IN ALL YOUR WEAKNESS, I MADE IT FOR YOU.
SO I AM OWED YOUR THANKS.

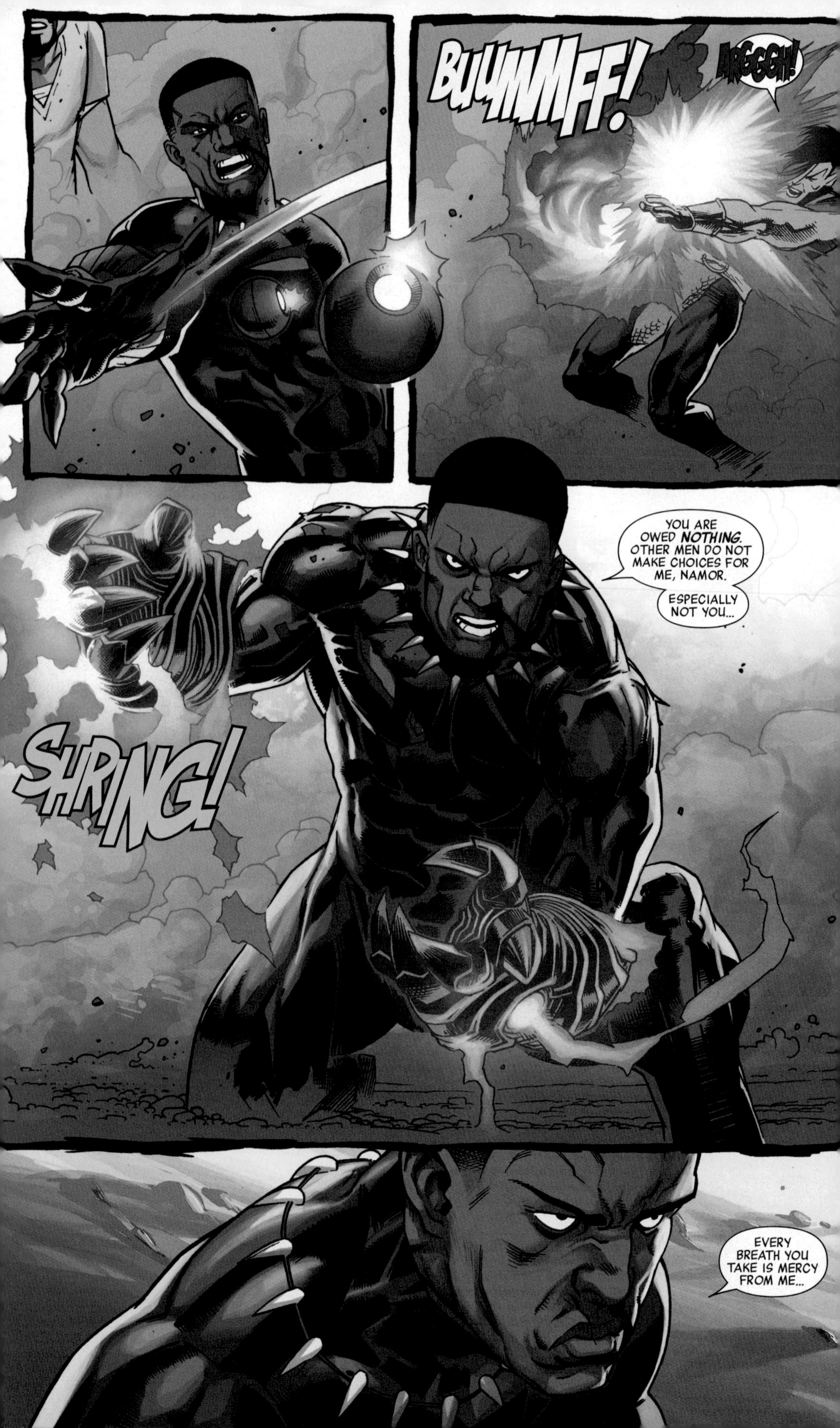
BUUMMFF!
ARGGGH!
YOU ARE OWED ***NOTHING***. OTHER MEN DO NOT MAKE CHOICES FOR ME, NAMOR.
ESPECIALLY NOT YOU...
SHRING!
EVERY BREATH YOU TAKE IS MERCY FROM ME...

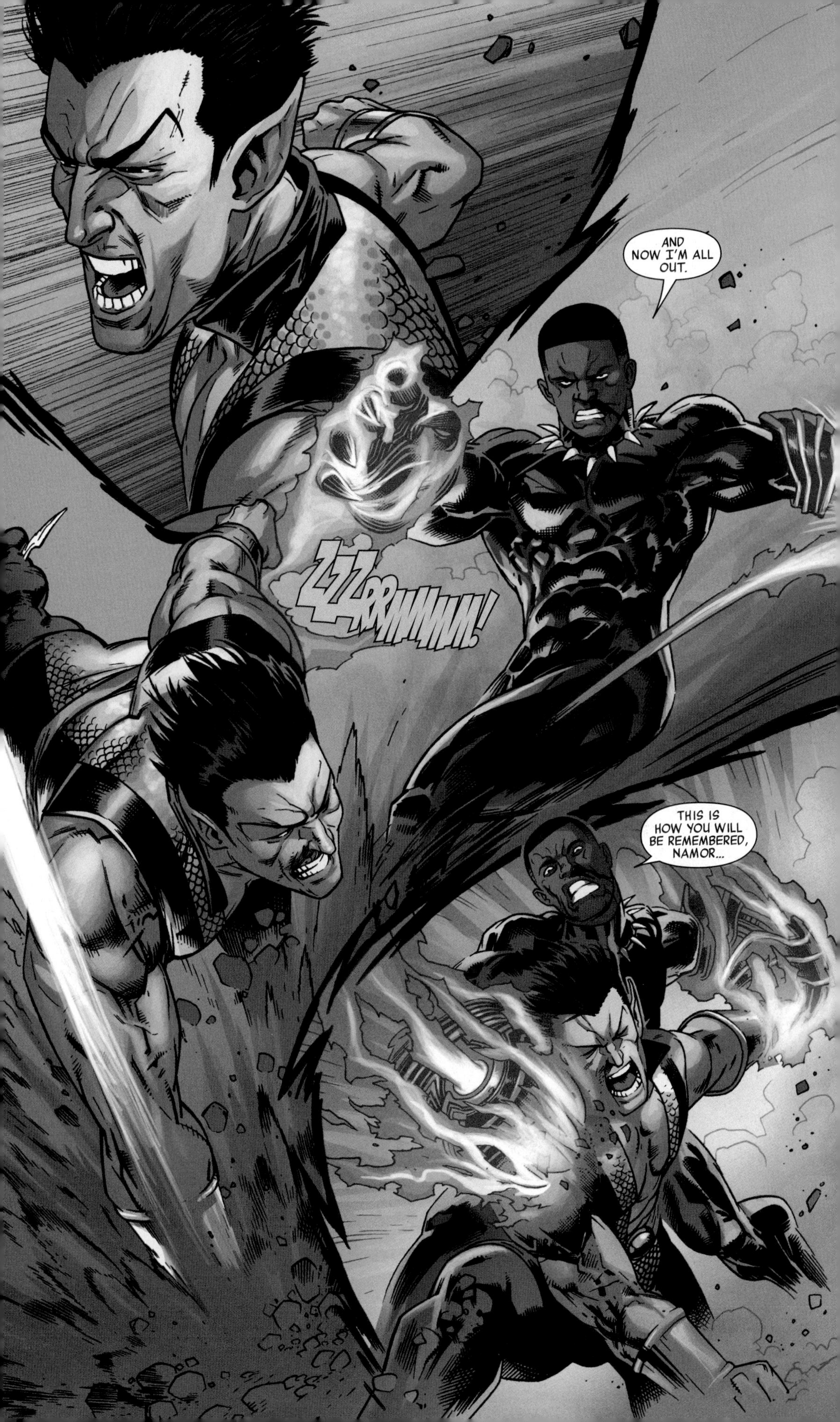
AND NOW I'M ALL OUT.
ZZZRRMMMM!
THIS IS HOW YOU WILL BE REMEMBERED, NAMOR...

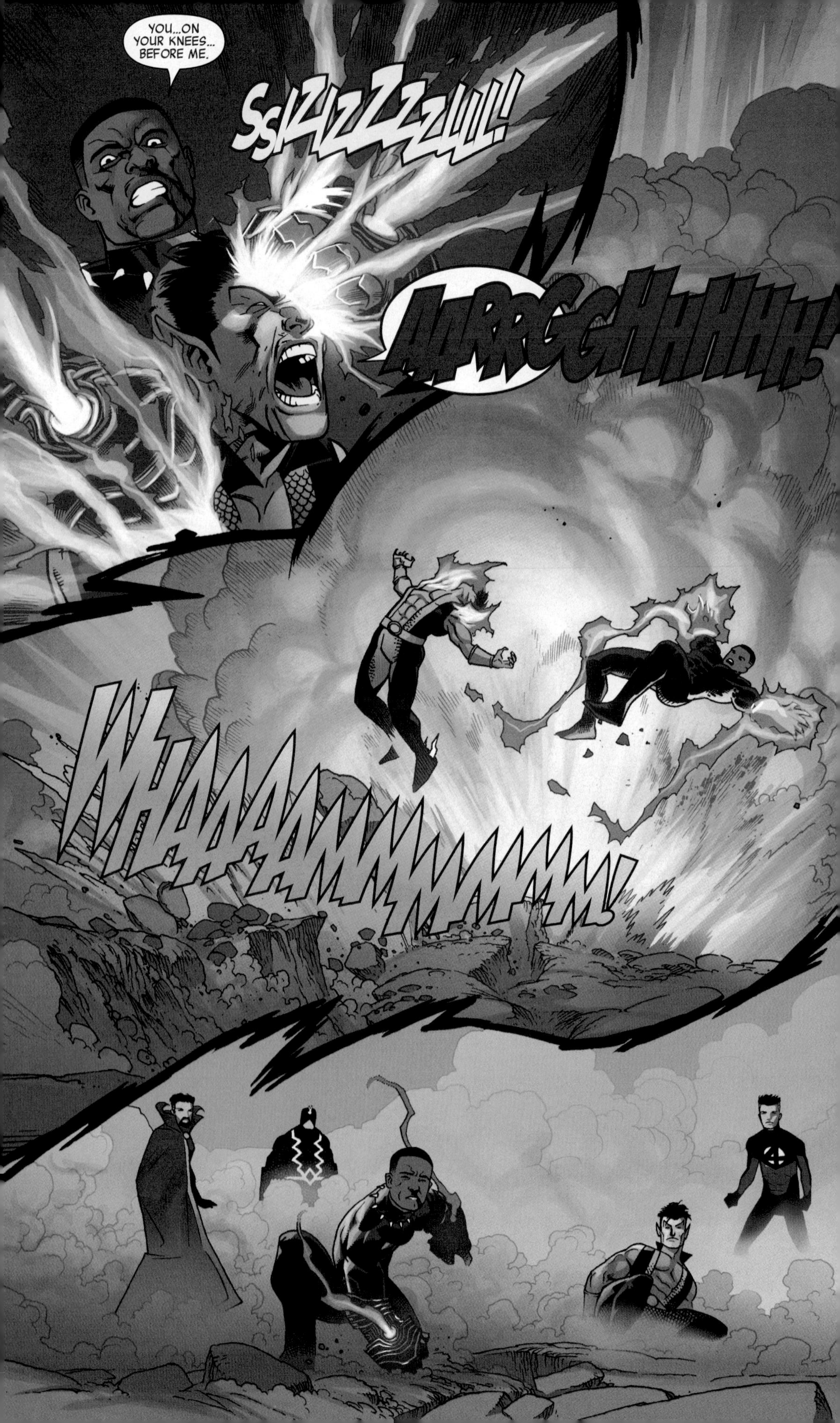
YOU...ON YOUR KNEES... BEFORE ME.
SsIZZIZZZZULL!
AARRGGHHHHH!
WHAAAMMMMM!

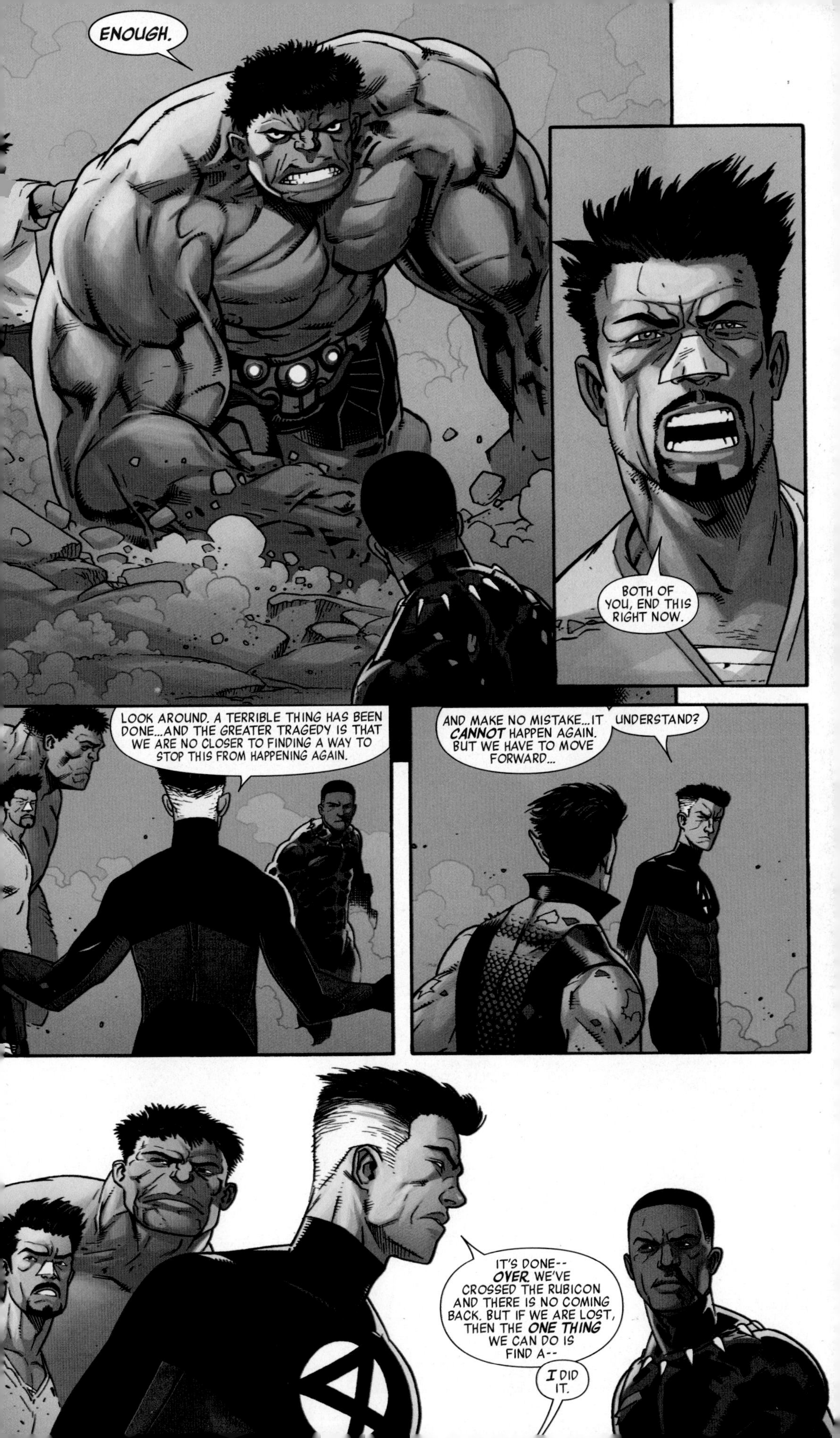
ENOUGH.
BOTH OF YOU, END THIS RIGHT NOW.
LOOK AROUND. A TERRIBLE THING HAS BEEN DONE...AND THE GREATER TRAGEDY IS THAT WE ARE NO CLOSER TO FINDING A WAY TO STOP THIS FROM HAPPENING AGAIN.
AND MAKE NO MISTAKE...IT *CANNOT* HAPPEN AGAIN. BUT WE HAVE TO MOVE FORWARD...
UNDERSTAND?
IT'S DONE-- *OVER.* WE'VE CROSSED THE RUBICON AND THERE IS NO COMING BACK. BUT IF WE ARE LOST, THEN THE *ONE THING* WE CAN DO IS FIND A--
I DID IT.

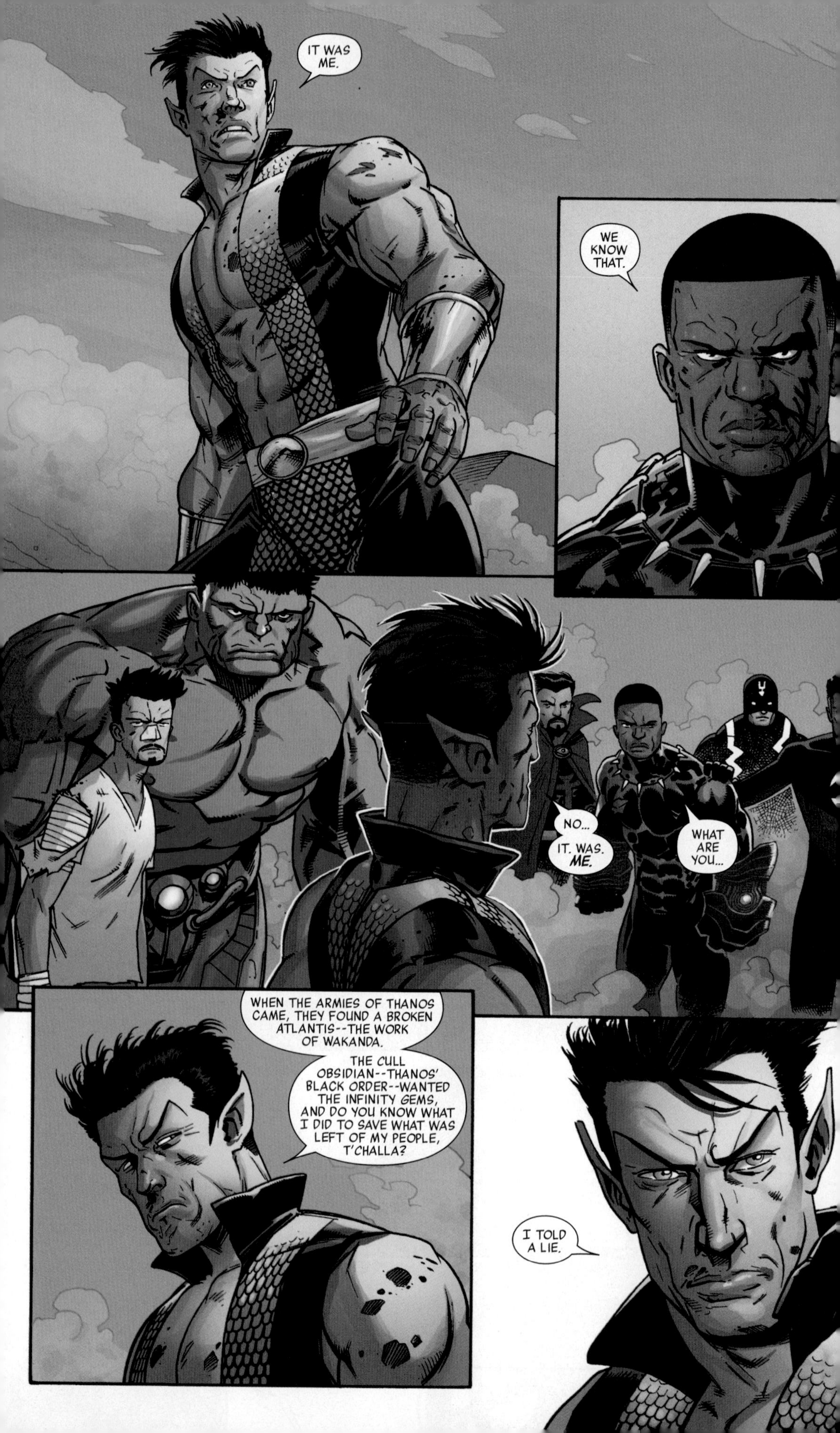
IT WAS ME.
WE KNOW THAT.
NO... IT. WAS. **ME.**
WHAT ARE YOU...
WHEN THE ARMIES OF THANOS CAME, THEY FOUND A BROKEN ATLANTIS--THE WORK OF WAKANDA.
THE CULL OBSIDIAN--THANOS' BLACK ORDER--WANTED THE INFINITY GEMS, AND DO YOU KNOW WHAT I DID TO SAVE WHAT WAS LEFT OF MY PEOPLE, T'CHALLA?
I TOLD A LIE.

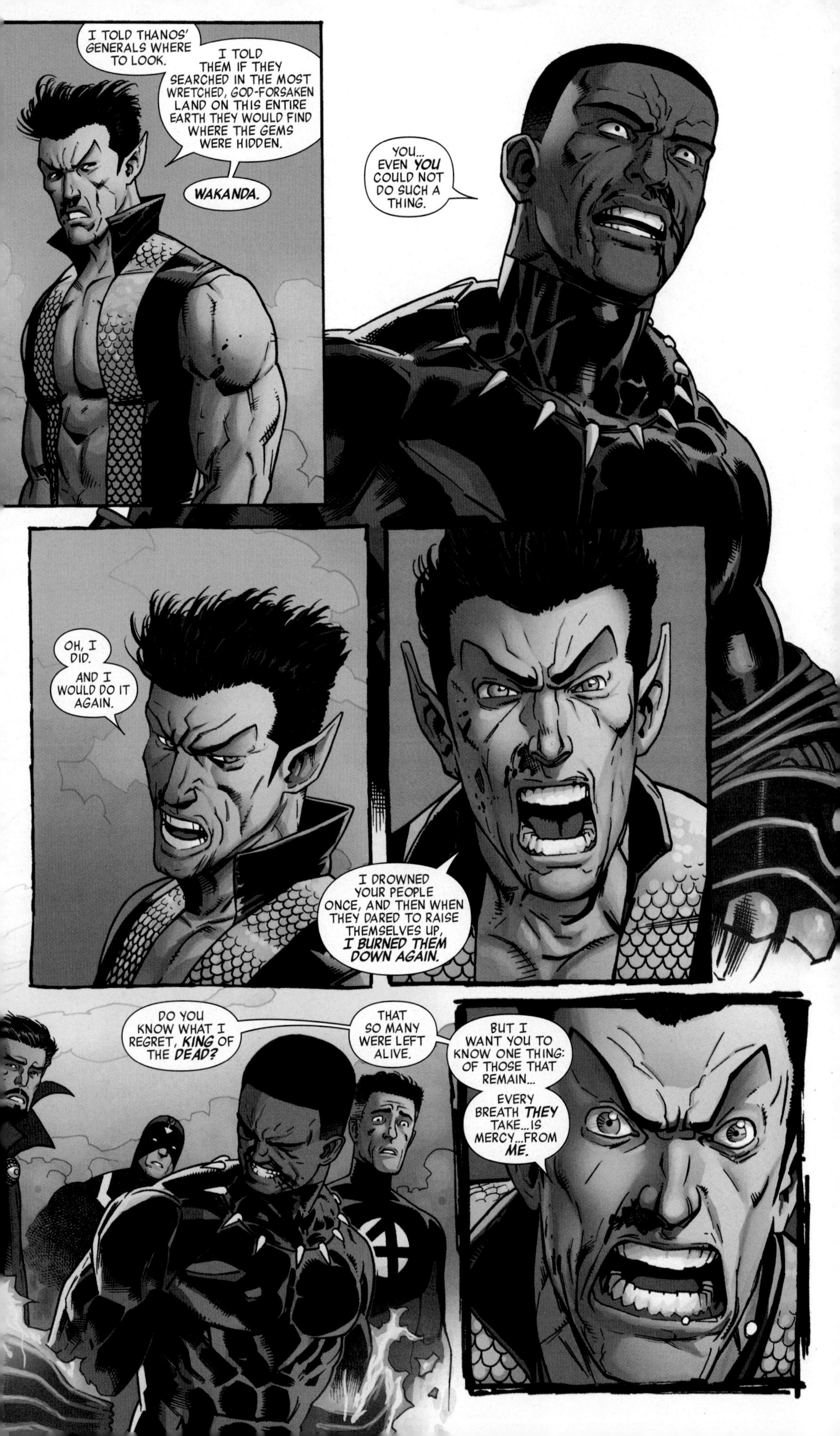

I TOLD THANOS' GENERALS WHERE TO LOOK.
I TOLD THEM IF THEY SEARCHED IN THE MOST WRETCHED, GOD-FORSAKEN LAND ON THIS ENTIRE EARTH THEY WOULD FIND WHERE THE GEMS WERE HIDDEN.
WAKANDA.
YOU... EVEN YOU COULD NOT DO SUCH A THING.
OH, I DID.
AND I WOULD DO IT AGAIN.
I DROWNED YOUR PEOPLE ONCE, AND THEN WHEN THEY DARED TO RAISE THEMSELVES UP, I BURNED THEM DOWN AGAIN.
DO YOU KNOW WHAT I REGRET, KING OF THE DEAD?
THAT SO MANY WERE LEFT ALIVE.
BUT I WANT YOU TO KNOW ONE THING: OF THOSE THAT REMAIN...
EVERY BREATH THEY TAKE...IS MERCY...FROM ME.

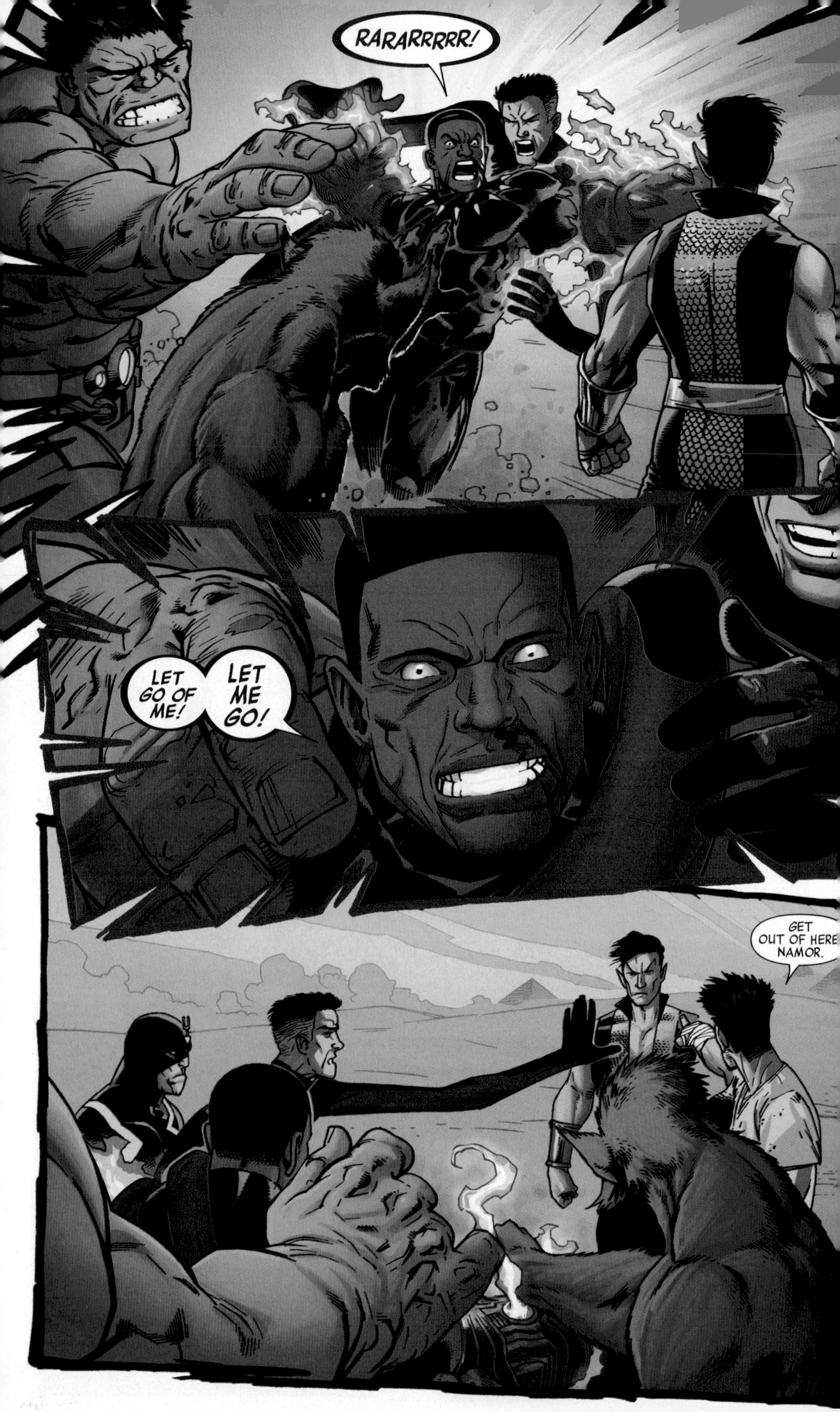
RARARRRRR!
LET GO OF ME!
LET ME GO!
GET OUT OF HERE NAMOR.

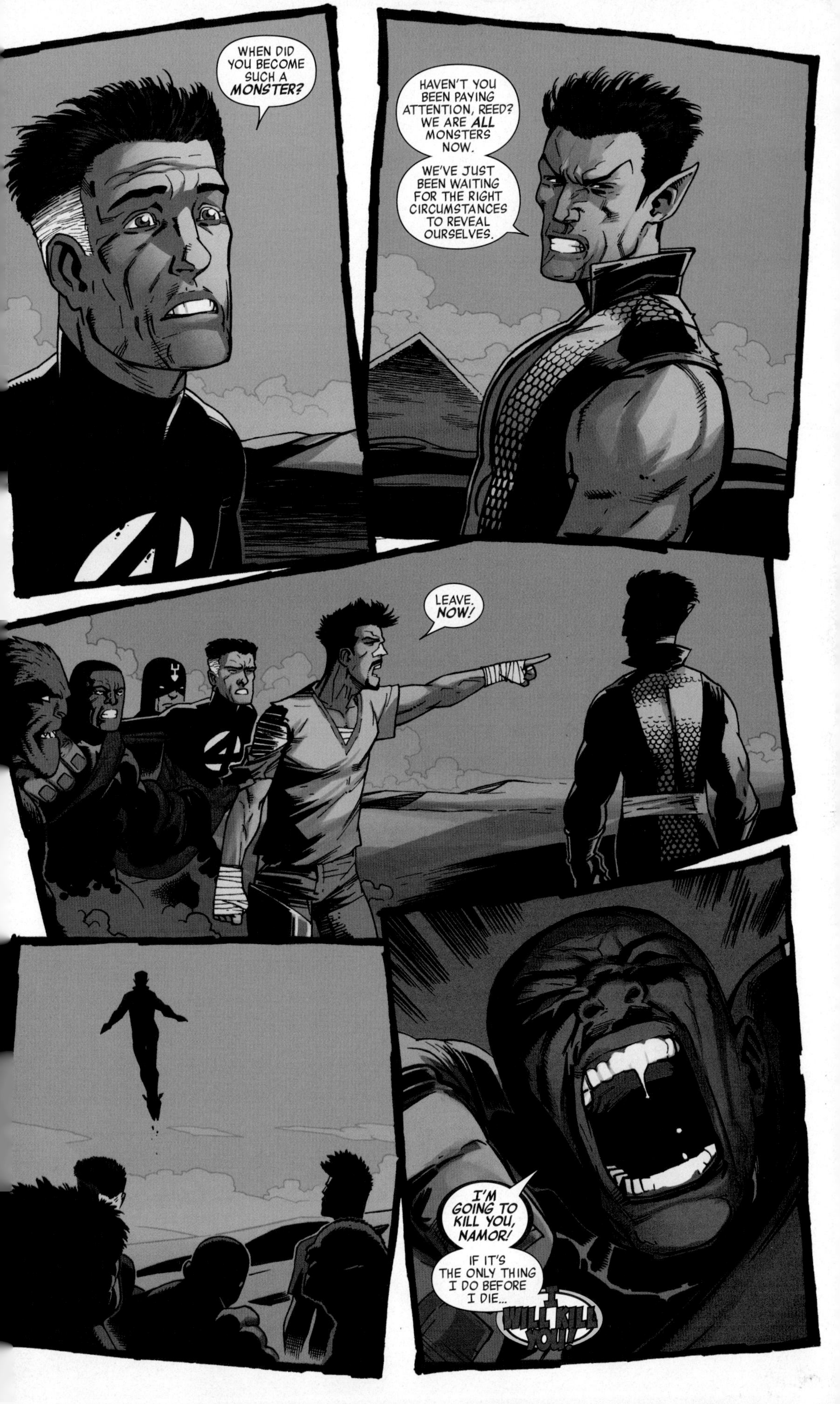
WHEN DID YOU BECOME SUCH A MONSTER?
HAVEN'T YOU BEEN PAYING ATTENTION, REED? WE ARE ALL MONSTERS NOW.
WE'VE JUST BEEN WAITING FOR THE RIGHT CIRCUMSTANCES TO REVEAL OURSELVES.
LEAVE. NOW!
I'M GOING TO KILL YOU, NAMOR!
IF IT'S THE ONLY THING I DO BEFORE I DIE...
I WILL KILL YOU!

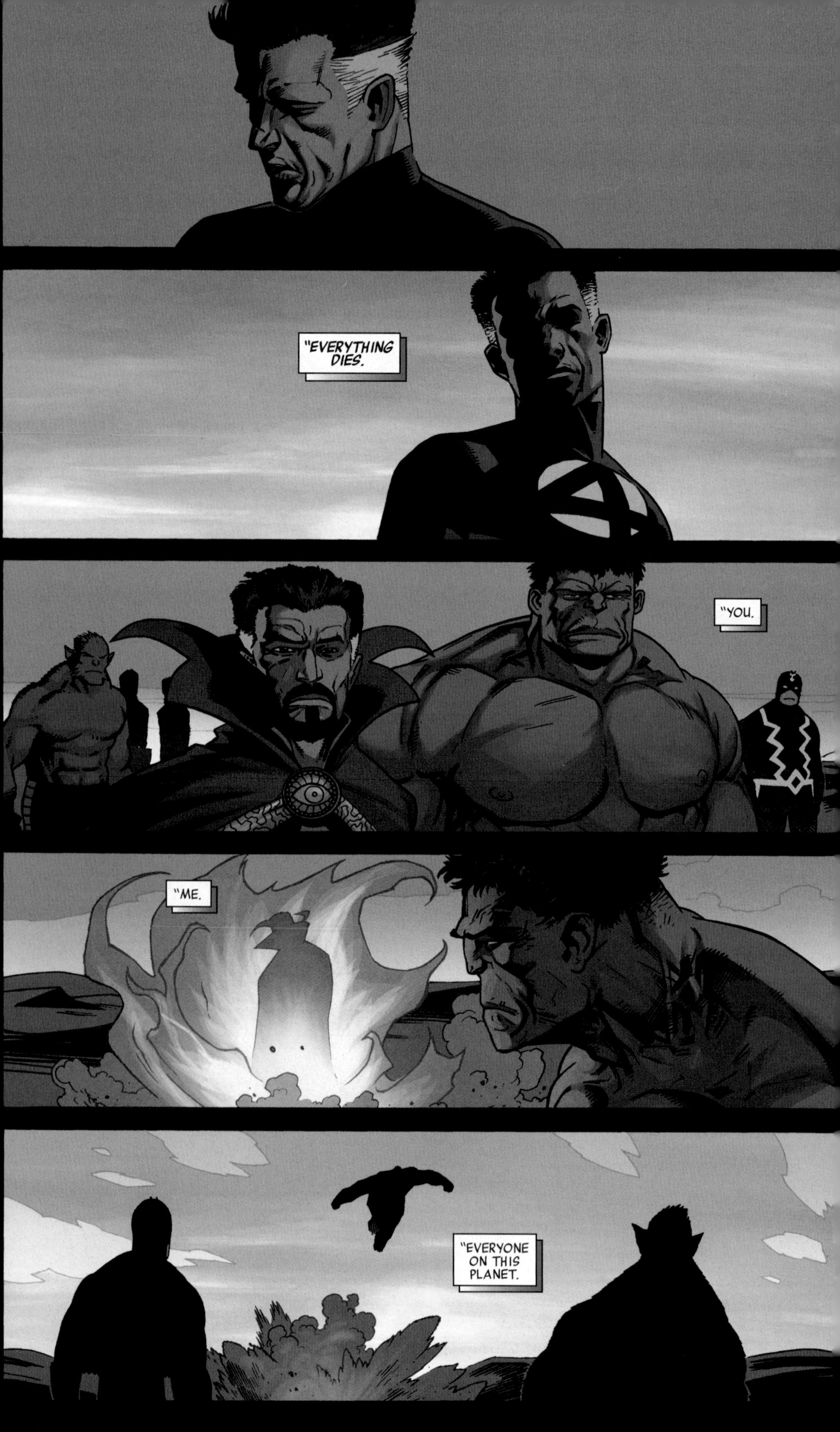
"EVERYTHING DIES.
"YOU.
"ME.
"EVERYONE ON THIS PLANET.

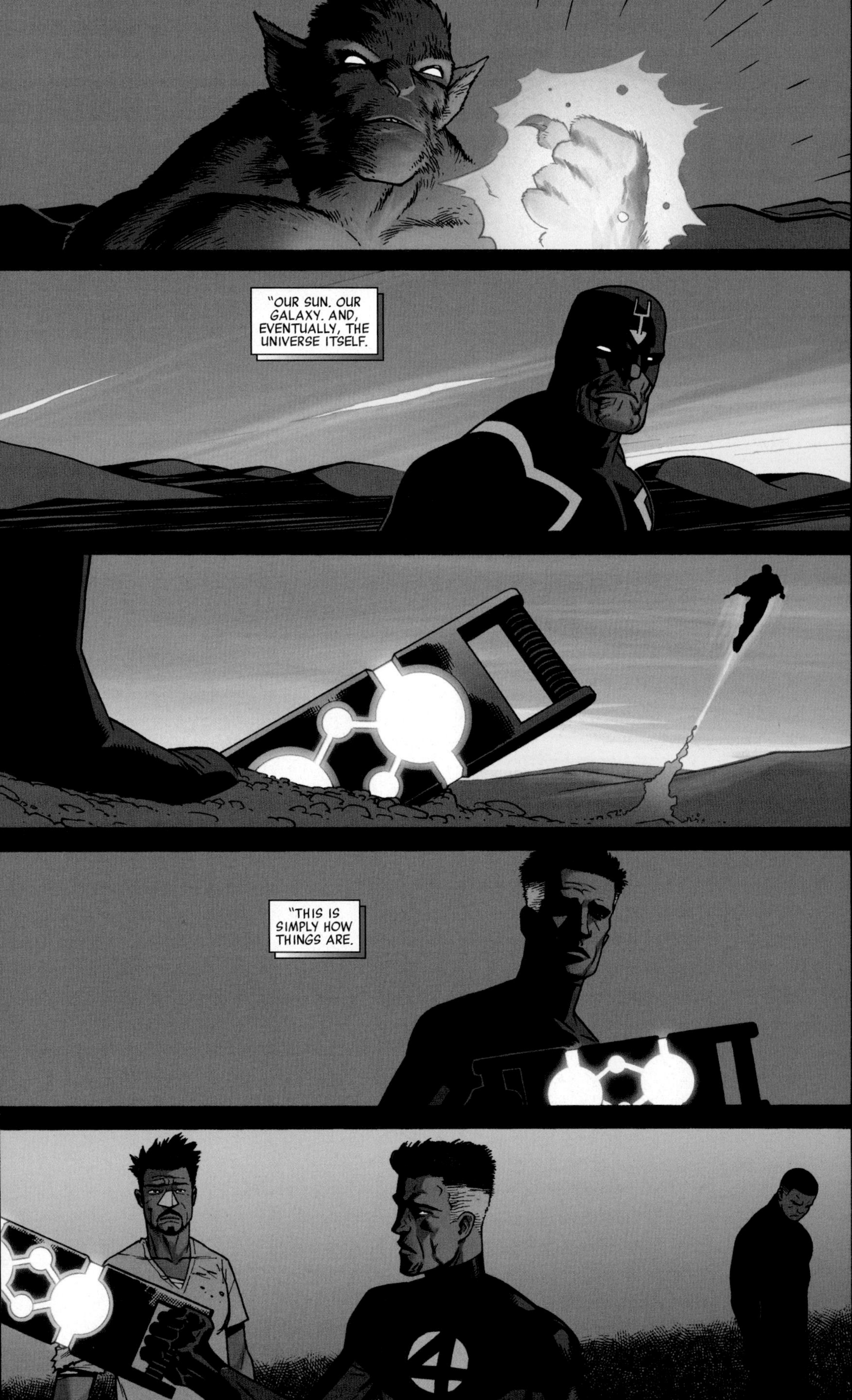
"OUR SUN. OUR GALAXY. AND, EVENTUALLY, THE UNIVERSE ITSELF.
"THIS IS SIMPLY HOW THINGS ARE.

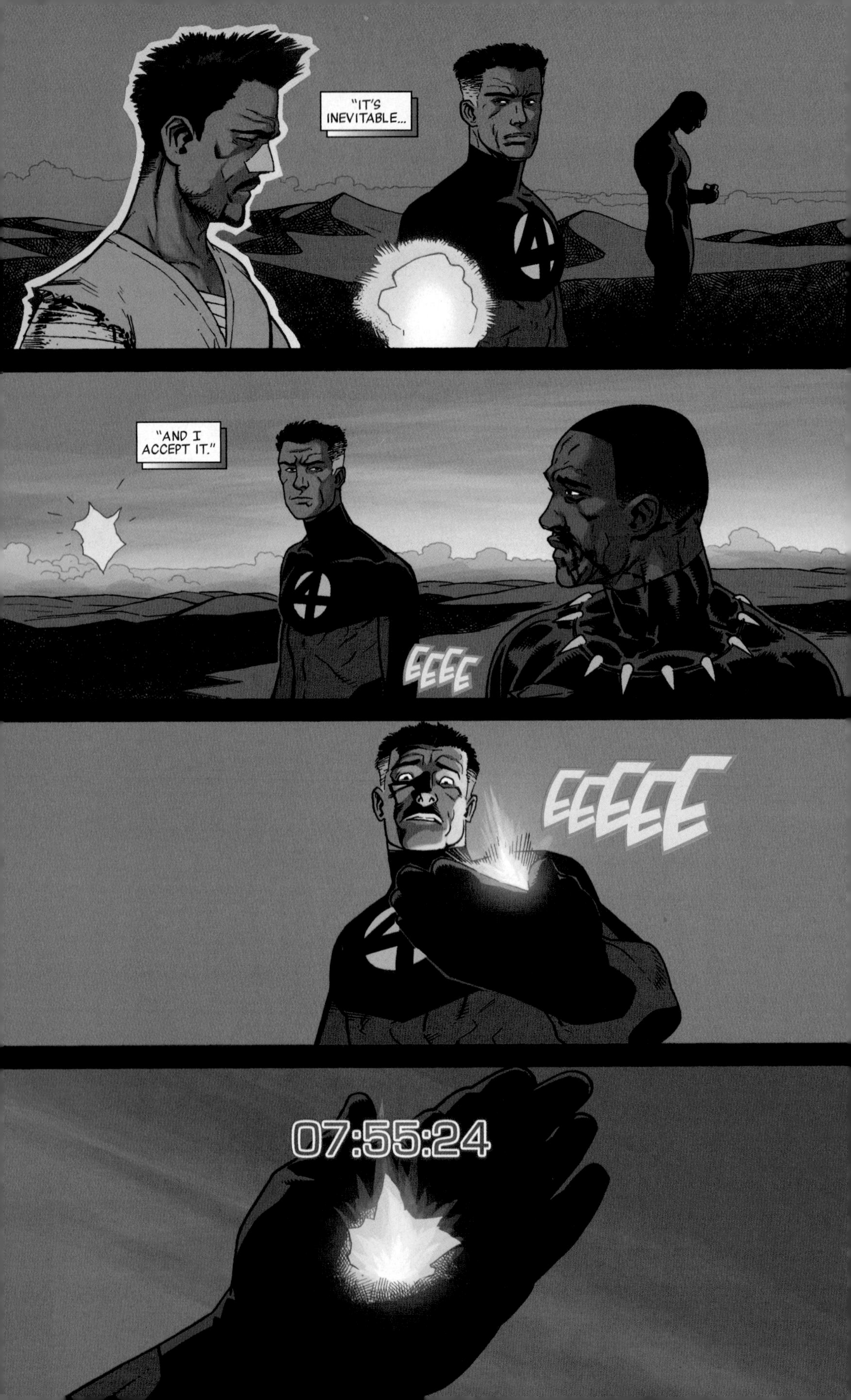
"IT'S INEVITABLE...
"AND I ACCEPT IT."
EEEE
EEEEE
07:55:24

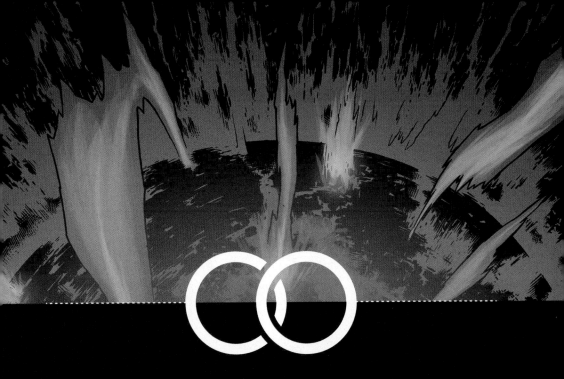

"ALL THE ANGELS HAVE FALLEN"

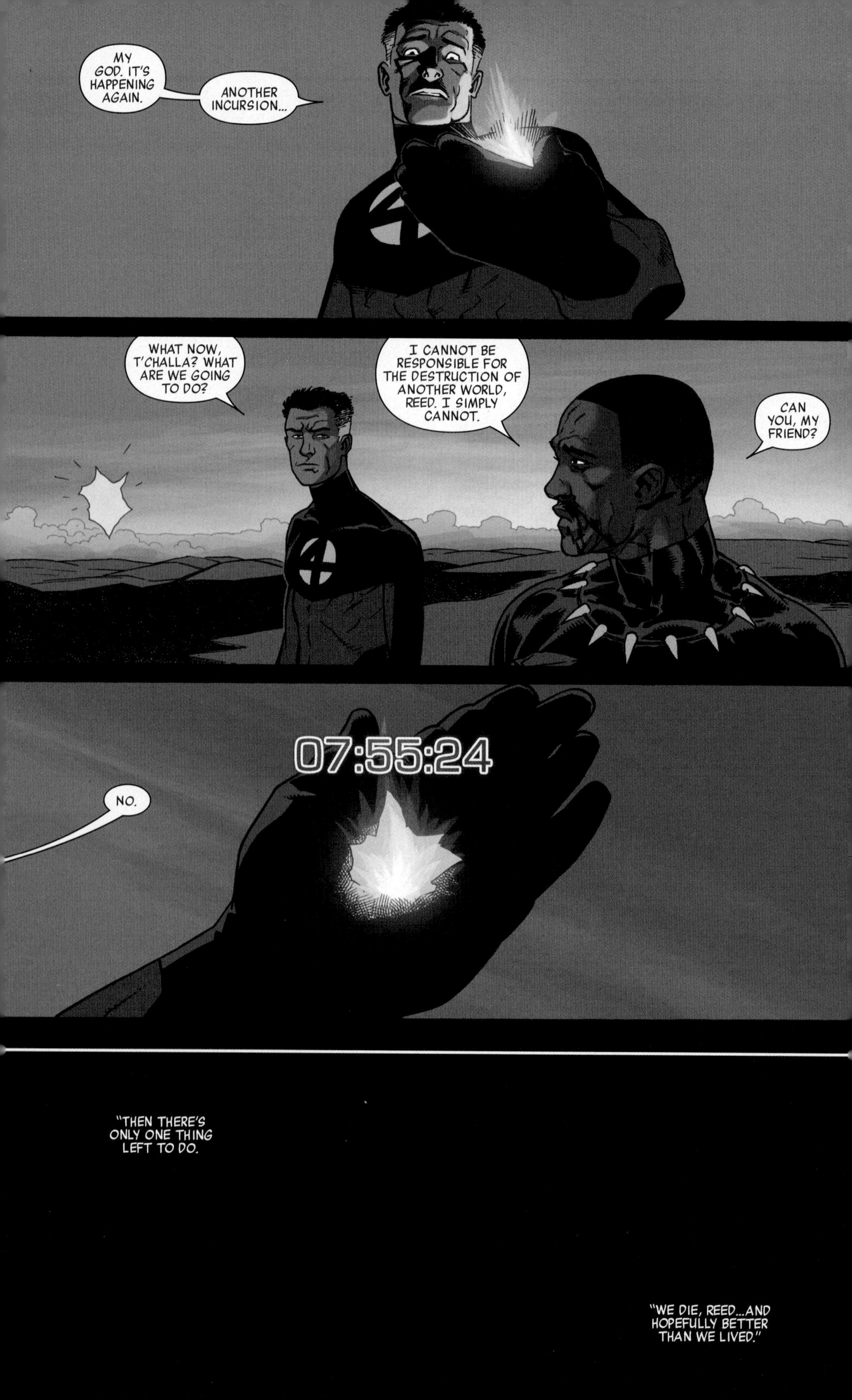
MY GOD. IT'S HAPPENING AGAIN.
ANOTHER INCURSION...
WHAT NOW, T'CHALLA? WHAT ARE WE GOING TO DO?
I CANNOT BE RESPONSIBLE FOR THE DESTRUCTION OF ANOTHER WORLD, REED. I SIMPLY CANNOT.
CAN YOU, MY FRIEND?
07:55:24
NO.
"THEN THERE'S ONLY ONE THING LEFT TO DO.
"WE DIE, REED...AND HOPEFULLY BETTER THAN WE LIVED."

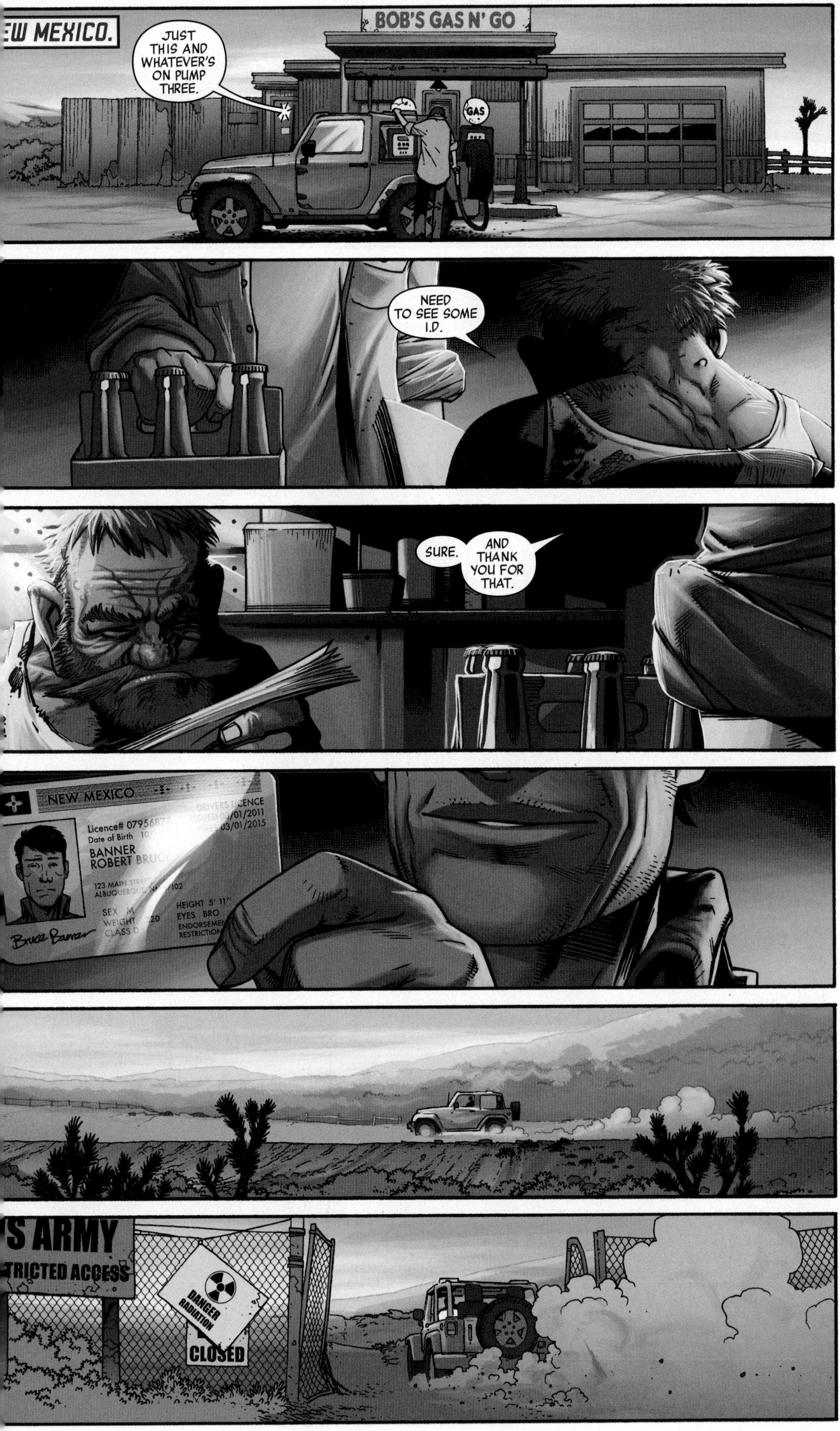

EW MEXICO.
BOB'S GAS N' GO
JUST THIS AND WHATEVER'S ON PUMP THREE.
GAS
NEED TO SEE SOME I.D.
SURE.
AND THANK YOU FOR THAT.
NEW MEXICO
DRIVERS LICENCE
Date of Birth
BANNER
HEIGHT 5' 11"
EYES BRO
'S ARMY
TRICTED ACCESS
DANGER RADIATION
CLOSED

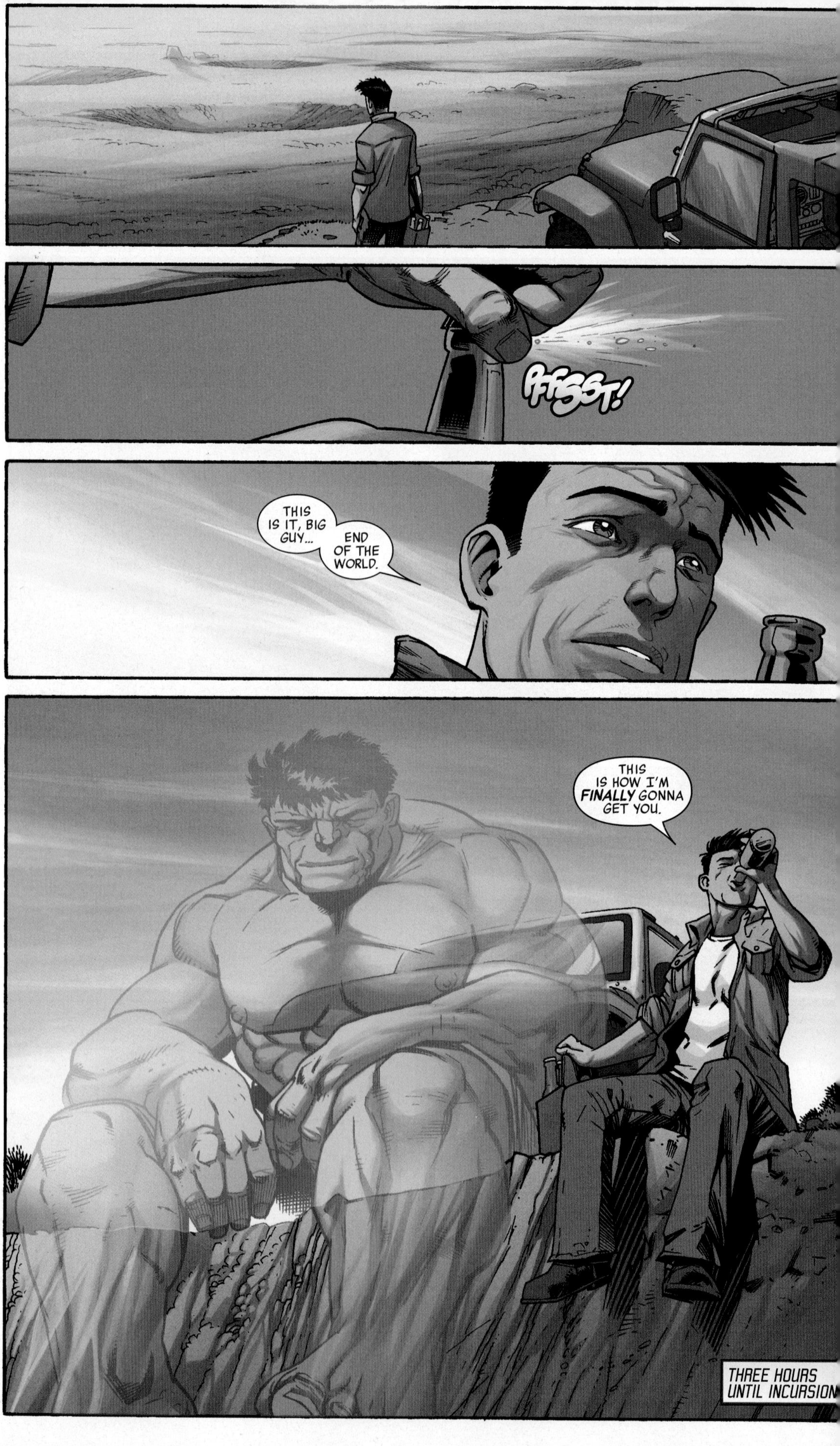
PFFSST!
THIS IS IT, BIG GUY...
END OF THE WORLD.
THIS IS HOW I'M FINALLY GONNA GET YOU.
THREE HOURS UNTIL INCURSION

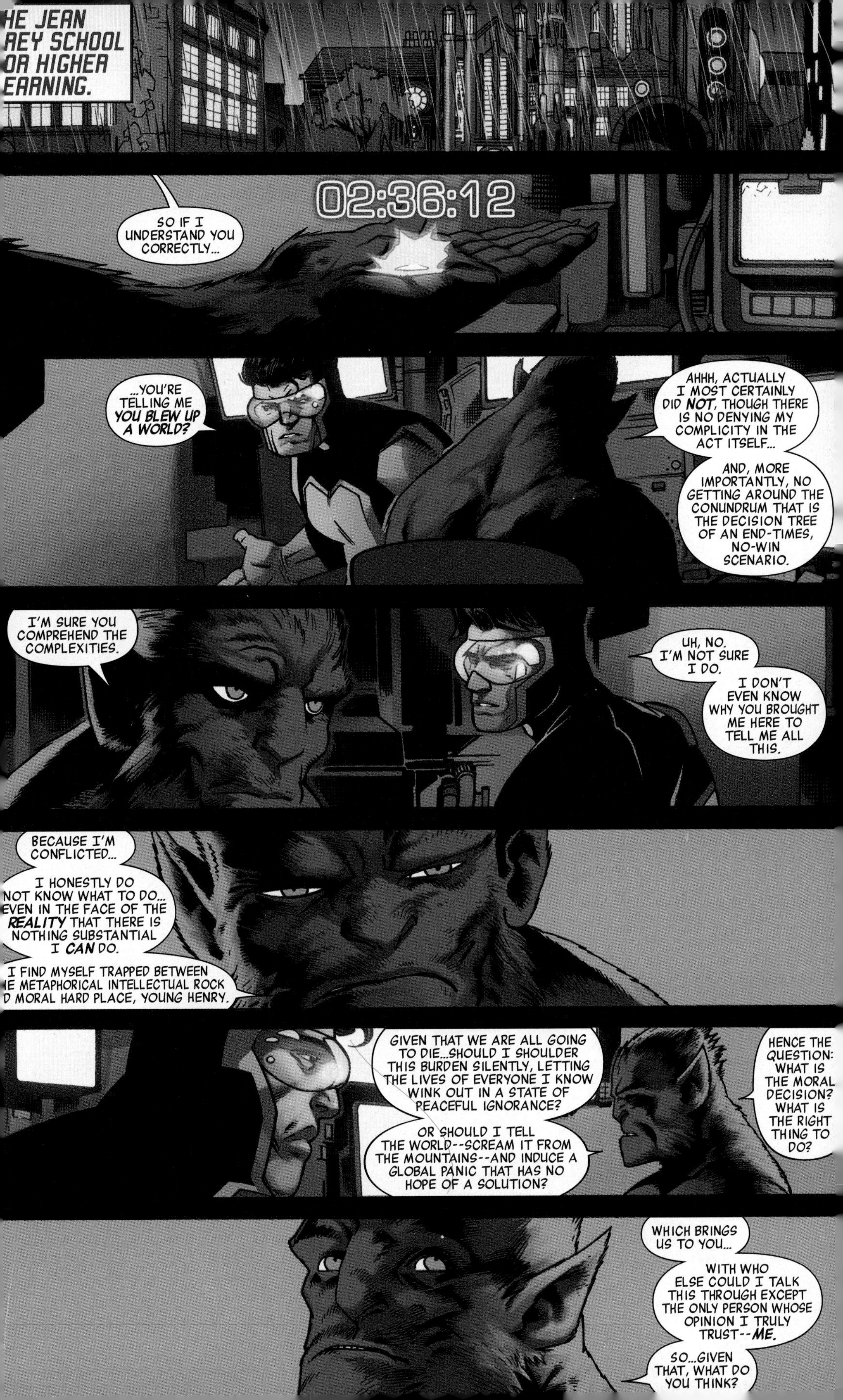
HE JEAN REY SCHOOL OR HIGHER EARNING.
02:36:12
SO IF I UNDERSTAND YOU CORRECTLY...
...YOU'RE TELLING ME YOU BLEW UP A WORLD?
AHHH, ACTUALLY I MOST CERTAINLY DID NOT, THOUGH THERE IS NO DENYING MY COMPLICITY IN THE ACT ITSELF...
AND, MORE IMPORTANTLY, NO GETTING AROUND THE CONUNDRUM THAT IS THE DECISION TREE OF AN END-TIMES, NO-WIN SCENARIO.
I'M SURE YOU COMPREHEND THE COMPLEXITIES.
UH, NO. I'M NOT SURE I DO.
I DON'T EVEN KNOW WHY YOU BROUGHT ME HERE TO TELL ME ALL THIS.
BECAUSE I'M CONFLICTED...
I HONESTLY DO NOT KNOW WHAT TO DO... EVEN IN THE FACE OF THE REALITY THAT THERE IS NOTHING SUBSTANTIAL I CAN DO.
I FIND MYSELF TRAPPED BETWEEN IE METAPHORICAL INTELLECTUAL ROCK D MORAL HARD PLACE, YOUNG HENRY.
GIVEN THAT WE ARE ALL GOING TO DIE...SHOULD I SHOULDER THIS BURDEN SILENTLY, LETTING THE LIVES OF EVERYONE I KNOW WINK OUT IN A STATE OF PEACEFUL IGNORANCE?
OR SHOULD I TELL THE WORLD--SCREAM IT FROM THE MOUNTAINS--AND INDUCE A GLOBAL PANIC THAT HAS NO HOPE OF A SOLUTION?
HENCE THE QUESTION: WHAT IS THE MORAL DECISION? WHAT IS THE RIGHT THING TO DO?
WHICH BRINGS US TO YOU...
WITH WHO ELSE COULD I TALK THIS THROUGH EXCEPT THE ONLY PERSON WHOSE OPINION I TRULY TRUST--ME.
SO...GIVEN THAT, WHAT DO YOU THINK?

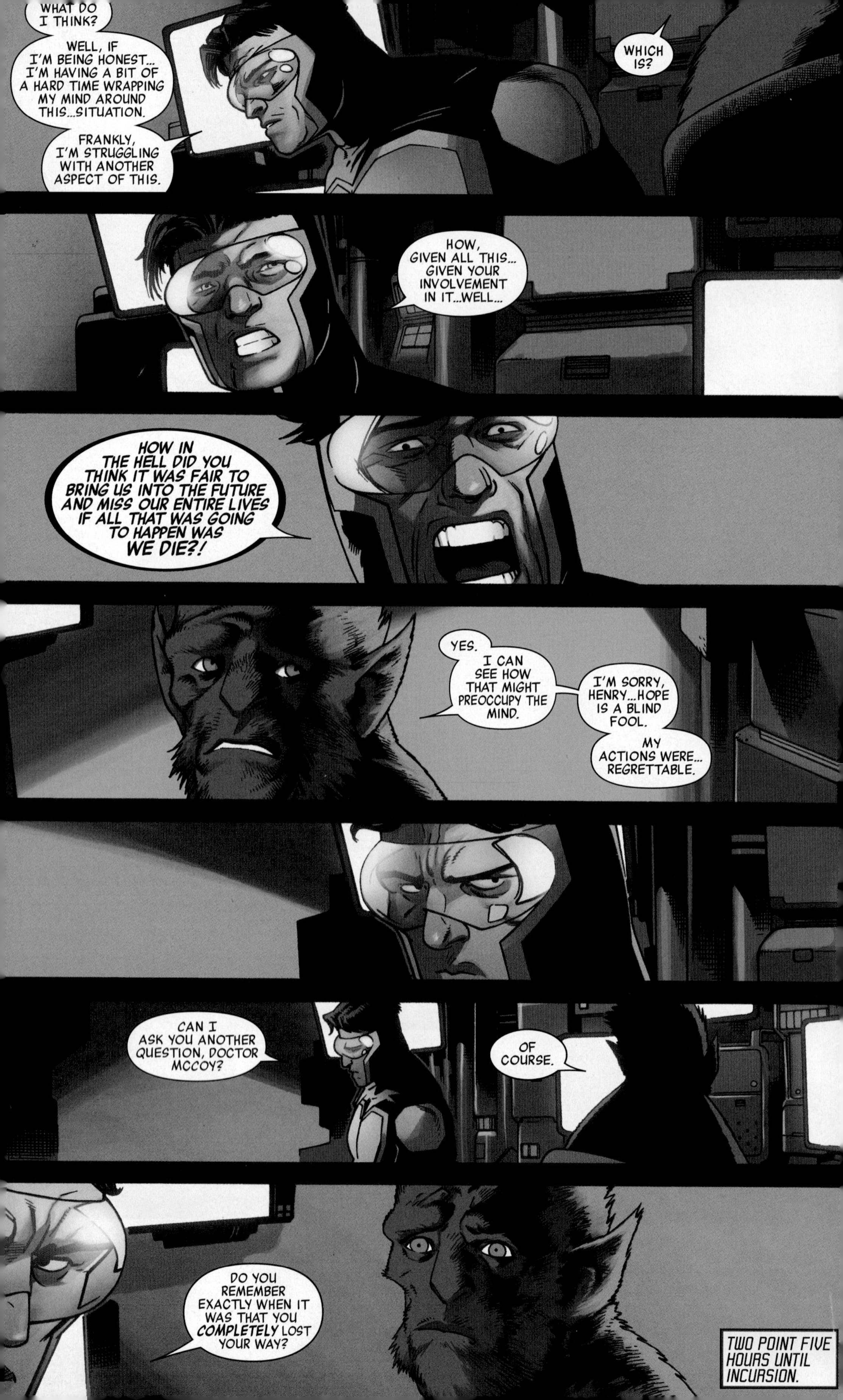
WHAT DO I THINK?
WELL, IF I'M BEING HONEST... I'M HAVING A BIT OF A HARD TIME WRAPPING MY MIND AROUND THIS...SITUATION.
WHICH IS?
FRANKLY, I'M STRUGGLING WITH ANOTHER ASPECT OF THIS.
HOW, GIVEN ALL THIS... GIVEN YOUR INVOLVEMENT IN IT...WELL...
HOW IN THE HELL DID YOU THINK IT WAS FAIR TO BRING US INTO THE FUTURE AND MISS OUR ENTIRE LIVES IF ALL THAT WAS GOING TO HAPPEN WAS WE DIE?!
YES.
I CAN SEE HOW THAT MIGHT PREOCCUPY THE MIND.
I'M SORRY, HENRY...HOPE IS A BLIND FOOL.
MY ACTIONS WERE... REGRETTABLE.
CAN I ASK YOU ANOTHER QUESTION, DOCTOR MCCOY?
OF COURSE.
DO YOU REMEMBER EXACTLY WHEN IT WAS THAT YOU COMPLETELY LOST YOUR WAY?
TWO POINT FIVE HOURS UNTIL INCURSION.

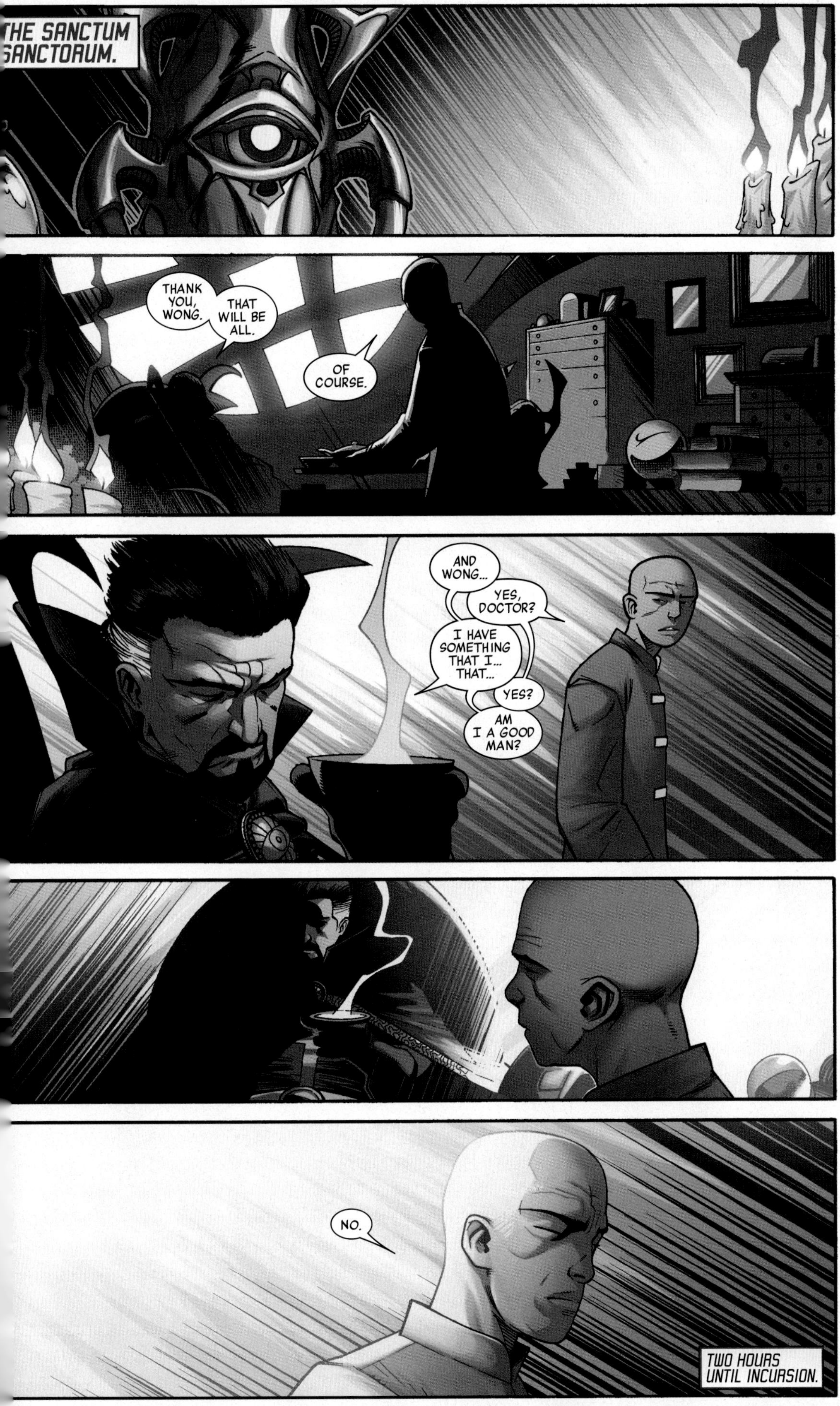
THE SANCTUM SANCTORUM.
THANK YOU, WONG.
THAT WILL BE ALL.
OF COURSE.
AND WONG...
YES, DOCTOR?
I HAVE SOMETHING THAT I... THAT...
YES?
AM I A GOOD MAN?
NO.
TWO HOURS UNTIL INCURSION.

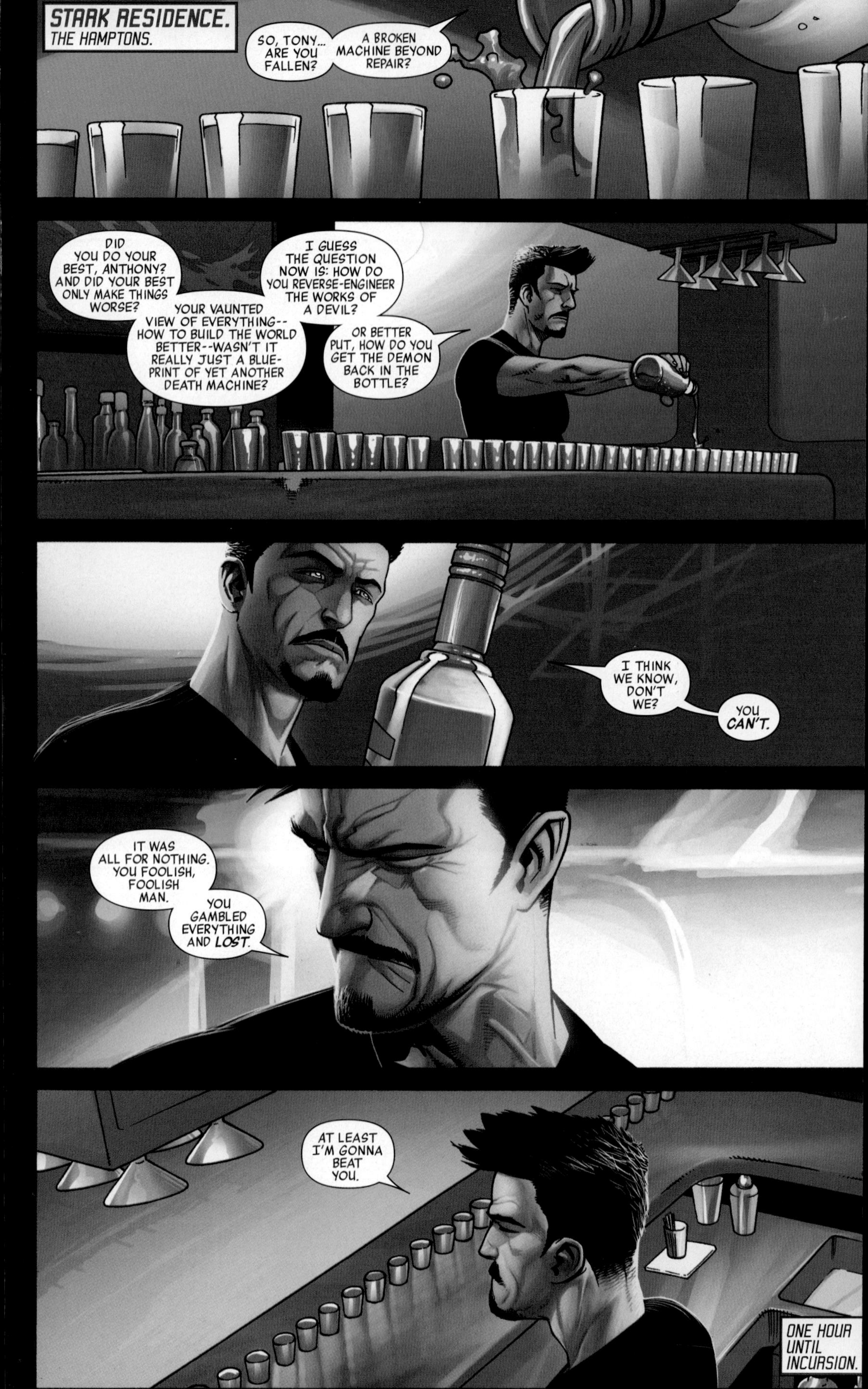
STARK RESIDENCE. THE HAMPTONS.
SO, TONY... ARE YOU FALLEN?
A BROKEN MACHINE BEYOND REPAIR?
DID YOU DO YOUR BEST, ANTHONY? AND DID YOUR BEST ONLY MAKE THINGS WORSE?
YOUR VAUNTED VIEW OF EVERYTHING--HOW TO BUILD THE WORLD BETTER--WASN'T IT REALLY JUST A BLUE-PRINT OF YET ANOTHER DEATH MACHINE?
I GUESS THE QUESTION NOW IS: HOW DO YOU REVERSE-ENGINEER THE WORKS OF A DEVIL?
OR BETTER PUT, HOW DO YOU GET THE DEMON BACK IN THE BOTTLE?
I THINK WE KNOW, DON'T WE?
YOU *CAN'T.*
IT WAS ALL FOR NOTHING. YOU FOOLISH, FOOLISH MAN.
YOU GAMBLED EVERYTHING AND *LOST.*
AT LEAST I'M GONNA BEAT YOU.
ONE HOUR UNTIL INCURSION.

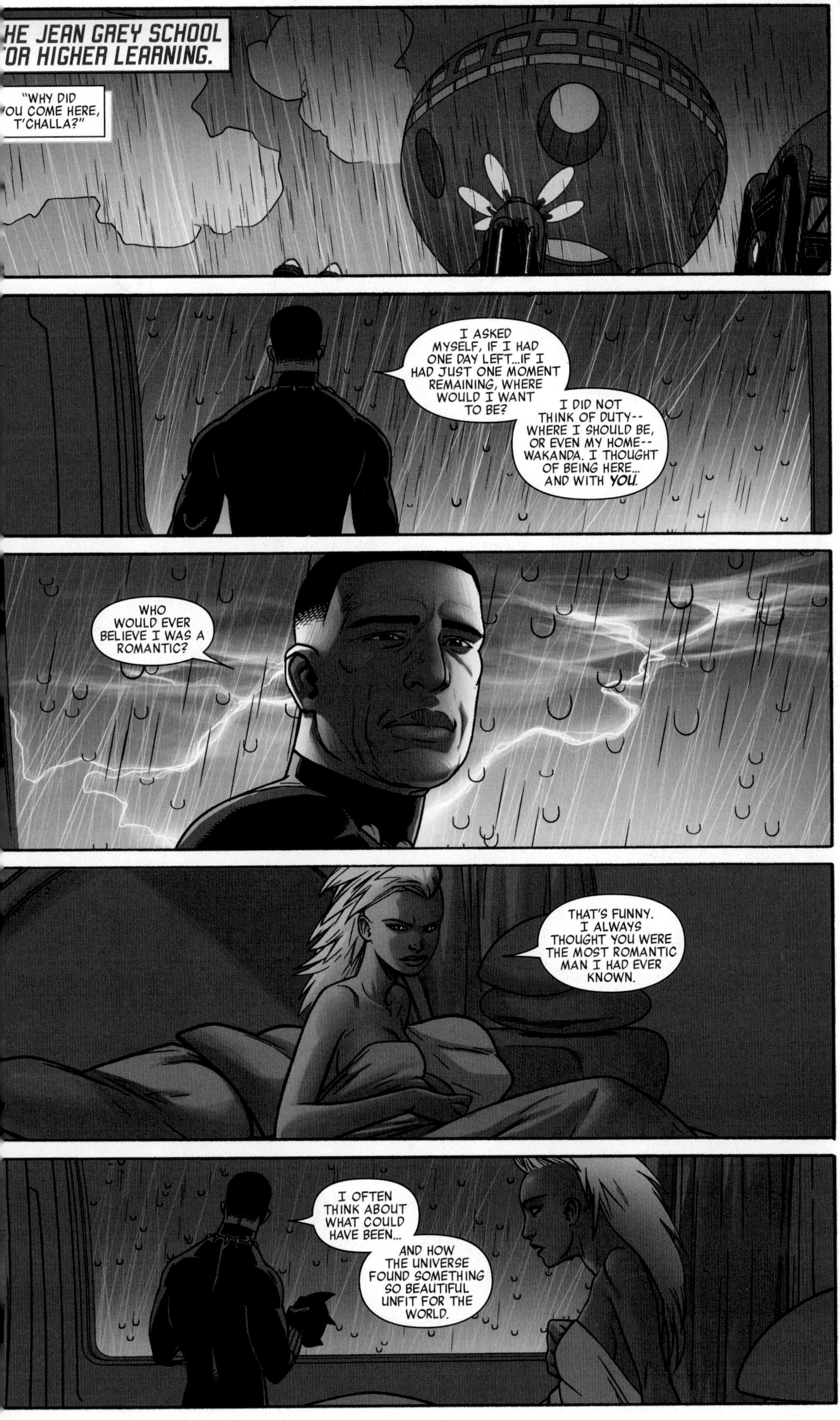
HE JEAN GREY SCHOOL
OR HIGHER LEARNING.
"WHY DID
OU COME HERE,
T'CHALLA?"
I ASKED MYSELF, IF I HAD ONE DAY LEFT...IF I HAD JUST ONE MOMENT REMAINING, WHERE WOULD I WANT TO BE?
I DID NOT THINK OF DUTY-- WHERE I SHOULD BE, OR EVEN MY HOME-- WAKANDA. I THOUGHT OF BEING HERE... AND WITH YOU.
WHO WOULD EVER BELIEVE I WAS A ROMANTIC?
THAT'S FUNNY. I ALWAYS THOUGHT YOU WERE THE MOST ROMANTIC MAN I HAD EVER KNOWN.
I OFTEN THINK ABOUT WHAT COULD HAVE BEEN...
AND HOW THE UNIVERSE FOUND SOMETHING SO BEAUTIFUL UNFIT FOR THE WORLD.

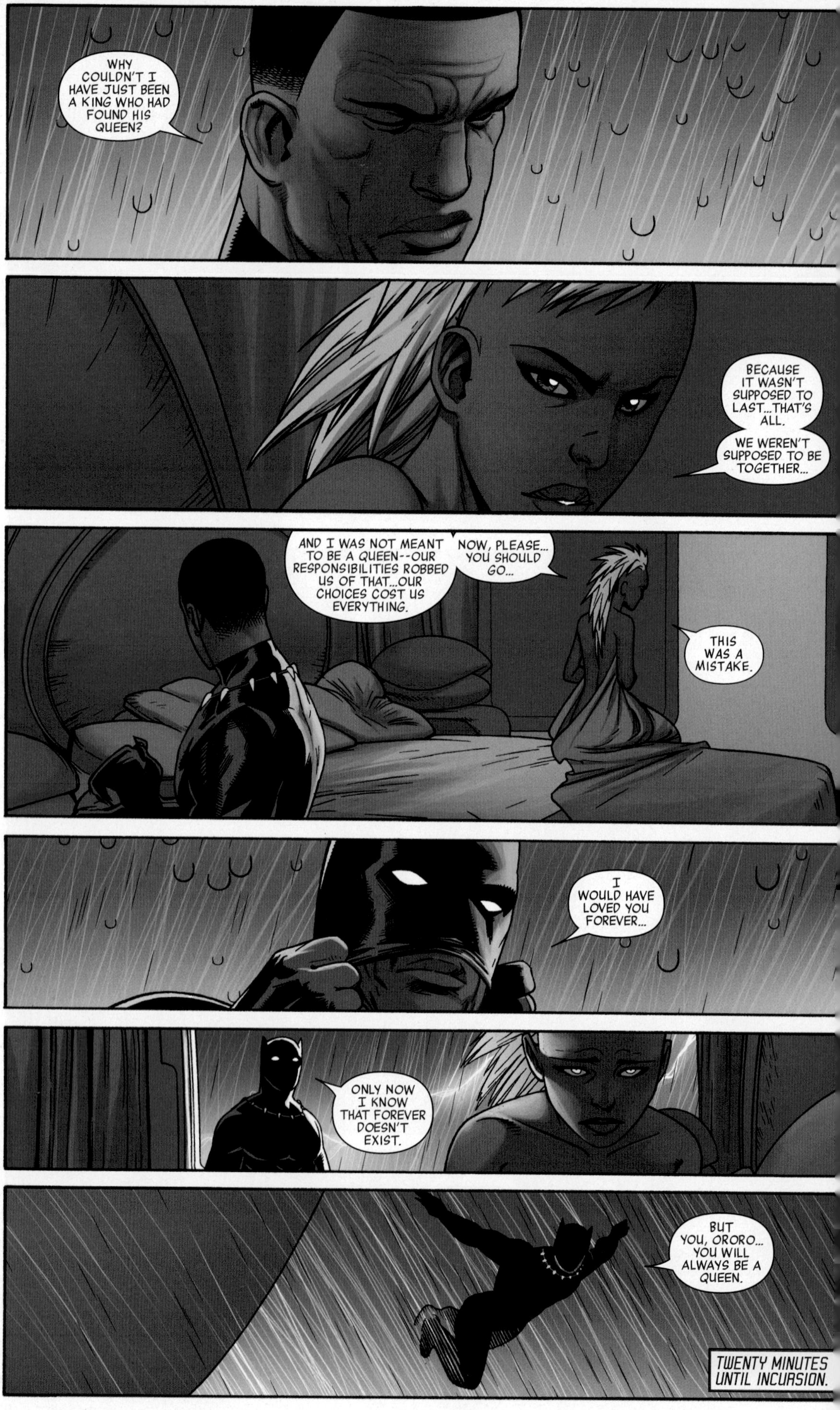
WHY COULDN'T I HAVE JUST BEEN A KING WHO HAD FOUND HIS QUEEN?
BECAUSE IT WASN'T SUPPOSED TO LAST...THAT'S ALL.
WE WEREN'T SUPPOSED TO BE TOGETHER...
AND I WAS NOT MEANT TO BE A QUEEN--OUR RESPONSIBILITIES ROBBED US OF THAT...OUR CHOICES COST US EVERYTHING.
NOW, PLEASE... YOU SHOULD GO...
THIS WAS A MISTAKE.
I WOULD HAVE LOVED YOU FOREVER...
ONLY NOW I KNOW THAT FOREVER DOESN'T EXIST.
BUT YOU, ORORO... YOU WILL ALWAYS BE A QUEEN.
TWENTY MINUTES UNTIL INCURSION.

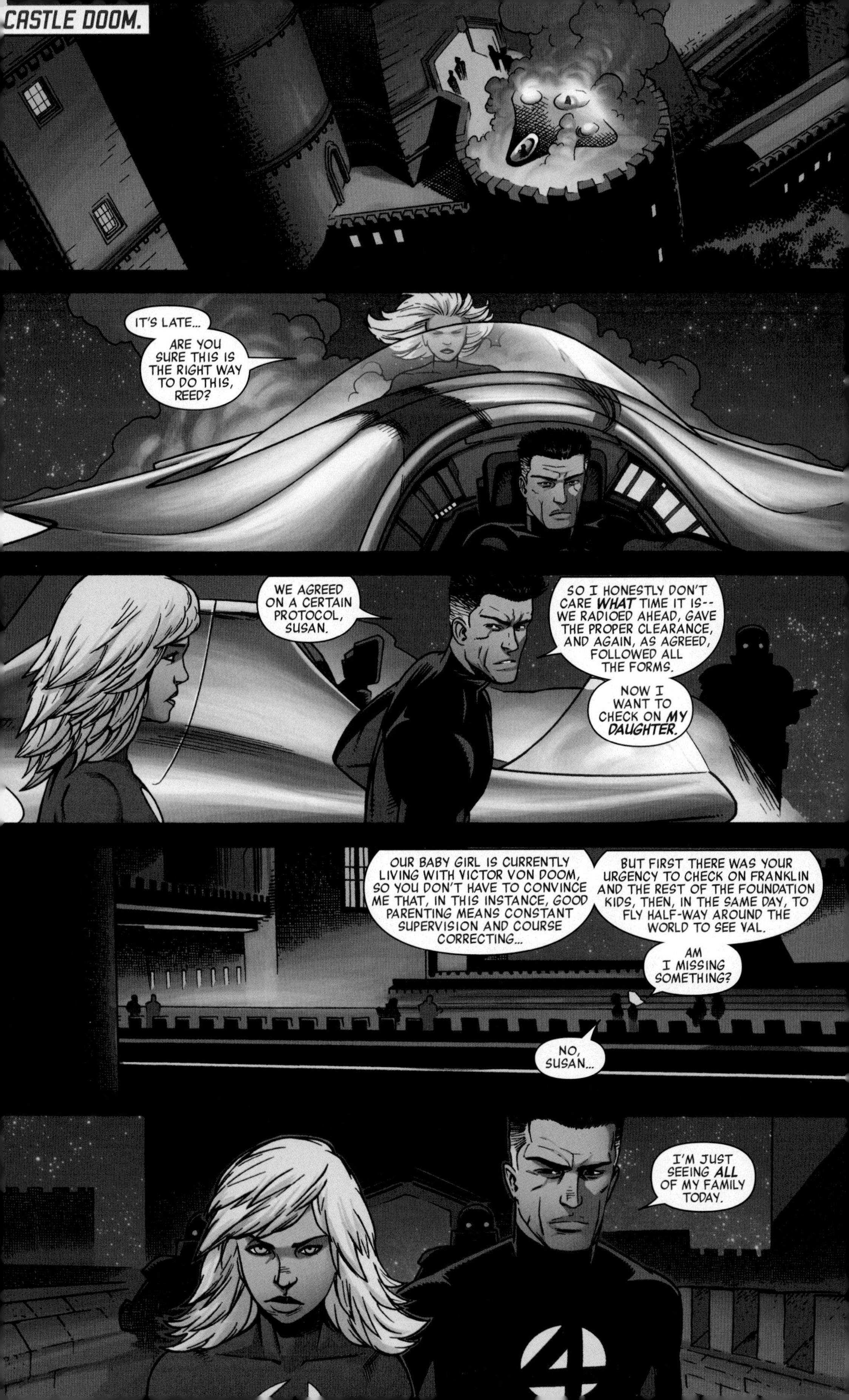
CASTLE DOOM.
IT'S LATE...
ARE YOU SURE THIS IS THE RIGHT WAY TO DO THIS, REED?
WE AGREED ON A CERTAIN PROTOCOL, SUSAN.
SO I HONESTLY DON'T CARE WHAT TIME IT IS-- WE RADIOED AHEAD, GAVE THE PROPER CLEARANCE, AND AGAIN, AS AGREED, FOLLOWED ALL THE FORMS.
NOW I WANT TO CHECK ON MY DAUGHTER.
OUR BABY GIRL IS CURRENTLY LIVING WITH VICTOR VON DOOM, SO YOU DON'T HAVE TO CONVINCE ME THAT, IN THIS INSTANCE, GOOD PARENTING MEANS CONSTANT SUPERVISION AND COURSE CORRECTING...
BUT FIRST THERE WAS YOUR URGENCY TO CHECK ON FRANKLIN AND THE REST OF THE FOUNDATION KIDS, THEN, IN THE SAME DAY, TO FLY HALF-WAY AROUND THE WORLD TO SEE VAL.
AM I MISSING SOMETHING?
NO, SUSAN...
I'M JUST SEEING ALL OF MY FAMILY TODAY.

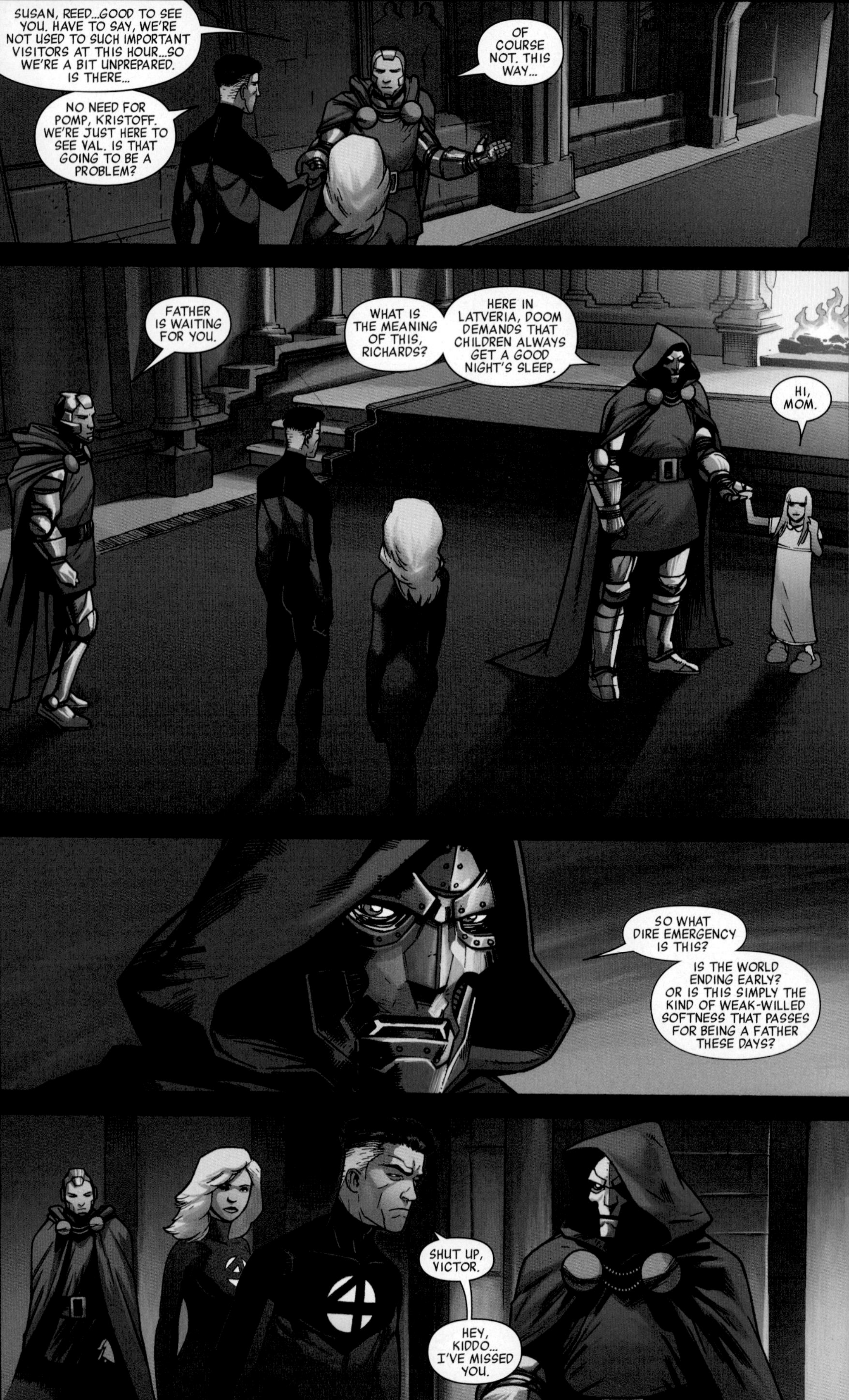
SUSAN, REED...GOOD TO SEE YOU. HAVE TO SAY, WE'RE NOT USED TO SUCH IMPORTANT VISITORS AT THIS HOUR...SO WE'RE A BIT UNPREPARED. IS THERE...
NO NEED FOR POMP, KRISTOFF. WE'RE JUST HERE TO SEE VAL. IS THAT GOING TO BE A PROBLEM?
OF COURSE NOT. THIS WAY...
FATHER IS WAITING FOR YOU.
WHAT IS THE MEANING OF THIS, RICHARDS?
HERE IN LATVERIA, DOOM DEMANDS THAT CHILDREN ALWAYS GET A GOOD NIGHT'S SLEEP.
HI, MOM.
SO WHAT DIRE EMERGENCY IS THIS?
IS THE WORLD ENDING EARLY? OR IS THIS SIMPLY THE KIND OF WEAK-WILLED SOFTNESS THAT PASSES FOR BEING A FATHER THESE DAYS?
SHUT UP, VICTOR.
HEY, KIDDO... I'VE MISSED YOU.

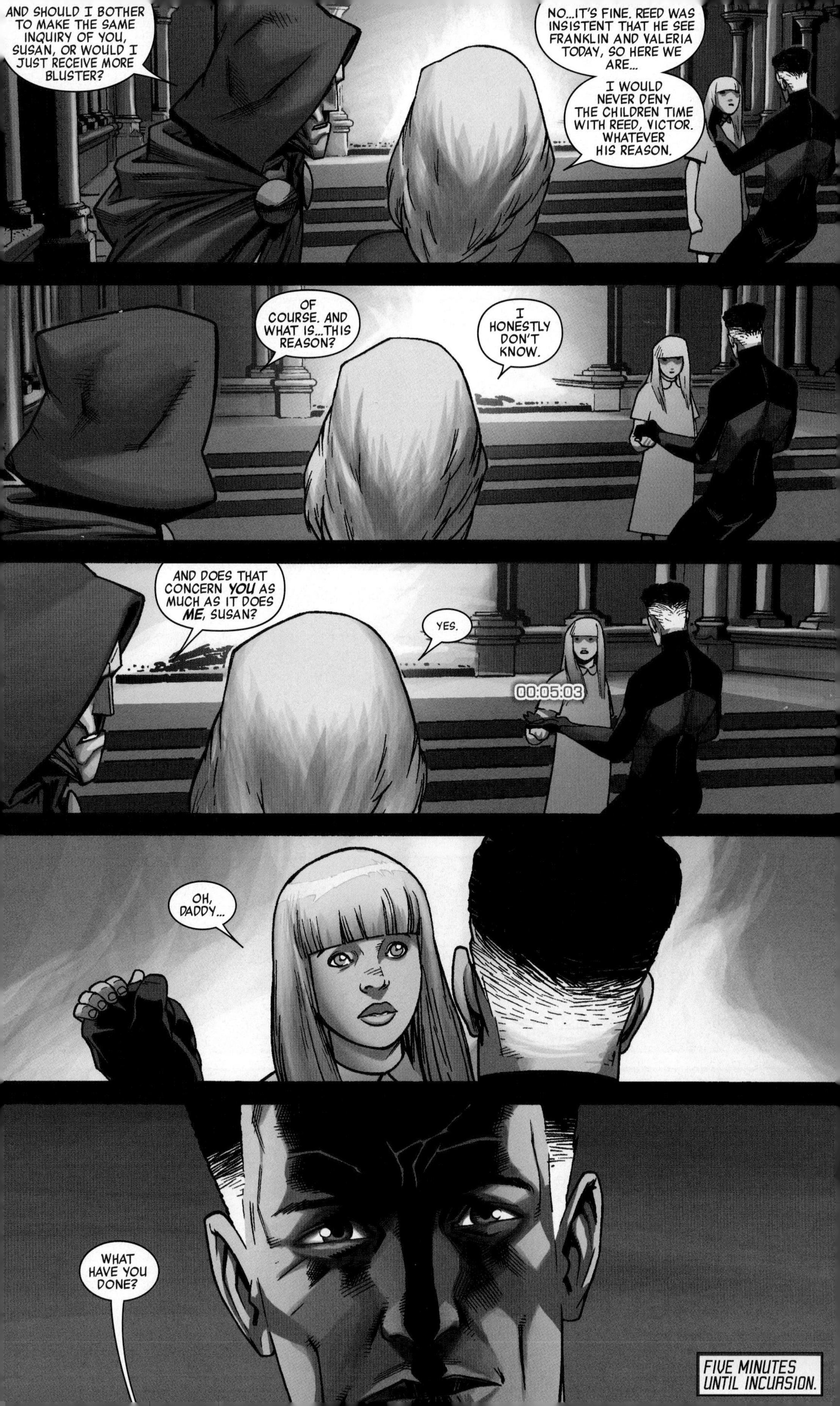
AND SHOULD I BOTHER TO MAKE THE SAME INQUIRY OF YOU, SUSAN, OR WOULD I JUST RECEIVE MORE BLUSTER?
NO...IT'S FINE. REED WAS INSISTENT THAT HE SEE FRANKLIN AND VALERIA TODAY, SO HERE WE ARE...
I WOULD NEVER DENY THE CHILDREN TIME WITH REED, VICTOR. WHATEVER HIS REASON.
OF COURSE. AND WHAT IS...THIS REASON?
I HONESTLY DON'T KNOW.
AND DOES THAT CONCERN YOU AS MUCH AS IT DOES ME, SUSAN?
YES.
00:05:03
OH, DADDY...
WHAT HAVE YOU DONE?
FIVE MINUTES UNTIL INCURSION.

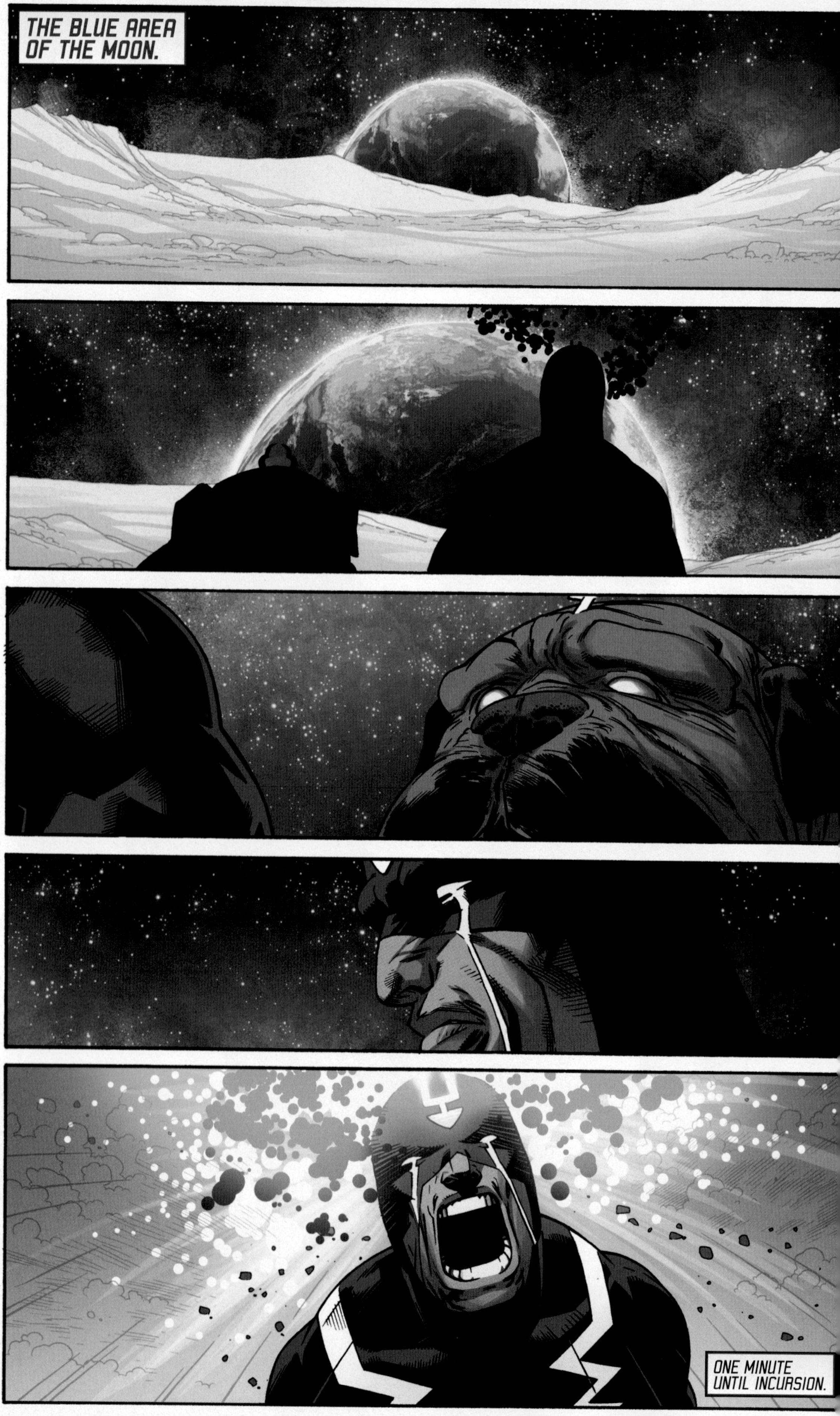
THE BLUE AREA OF THE MOON.
ONE MINUTE UNTIL INCURSION.

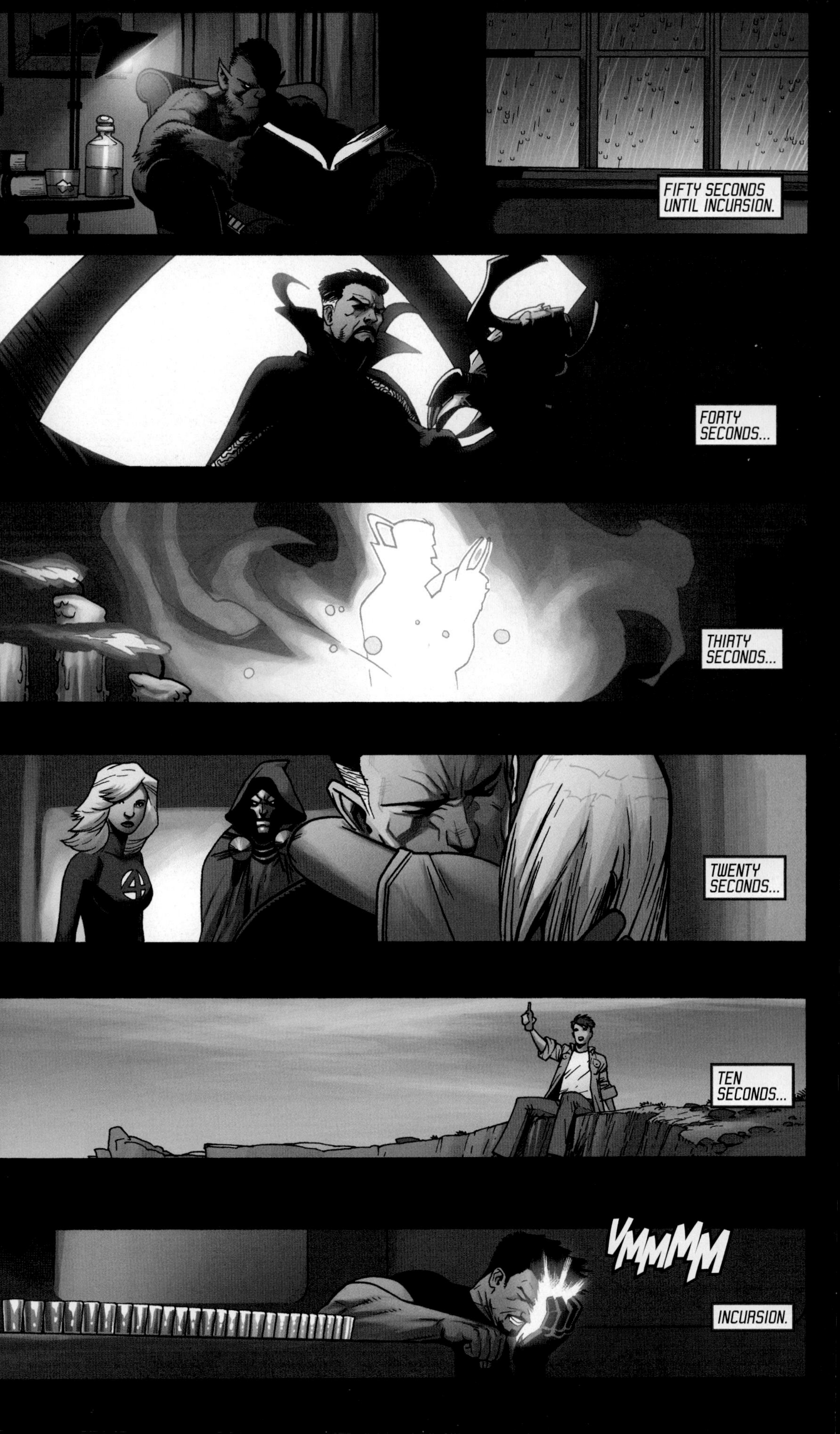
FIFTY SECONDS UNTIL INCURSION.
FORTY SECONDS...
THIRTY SECONDS...
TWENTY SECONDS...
TEN SECONDS...
VMMMM
INCURSION.

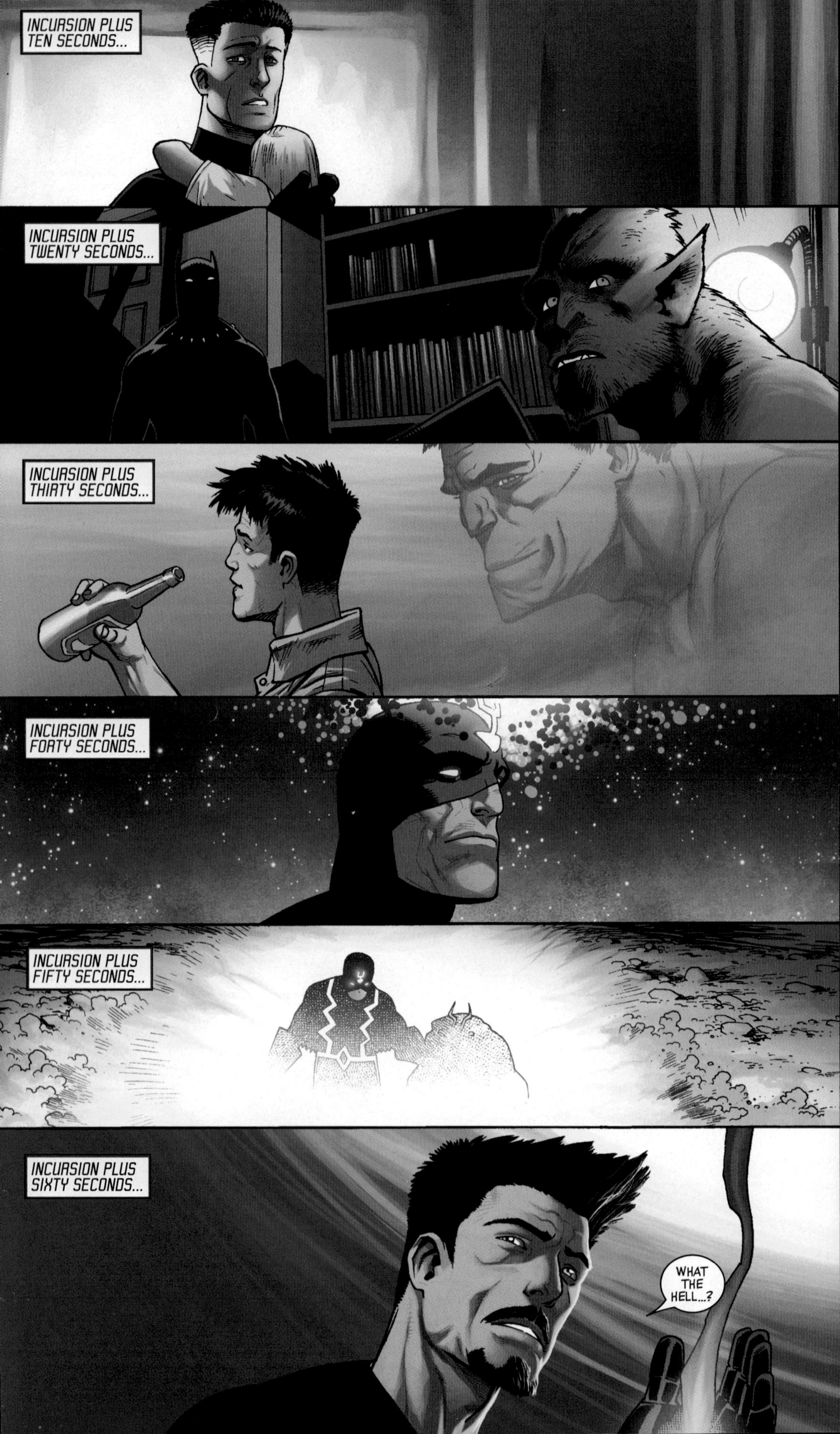
INCURSION PLUS TEN SECONDS...
INCURSION PLUS TWENTY SECONDS...
INCURSION PLUS THIRTY SECONDS...
INCURSION PLUS FORTY SECONDS...
INCURSION PLUS FIFTY SECONDS...
INCURSION PLUS SIXTY SECONDS...
WHAT THE HELL...?

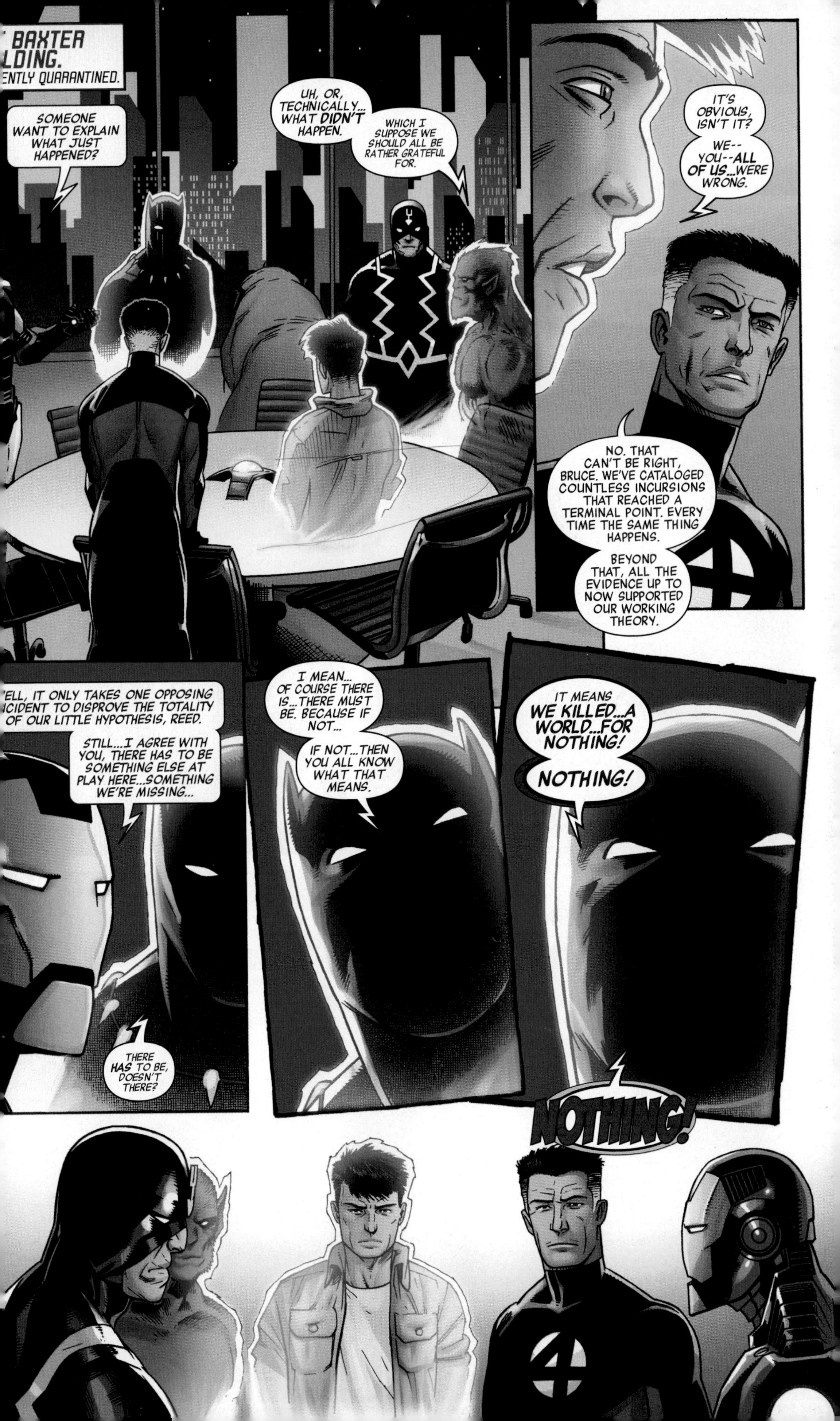

BAXTER
LDING.
ENTLY QUARANTINED.
SOMEONE WANT TO EXPLAIN WHAT JUST HAPPENED?
UH, OR, TECHNICALLY... WHAT DIDN'T HAPPEN.
WHICH I SUPPOSE WE SHOULD ALL BE RATHER GRATEFUL FOR.
IT'S OBVIOUS, ISN'T IT?
WE-- YOU--ALL OF US...WERE WRONG.
NO. THAT CAN'T BE RIGHT, BRUCE. WE'VE CATALOGED COUNTLESS INCURSIONS THAT REACHED A TERMINAL POINT. EVERY TIME THE SAME THING HAPPENS.
BEYOND THAT, ALL THE EVIDENCE UP TO NOW SUPPORTED OUR WORKING THEORY.
ELL, IT ONLY TAKES ONE OPPOSING NCIDENT TO DISPROVE THE TOTALITY OF OUR LITTLE HYPOTHESIS, REED.
STILL...I AGREE WITH YOU, THERE HAS TO BE SOMETHING ELSE AT PLAY HERE...SOMETHING WE'RE MISSING...
THERE HAS TO BE, DOESN'T THERE?
I MEAN... OF COURSE THERE IS...THERE MUST BE. BECAUSE IF NOT...
IF NOT...THEN YOU ALL KNOW WHAT THAT MEANS.
IT MEANS WE KILLED...A WORLD...FOR NOTHING!
NOTHING!
NOTHING!

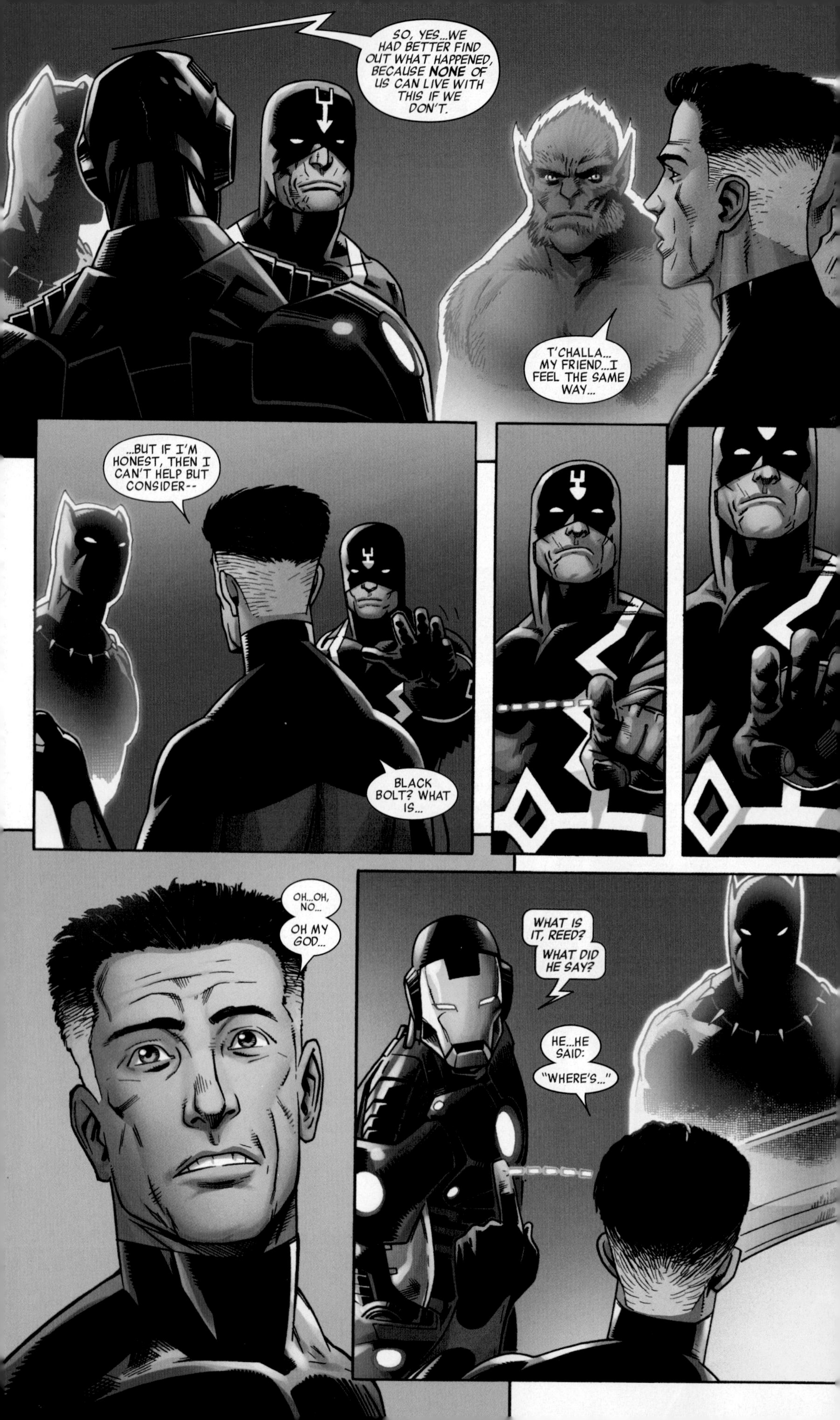
SO, YES...WE HAD BETTER FIND OUT WHAT HAPPENED, BECAUSE **NONE** OF US CAN LIVE WITH THIS IF WE DON'T.
T'CHALLA... MY FRIEND...I FEEL THE SAME WAY...
...BUT IF I'M HONEST, THEN I CAN'T HELP BUT CONSIDER--
BLACK BOLT? WHAT IS...
OH...OH, NO...
OH MY GOD...
WHAT IS IT, REED?
WHAT DID HE SAY?
HE...HE SAID:
"WHERE'S..."

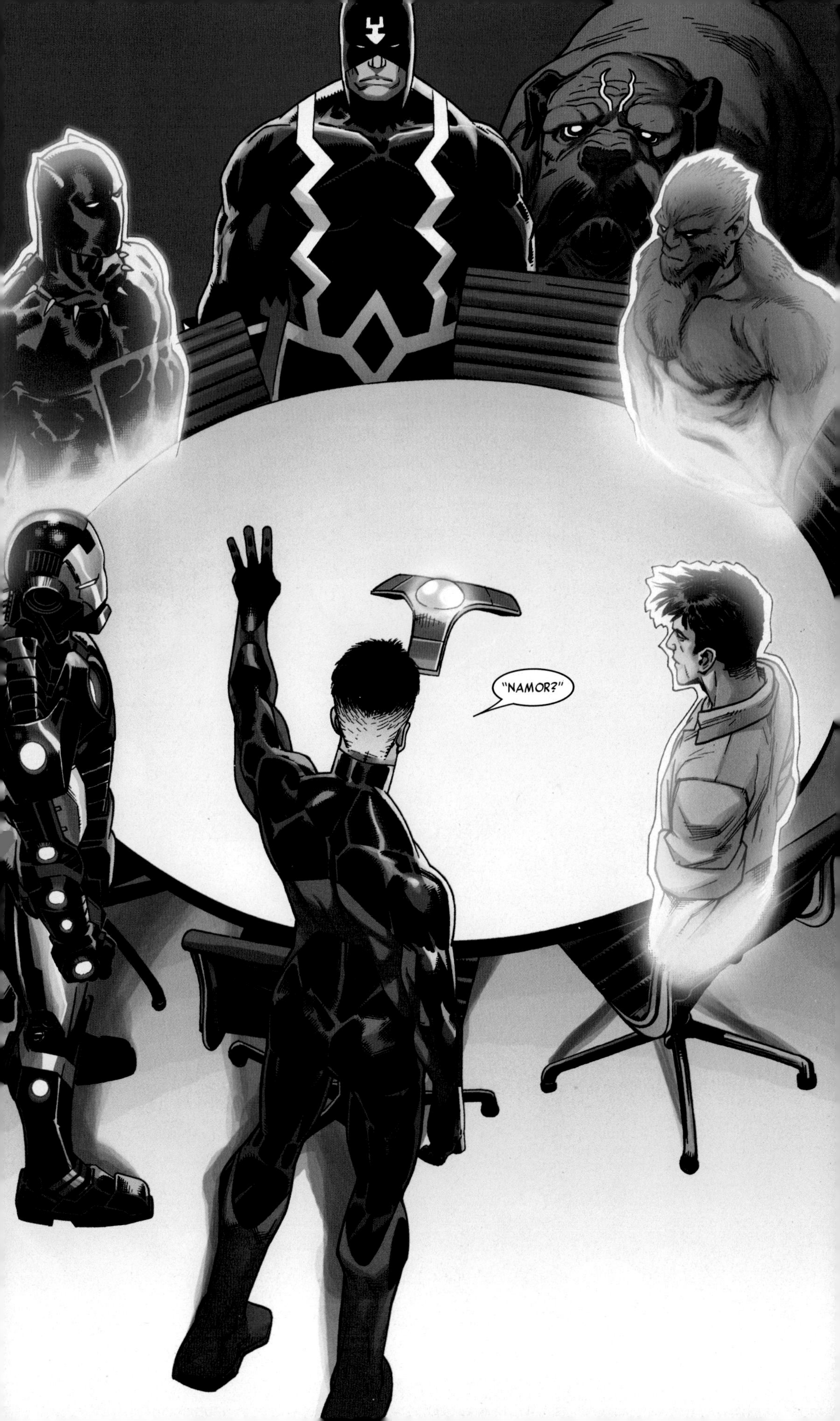
"NAMOR?"

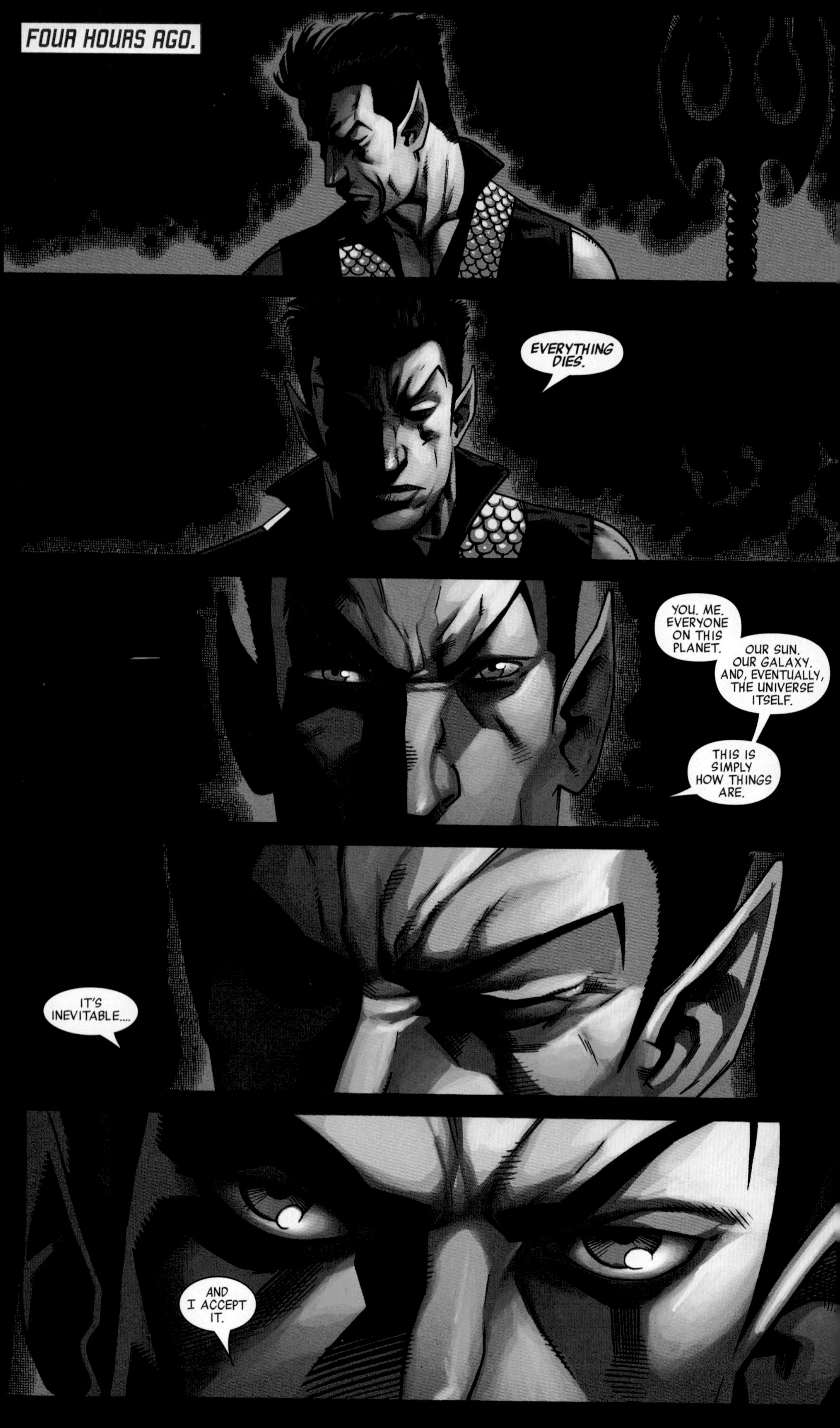
FOUR HOURS AGO.
EVERYTHING DIES.
YOU. ME. EVERYONE ON THIS PLANET.
OUR SUN. OUR GALAXY. AND, EVENTUALLY, THE UNIVERSE ITSELF.
THIS IS SIMPLY HOW THINGS ARE.
IT'S INEVITABLE....
AND I ACCEPT IT.

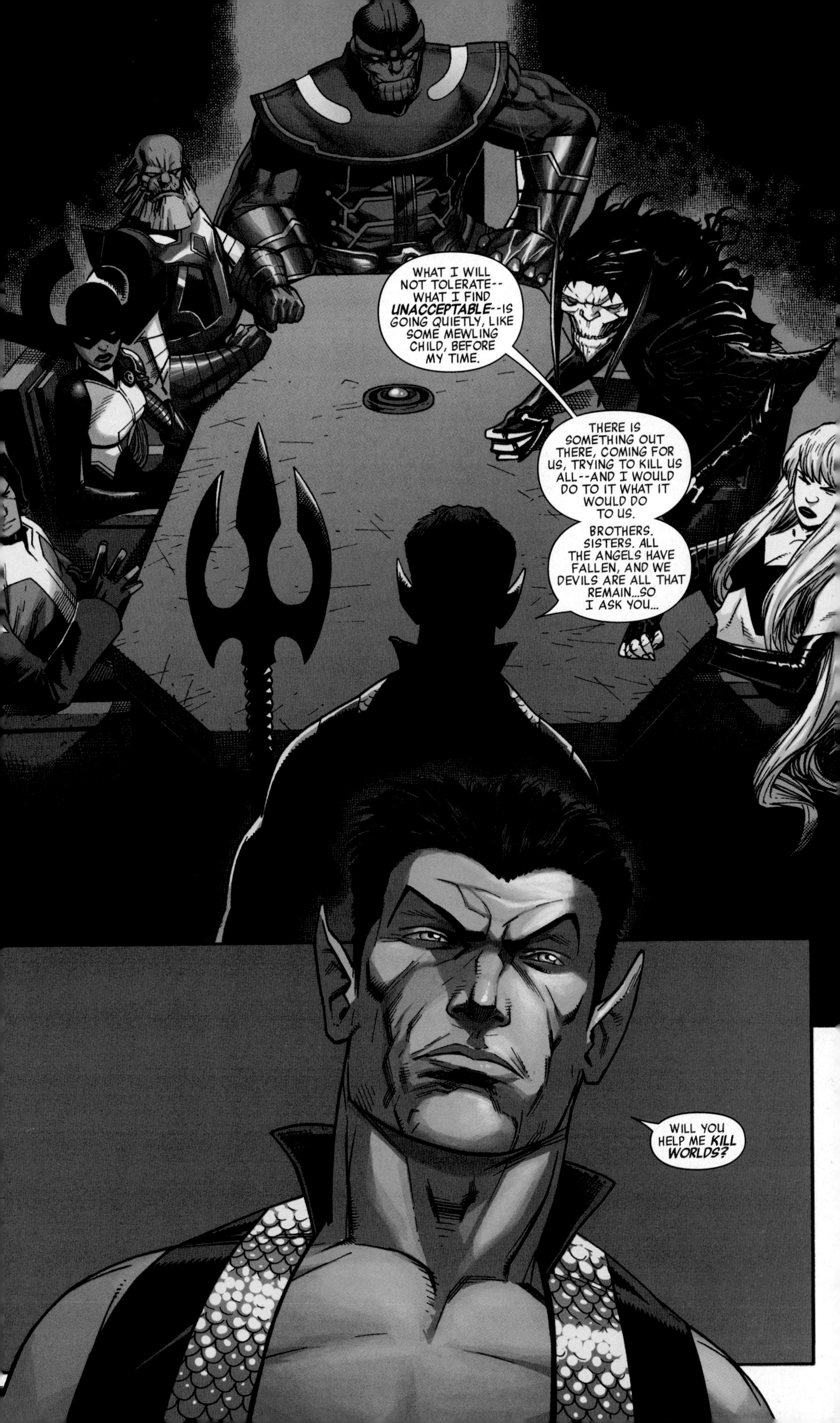
WHAT I WILL NOT TOLERATE-- WHAT I FIND **UNACCEPTABLE**--IS GOING QUIETLY, LIKE SOME MEWLING CHILD, BEFORE MY TIME.
THERE IS SOMETHING OUT THERE, COMING FOR US, TRYING TO KILL US ALL--AND I WOULD DO TO IT WHAT IT WOULD DO TO US.
BROTHERS. SISTERS. ALL THE ANGELS HAVE FALLEN, AND WE DEVILS ARE ALL THAT REMAIN...SO I ASK YOU...
WILL YOU HELP ME **KILL WORLDS?**

RISE, THE CABAL.

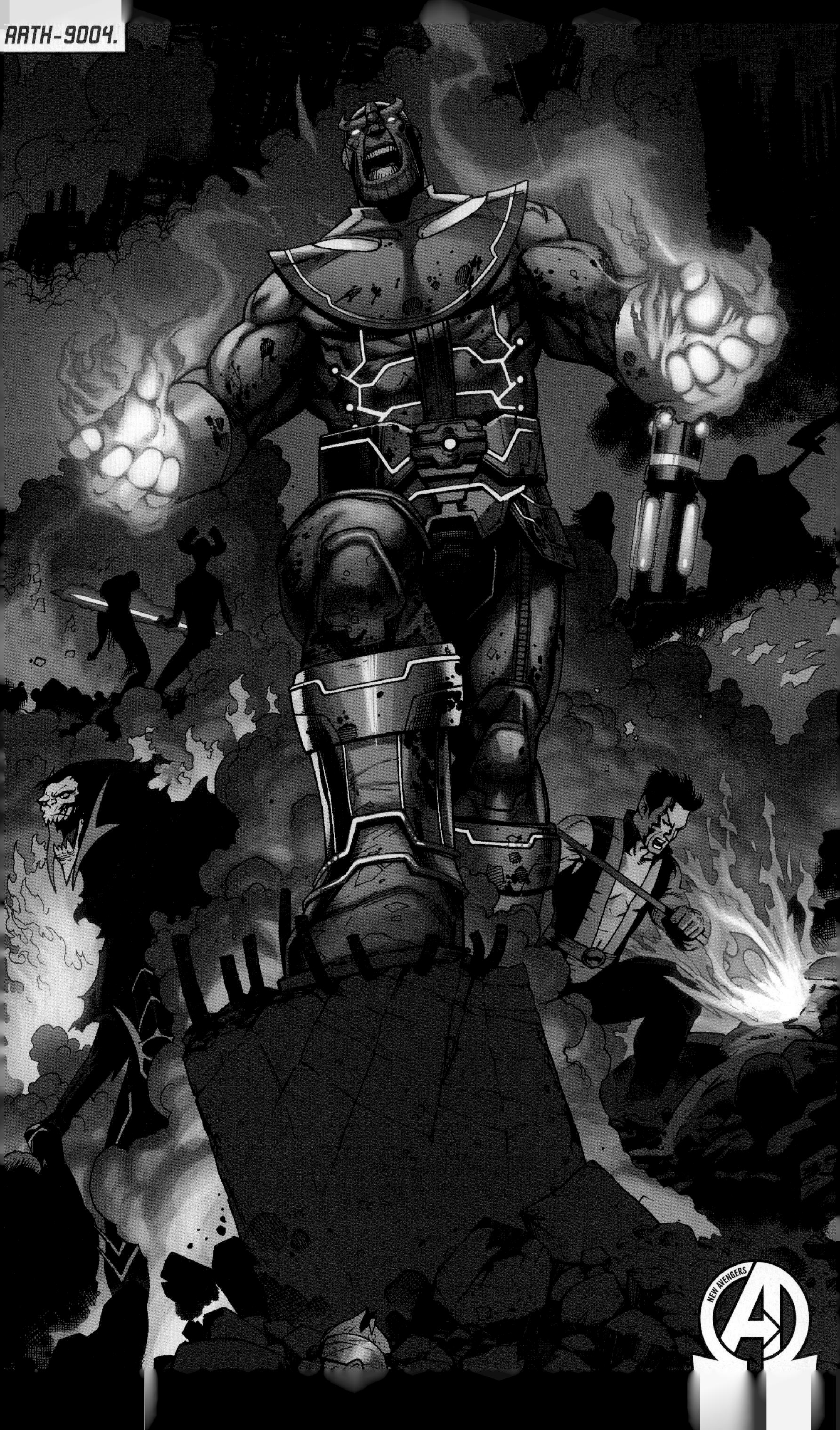
ARTH-9004.
NEW AVENGERS

COVER GALLERY

#18

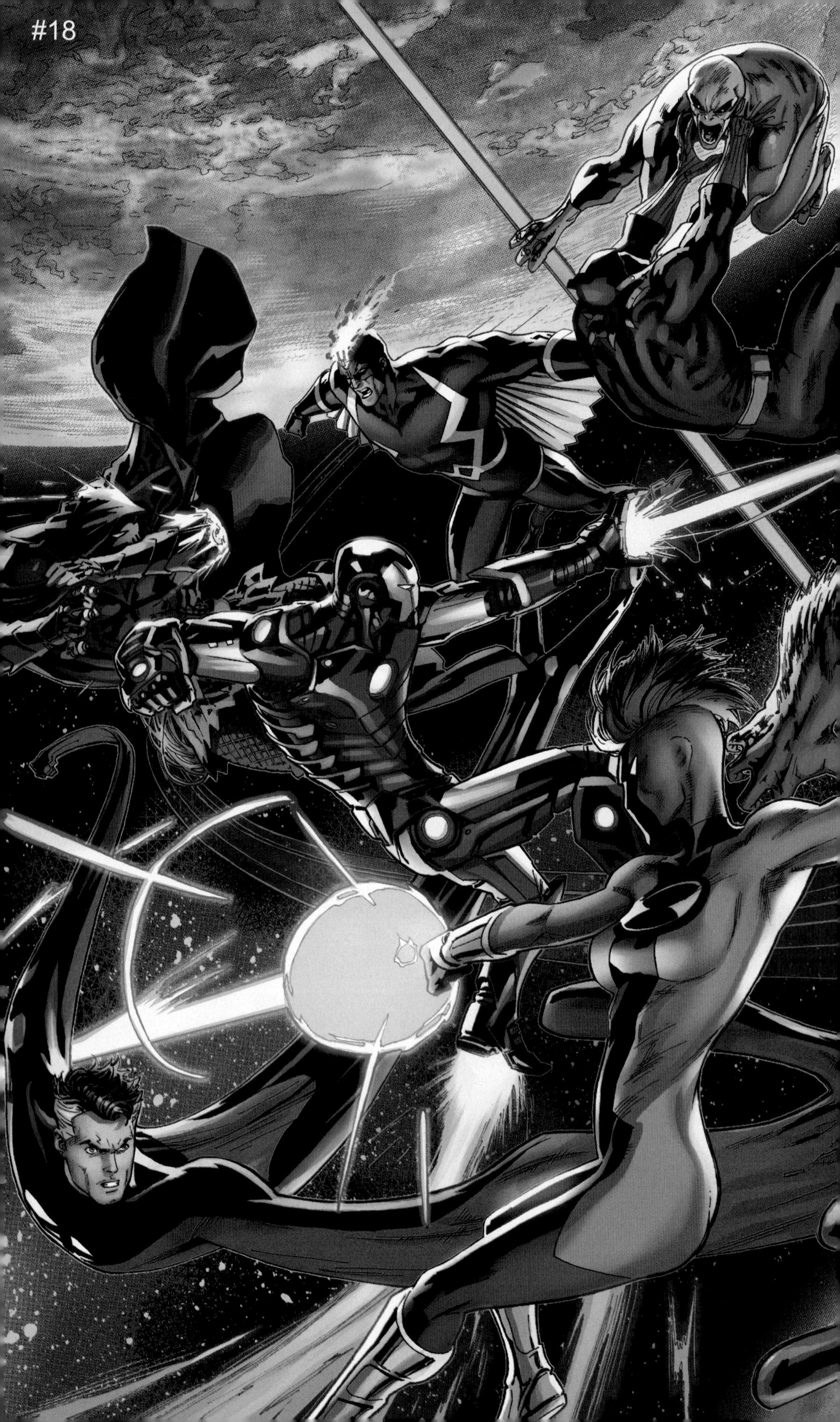

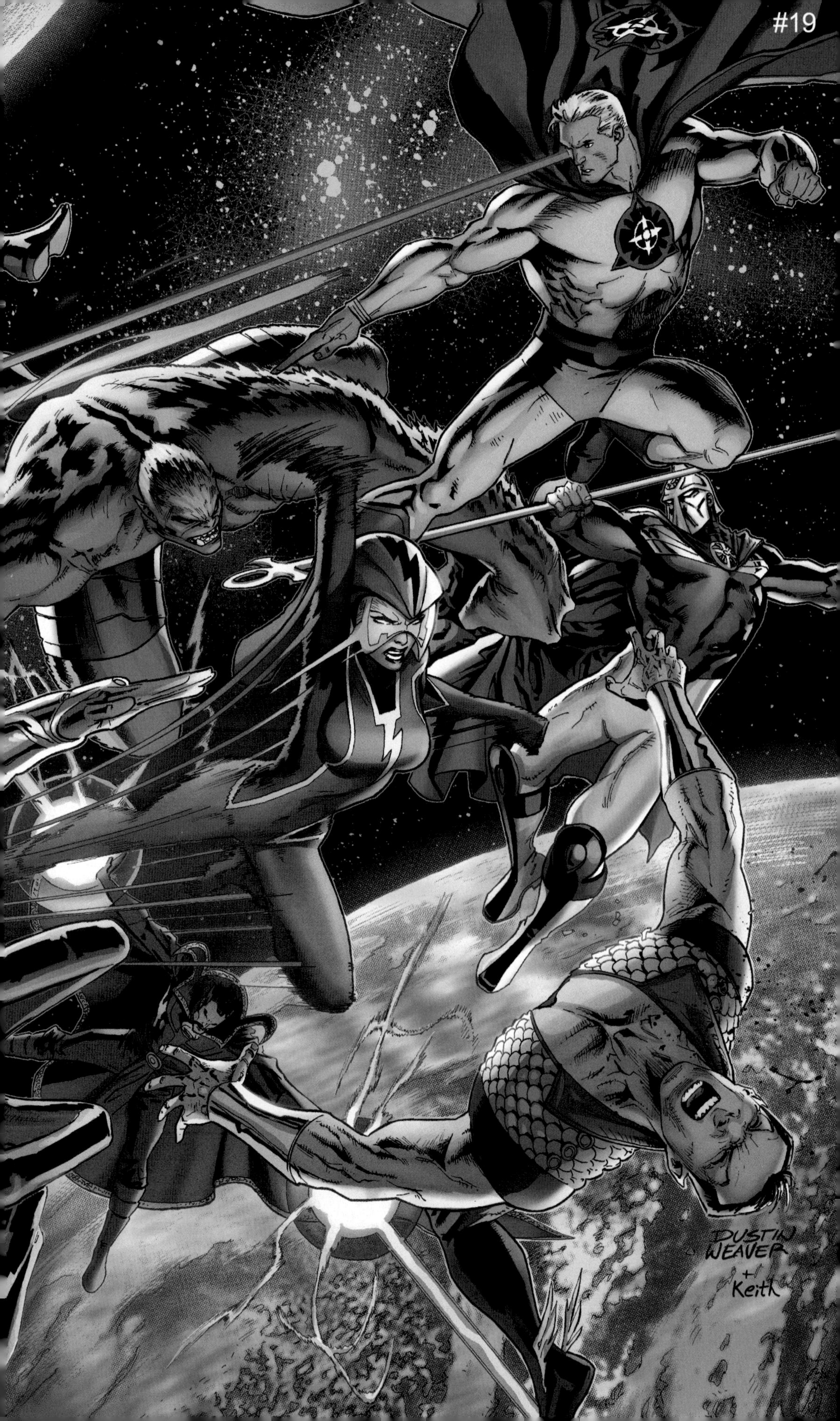
DUSTIN WEAVER + Keith

#20

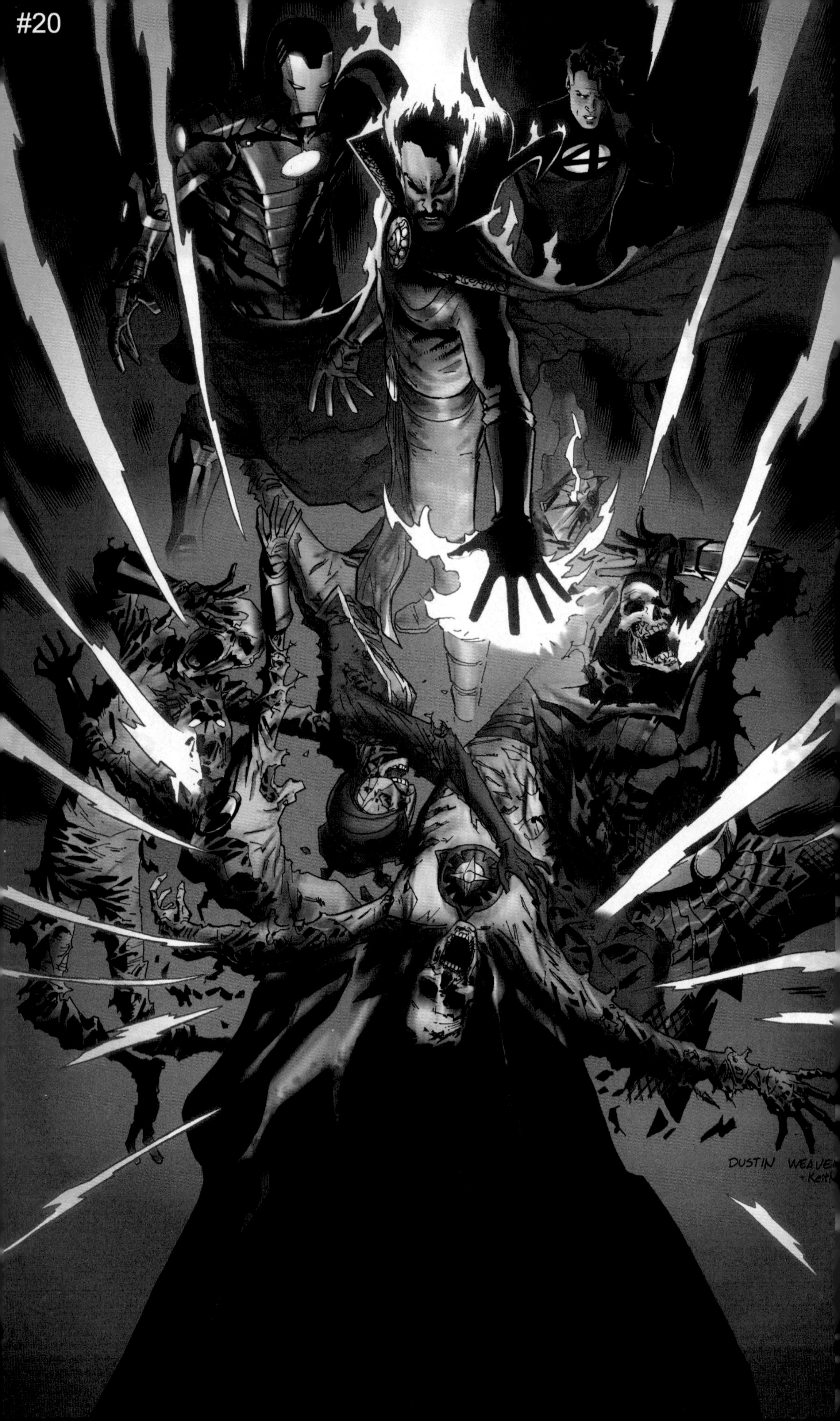
DUSTIN WEAVE
+ Keith

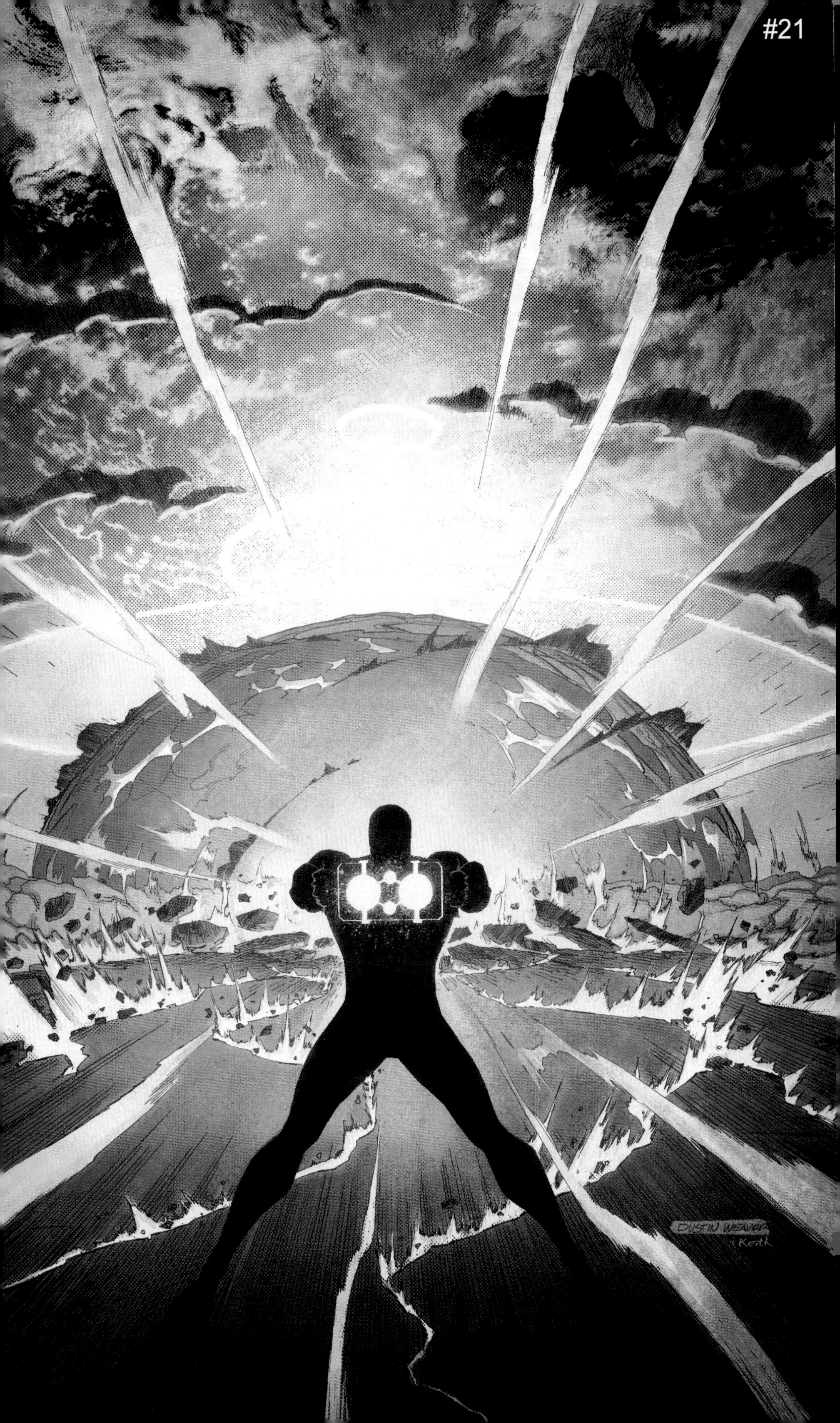
#21
DUSTIN WEAVER
+ Keith

#22

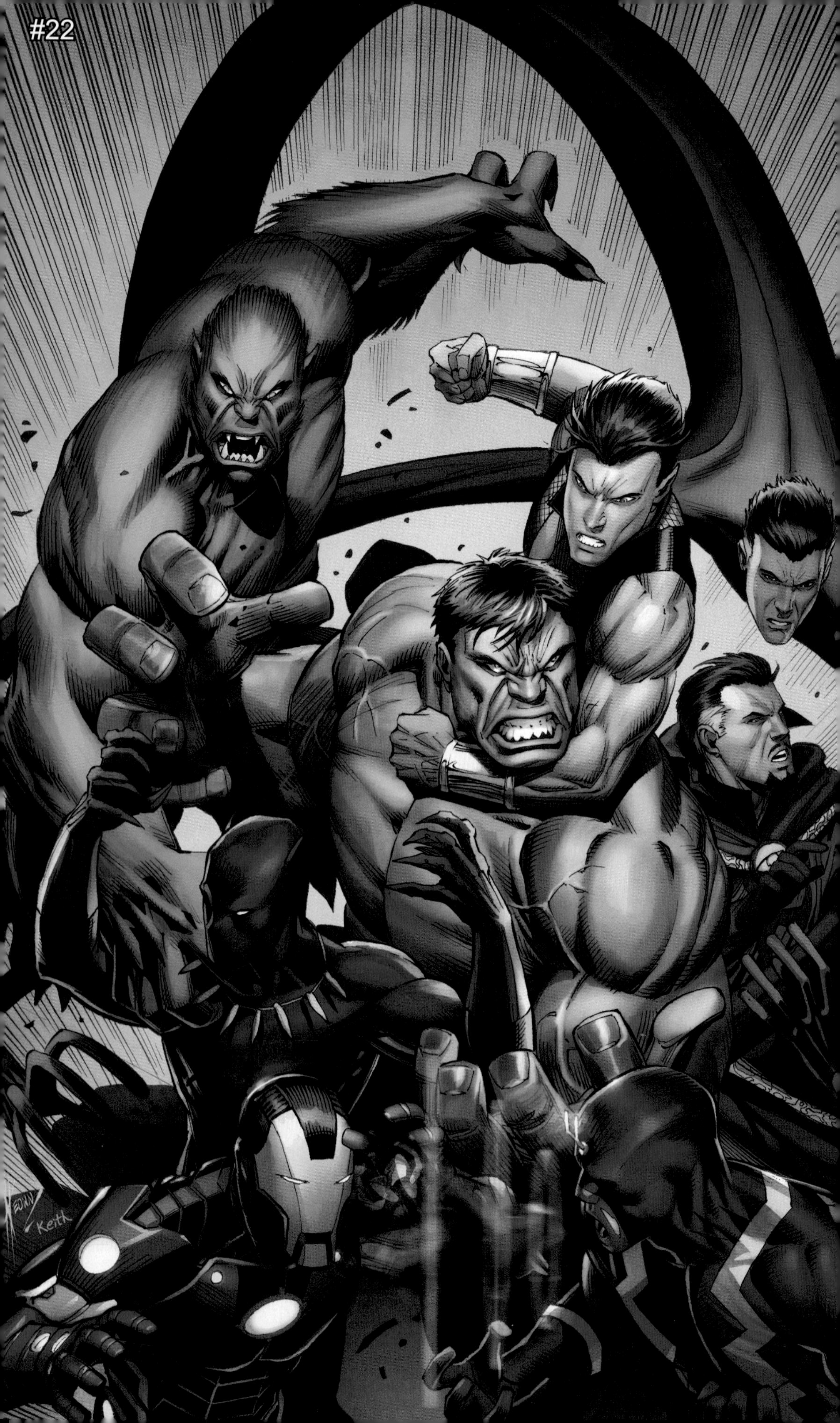

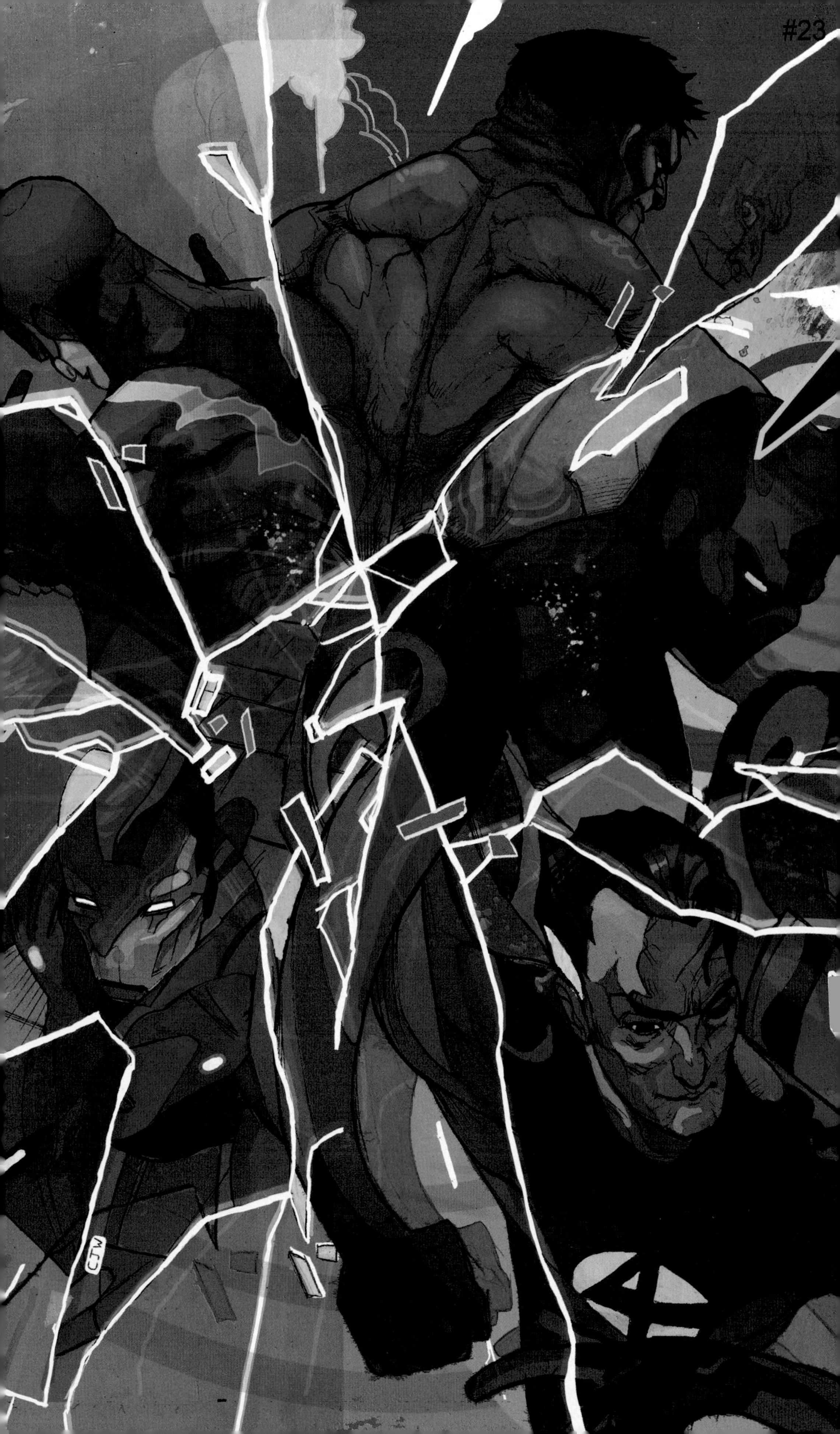
#23

#18 VARIANT BY **CHRISTIAN WARD**

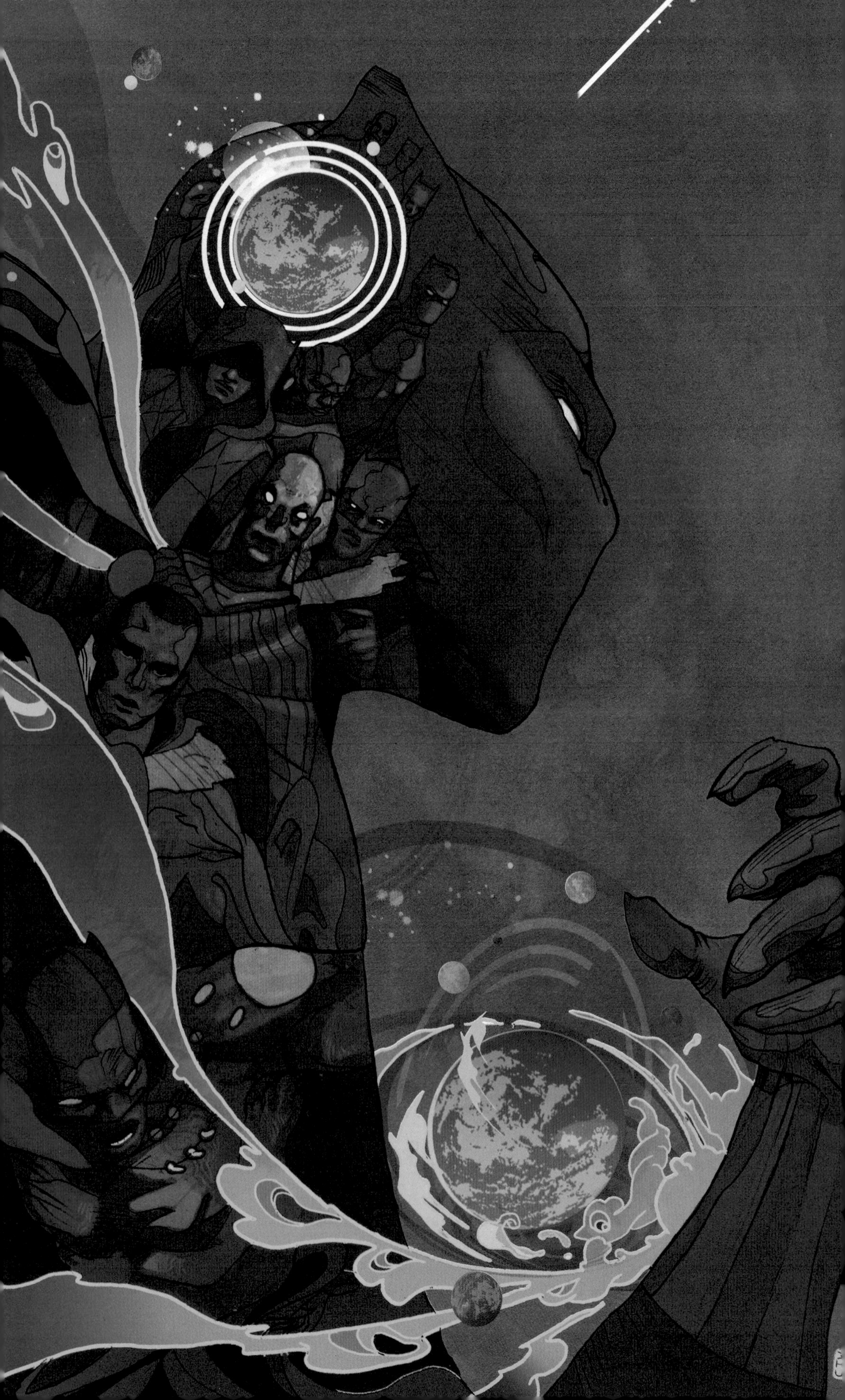

#21 GUARDIANS OF THE GALAXY VARIANT BY
PASQUAL FERRY & JASON KEITH

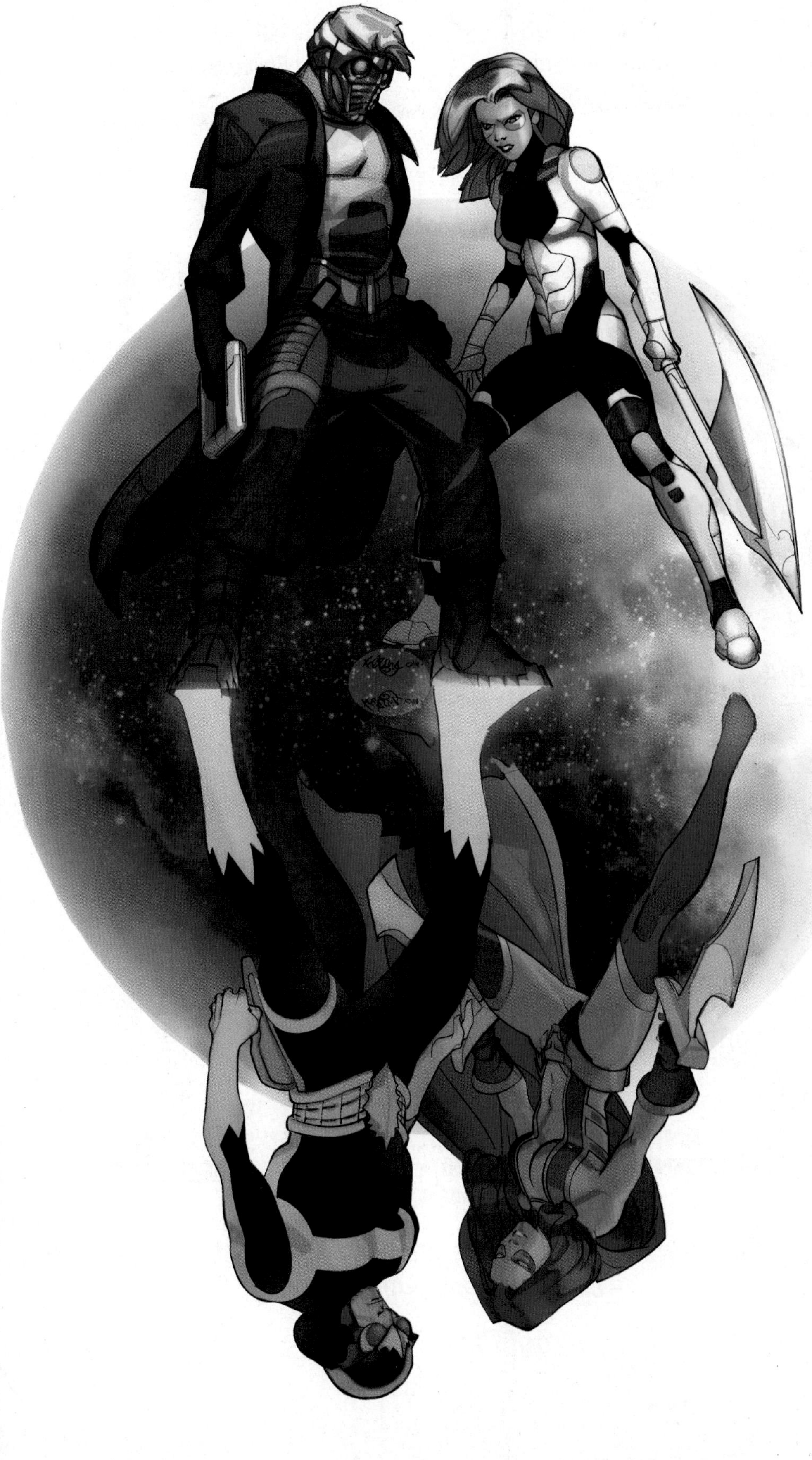

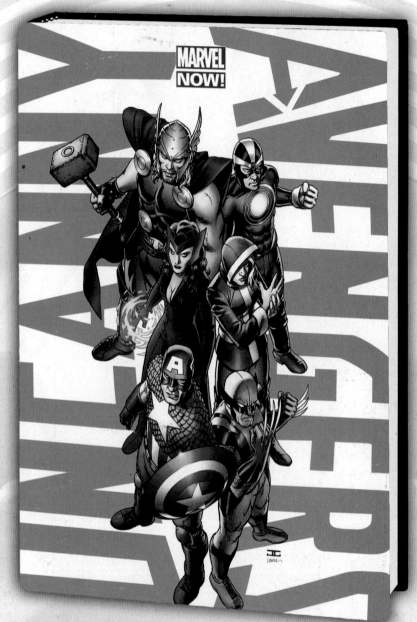